CHELTEN...

3

Springer

London
Berlin
Heidelberg
New York
Barcelona
Budapest
Hong Kong
Milan
Paris
Santa Clara
Singapore
Tokyo

3

Other titles in this series:

The Project Management Paradigm
K. Burnett
3-540-76238-8

Electronic Commerce and Business Communications
M. Chesher and R. Kaura
3-540-19930-6

Key Java
J. Hunt and A. McManus
3-540-76259-0

Distributed Applications Engineering
I. Wijegunaratne and G. Fernandez
3-540-76210-8
Publication due Autumn, 1998

Finance for IT Decision Makers
M. Blackstaff
3-540-76232-9
Publication due Autumn, 1998

Using Interface Design: Conceptual Modelling using ERMIA
D. Benyon, D. Bental and T. Green
1-85233-009-0
Publication due Autumn, 1998

Middleware
D. Serain
1-85233-011-2
Publication due Autumn, 1998

Lesley Trenner and Joanna Bawa

The Politics of Usability

A Practical Guide to Designing Usable Systems in Industry

 Springer

Lesley Trenner
Glaxo Wellcome Medicines Research Centre
Gunnels Wood Road
Stevenage, UK

Joanna Bawa
PO Box 578
Watford
WD2 8ZD, UK

ISBN 3-540-76181-0 Springer-Verlag Berlin Heidelberg New York

British Library Cataloguing in Publication Data
The politics of usability: a practical guide to designing usable systems in industry.
(Practitioner series)
1. Computer software - Standards
I. Trenner, Lesley II. Bawa, Joanna
005
ISBN 3540761810

Library of Congress Cataloging-in-Publication Data
Trenner, Lesley, 1957–
    The politics of usability / Lesley Trenner and Joanna Bawa.
    p. cm. – (Practitioner series)
    Includes bibliographical references and index.
    ISBN 3-540-76181-0 (pbk. : alk. paper)
    1. System design. 2. Management information systems. I. Bawa, Joanna. II. Title. III. Series:
    Practitioner series (Springer-Verlag)
    QA76.9.S88T76 1998
    658'.05--dc21

                                                                                    98-4708

Typesetting: Elaine Bingham, 30 Wentworth Road, Dronfield, UK.
Printed and bound at the Athenæum Press Ltd, Gateshead, Tyne and Wear, UK.
34/3830-543210 Printed on acid-free paper

Contents

The Authors

Alan Arnfeld

Alan Arnfeld is a Chartered Psychologist and Director of User Centred Ltd, an independent consultancy supporting the integration of usability within business culture, the life cycle of software and product development, and the analysis and improvement of business processes. Prior to working for Thames Water, Alan performed research in training, HCI, synthetic environments and human performance within complex systems. He also participated in UK National Standards.

Alan Arnfeld, User Centred Ltd, PO Box 4226, Goring, Berkshire, RG8 0XX, UK
Telephone: +44 (0)1491 875765; Email: user.centred@btinternet.com

Joanna Bawa

Joanna Bawa is an independent human factors consultant and technology writer. She started her career at British Telecom's Human Factors Research Centre, then moved to an agency where she gained experience in technical writing for the IT industry. She joined PC Magazine in 1991 where she developed PC Magazine's comparative usability evaluation methodology. She remains a Contributing Editor to the magazine.

Joanna Bawa, PO Box 578, Watford, WD2 8ZD, UK
Telephone: +44 (0)1923 857106; Email: joanna_bawa@zd.com

David Benyon

David Benyon is Professor of Human-Computer Systems at Napier University, Edinburgh. His main research interests are in HCI, particularly in the application of knowledge-based techniques to HCI, and information systems design. David takes a very practical approach to the application of theory: through his experience in industry and his continuing involvement as a consultant, he has developed a broad-based understanding of both the problems of introducing information technology into business and the ways in which these problems can be overcome.

David Benyon, Computing Department, Napier University, 219 Colinton Road, Edinburgh EH14 1DJ, UK
Telephone: +44 (0)131 455 5317; Fax: +44 (0)131 455 4552
Email: d.benyon@dcs.napier.ac.uk; http://www.dcs.napier.ac.uk/~dbenyon

Dermot Browne

Dermot Browne has worked in the software development industry for over twelve years. He has worked for a software house, a management consultancy and is now the managing director of a consultancy specializing in the application of Human Factors for the betterment of systems. During his career, Dermot has worked on major research projects and commercial developments with many companies in a variety of business sectors. He holds degrees in Psychology, Ergonomics, and Computer Science and a PhD in Human Computer Interaction.

Dermot Browne, Corporate Solutions Consulting (UK) Limited, 84–88 Pinner Road, Harrow, Middlesex, HA1 4LQ, UK
Telephone: +44 (0)181 427 7795; Fax: +44 (0)181 423 7730
Email: Corporate_Solutions@consult-me.co.uk

Alison Crerar

Alison Crerar is a Senior Lecturer in Computing at Napier University, Edinburgh. Her main research interests are in HCI, particularly in the areas of usability evaluation, interface design for special needs and software for cognitive diagnosis and rehabilitation. In 1991 she won a British Computer Society IT Award for 'Microworld for Aphasia' a system to diagnose and treat language problems in stroke victims. Alison provides HCI consultancy for both private and public sector organizations.

Alison Crerar, Computing Department, Napier University, 219 Colinton Road, Edinburgh, EH14 1DJ, UK
Telephone: +44 (0)131 455 4623; Fax: +44 (0)131 455 4552
Email: a.crerar@dcs.napier.ac.uk

Patricia Dorazio

Patricia Dorazio is a tenured faculty member and chairperson of the Communication and Humanities Department at the State University of New York Institute of Technology @Utica/Rome, New York, USA. She teaches courses in technical communication, online information design, technical editing, and usability testing. She is a Senior Member of the Society for Technical

Communication (STC) and has published a number of articles in various refereed journals. Additionally, she has conducted numerous workshops and seminars on usability testing for many companies and STC, the Association for Computing Machinery (ACM) Special Interest Group on Documentation (SIGDOC), and the Usability Professionals' Association (UPA). Furthermore, she is principal of PATent Solutions, a technical writing and usability consulting firm in Syracuse, NY.

Pat Dorazio, Chair, Communication and Humanities, State University of New York Institute of Technology, School of Arts and Sciences, Donovan Hall/2131, Utica/ NY 13504, USA
Telephone: +1 (315) 792-7315; Fax: +1 (315) 792-7503
Email: fpad@sunyit.edu; http://www.ntcnet.com/usabilitytesting

Susan Dray

Susan Dray has worked for nearly 20 years as a Human Factors professional, both as a researcher and manager in Honeywell and American Express, and as a consultant. She specializes in user-centred design of products, including helping her clients to understand all aspects of users and their work, using a variety of methods from customer visits to usability evaluation. Much of her work is international.

Susan Dray, Dray & Associates, 2007 Kenwood Parkway, Minneapolis, MN 55405, USA
Telephone: +1 (612) 377-1980; Fax: +1 (612) 377-0363
Email: sdray@mr.net; dray.@acm.org

John Friend

John Friend has over ten years' experience with Human Computer Interaction and Object Technology in commercial environments. John was one of the earliest users of both Smalltalk and NEXTSTEP in the UK, using both to deliver bespoke GUI applications. John has been using the STUDIO™ method since its inception and is acutely aware that HCI practices have to be tailored to the organization that applies them. His commercial experience has been gained in a variety of contexts including those of a software house and a large British law firm. He is currently part of the team working on Fidelity Investments developments on the Internet.

John Friend, Fidelity Investments, Oakhill House, 130 Tonbridge Road, Hildenbrough, Nr Tonbridge, Kent, TN11 9DZ, UK
Telephone: +44 (0)1732 777495
Email: John.Friend@uk.fid-intl.com

Tasnim Kaderbhai

Tasnim Kaderbhai is currently working as a Business Systems Analyst for Warner Music UK Ltd. Her final year project for a BA in Computing in Business specialized in "organizational factors and usability". Her chapter is based on her experiences as an industrial trainee within the IT division of Glaxo R&D UK (now the global organization GlaxoWellcome R&D). Tasnim used Glaxo as a case study of how to introduce usability to an organization.

Tasnim Kaderbhai, 5 Harwell Close, Ruislip, Middlesex, HA4 7EA, UK
Telephone: +44 (0)1895 623734

Chris Nodder

Chris Nodder works for Microsoft Corporation where he is focusing on the usability issues associated with group communication across the Internet. He was formerly the Manager of National Westminster Bank's Usability Group and his chapter is based on his experiences there.

Chris Nodder, Microsoft Corporation, 1 Microsoft Way, Redmond, WA 98052, USA
Telephone: +1 (425) 703 4685
Email: cnodder@microsoft.com

Larry Rowland

Larry Rowland is currently a software quality engineer, working on improving processes for designing and producing complex technology. His chequered past includes technical writing and broadcast engineering in radio and TV. He is passionately committed to humanistic use of computers and volunteers in local schools to teach children and their teachers how to use science and computers for interesting, unpredictable things.

Larry Rowland, Software Quality Engineering, Hewlett-Packard, 3404 East Harmony Road, Fort Collins, CO 80525, USA
Telephone: +1 (970) 229-2280; Fax: +1 (970) 229-4556
Email: lrr@hpswqe.fc.hp.com; CrazyLarry@aol.com (home)

Janet Saunders

Janet Saunders is an independent consultant in software usability and HCI. Since establishing Datawyse Ltd in early 1995, she has provided usability expertise, advice and training to a variety of clients, from software houses to major organizations. Her expertise includes requirements analysis, usability testing and evaluation, advice on interface design and help with introducing usability into the development cycle.

Janet Saunders, Datawyse Ltd, 43 Paradise Street, Warwick, CV34 5BT, UK
Telephone: +44 (0)1926 499066; Email: JanetSaunders@compuserve.com.

Nichole Simpson

Nichole Simpson is a principal consultant with Corporate Solutions Consulting (UK) Limited. Nichole has worked as a human factors specialist for nearly 10 years, providing consultancy in the areas of user requirements analysis, user interface design and usability evaluation. For five years she operated as an internal consultant to the telecommunications organization described in the site study. Among Nichole's current assignments is a project that combines market research and usability testing techniques in order to speed the uptake of user feedback into the product design process.

Nichole Simpson, Corporate Solutions Consulting (UK) Limited, 84-88 Pinner Road, Harrow, Middlesex, HA1 4LQ, UK
Telephone: +44 (0)181 427 7795; Fax: +44 (0)181 423 7730
Email: Corporate_Solutions @consult-me.co.uk; http://www.consult-me.co.uk

Tom Stewart

Tom Stewart has nearly 30 years' experience as a psychologist and ergonomist helping individuals and organizations make effective use of technology. He is currently Managing Director of System Concepts, one of the UK's leading consultancies specializing in ergonomics and human factors. He advises a number of major private and public sector organizations, including Marks and Spencer, the Employment Service and the Guardian/Observer Group. In addition to his consultancy work, he chairs the British Standards Applied Ergonomics Committee and also the International and European Standards Committees responsible for ergonomics standards for user interfaces.

Tom Stewart, System Concepts Limited, 2 Savoy Court, Strand, London WC2R 0EZ
Telephone: +44 (0)171 240 3388; Fax: +44 (0)171 240 5212
Email: tom@system-concepts.com; URL: http://www.system-concepts.com

Cathy Thomas

Cathy Thomas is a registered ergonomist and has been involved in HCI issues for 14 years. She was inspired to write her chapter after attending a conference where dissatisfaction was expressed with management consultants. As a usability consultant Cathy is concerned to ensure that HCI consultancy addresses clients' needs. She works for NPL Usability Services and is a specialist in software evaluation and usability metrics.

Cathy Thomas, NPL Usability Services, National Physical Laboratory, Teddington, Middlesex, TW11 0LW, UK
Telephone: +44 (0)181 943 6261; Fax: +44 (0)181 977 7091
Email: cathy@hci.npl.co.uk; http://www.co.uk/npl/sections/cise/us

Ingrid K. Towey

Ingrid K. Towey has been a user interface designer and usability specialist for the US division of Glaxo Wellcome for over five years. She is a strong advocate of customer-centered design and has acted as a facilitator for a number of Contextual Inquiry and Design teams. Most of her work has been in support of Glaxo Wellcome's research scientists.

Ingrid Towey, GUI & Usability Specialist, Information Systems, 5 Moore Drive, PO Box 13398, RTP, North Carolina 27709, USA
Telephone: +1 (919) 483-7632 (work); Email: it9371@glaxowellcome.co.uk

Lesley Trenner

Lesley Trenner is currently working as Business Benefits Manager for an international project to roll out a new PC desktop at GlaxoWellcome R&D. She has published widely on usability issues and has an academic background but since working for a multi-national pharmaceutical company has become increasingly interested in the practical issues associated with "doing usability" in industry.

Lesley Trenner, IT Strategic Planning, Glaxo Wellcome Medicines Research Centre, Gunnels Wood Road, Stevenage, UK
Telephone: +44 (0)1438 763294; Email: LT8571@GlaxoWellcome.co.uk

Maggie Williams

Maggie Williams has been working in the HCI field for six years. She is Usability Editor for PC Magazine where she carries out comparative usability testing on both hardware and software products. Prior to that, she worked for a financial institution as a consultant, assisting in establishing an in-house Human Factors department and providing usability support to software developments.

Maggie Williams, PC Magazine, Ziff-Davis UK Ltd, 1 St Katharine's Way, London, E1 9UN, UK
Telephone: +44 (0)171 903 6828; Email: Maggie_Williams@zd.com

Introduction

Why This Book, Why Now?

It is now widely recognized that in the development of IT systems, the technology-driven focus of the past has been eclipsed by a concern for user satisfaction and user productivity. It is well known that usability engineering helps make systems easier to use and more relevant to business needs. The benefits of producing usable computer systems have been proven in careful dollar or pound calculations and any computer user who has interacted with a system designed for usability will enthuse about the benefits and refuse to go back to the bad old days.

More and more organizations are starting to take usability seriously. Along with Microsoft and Apple and other IT organizations, we now find banks, insurance companies, multi-national pharmaceuticals and many other non-IT corporations starting to "do something about usability". It seems as if there is plenty of material explaining how to do it. HCI (Human Computer Interaction – or CHI, Computer Human Interaction in the USA) has been studied in academia for several years and there are a range of books on usability engineering for practitioners from systems engineering and user interface design to usability evaluation. However, as many practitioners have found, although you do need to understand the theories and be familiar with the techniques, applying them in a commercial context is not a straightforward matter.

Corporate politics is a reality of corporate life. Whilst we might want to "get on with our jobs" most of us recognize that working in the industrial world means learning how to influence opinion and behaviour and acquiring a number of inter-personal skills to complement the technical ones. Before you can do any useful work at all, you have to convince the right people that usability is a good idea in your organization and think of persuasive arguments why your request for a budget is more important than your colleague's. You then have to work within the constraints of a dynamic organization where priorities, objectives and deadlines will be constantly shifting. Whilst trying to assist a particular IT project, you might find that the budget and timescales change, that users are unavailable and that the developers resent your intrusion. Reviewing a new system is sometimes like the story of the Emperor's new clothes. Everyone knows there is a problem but no-one will thank you for pointing it out. How can you do meaningful usability work when faced with these hurdles?

"The Politics of Usability" is written by usability professionals from a variety of non-IT organizations who have dealt with these issues first hand. They explain how you need a range of skills and techniques from an understanding of usability metrics to the ability to persuade and influence, and an understanding of team dynamics. They caution that as a usability professional you need a thick skin and often have to be resourceful, flexible, tactful and patient. These softer skills are as important in industry as the "hard" knowledge of usability methods and techniques. Time spent "politicking" will not be wasted – it will oil the wheels for doing the "real" work.

Who Is This Book for?

This book will be of great interest to usability professionals and practitioners. It will help those who are moving from academia to the commercial world and others who are starting out in industry. It will also be useful for the "old timers" who have struggled with the political problems to see some new solutions.

The case studies will help IT managers, quality specialists and project managers to have a greater understanding of the problems of introducing best practice into the software development process.

Finally, we would encourage business managers and computer users to read the book. We hope that the themes and lessons learned will help them fight for more usable systems and to co-operate in processes aimed at making that possible.

Themes and Issues

Part 1 – The Politics of Funding: Justifying Your Existence

When "doing usability" in industry, the first hurdle you will have to face, and arguably the most difficult one, is to secure funding. Whether you are looking for human resources, a budget to buy expertise or training, funds to set up a usability lab, or all of these things, you need persuasive arguments and ready answers for all the possible objections that will be raised. You need a clear business case based around the culture of your organization. As Chris Nodder's chapter about the National Westminster Bank shows, in a financial organization, nothing less than a full cost benefit justification will do. As a comparison, in the later section on "Set up", Tasnim Kaderbhai found that in a R&D organization, there was less emphasis on pure cost benefit and that arguments relating to user satisfaction and user productivity were more influential.

Finding money for external consultants may prove harder to justify as the expenditure is more visible than the "hidden" costs of using internal staff. Some organizations are uncomfortable using external help and your justification will need to tackle questions like: "why can't our own internal staff do this work?"; "if we take on a contractor will we get dependent on their skills?" (and, by implication be tied into paying for their services for years to come). Dermot Browne's chapter will help you supply valid answers to these concerns. On the other hand, in some cultures, inviting contractors to help with IT projects is seen as a cost effective way of buying in objective consultancy and much needed expertise. In this case, as Dermot points out, your arguments will need to focus on the fact that the introduction of Windows technology has made the design of user interfaces more complicated, not less so, and that new skills are required that the organization needs to buy in.

Unfortunately, the argument for funding is not a decisive war but rather a series of skirmishes that break out sporadically. Even if you have secured funding for this year, you may have to fight the case again next year. If IT budgets are tight, someone will look at the usability expenditure with beady eyes. As Chris Nodder points out, you need to be constantly measuring and monitoring the effectiveness of your own function and promoting awareness of your services across the organization to avoid being a target for cutbacks.

Part 2 – The Politics of Set Up: What to Do with the Money once You Have Got it

Even if you have the green light for doing usability within your organization, there seems to be an inertia that slows down progress and throws up obstacles. Tasnim Kaderbhai outlines some factors that can limit the uptake of usability in industry:

- the difficulty of quantifying the cost benefits;
- a perception that usability activities are "optional extras" that will lengthen project life cycles;
- lack of management support;
- resistance by developers and/or a distrust of usability personnel;
- limited access to users;
- lack of awareness of usability by the business and therefore lack of demand.

Tasnim examines how far each of these factors slowed down the progress of the Usability Group at Glaxo R&D (UK) when it was originally set up and evaluates some other early initiatives to see which were most successful. Her chapter highlights a recurrent theme in dealing with the politics of usability – the need for senior management sponsorship. This is especially true if the corporate culture is not receptive to usability, or where IT middle managers act in a parochial way with a vested interest in either development or support. Arguments about cost savings will be better appreciated more by someone senior with an understanding of the overall cost of developing, supporting and maintaining systems.

Corporate culture is one of the main themes of Janet Saunders and Alan Arnfeld's chapter. Their account of working with Thames Water reveals the successes and challenges of attempting to introduce a formal "usability culture" into a large organization. The initiative was triggered by a software development project and began with awareness-raising and the eventual construction of a usability lab. It was followed by a major drive to get usability incorporated into every stage of software development across a wide range of projects. Co-operation, communication and "giving usability away", says Arnfeld, form the keystones to maintaining and even growing a successful usability-orientated corporate culture.

Alison Crerar and David Benyon's chapter gives useful advice on how to maximize the value of your budget by providing a critical review of usability resources from books and web sites to training courses and methods. As the other chapters make clear, instituting methods to get usability into the design cycle is one of the key tasks for usability people. David examines the benefits of using a standard systems development methodology and discusses ways you can adapt methods to suit your organization without reinventing the wheel for every project. He also looks at how you can effectively tap into existing resources such as internal expertise and the relevant professional associations, and when you need to pay for external consultancy.

John Friend and Dermot Browne discuss the need for a structured method to make sure that user-centred design is a reality not just a nice idea. They agree that there is a fine balance between using consistent and workable methods such as STUDIO™ or MUSiC and remaining flexible and open to the inevitable changes in the political landscape. However, they stress that system development methodologies should be applied flexibly. Their chapter stresses the importance of linking usability objectives to the business case for a project so that usability work is directly linked with the overall goals of the organization. They also highlight the problems of gaining access to users. In their case study of Linklaters & Paines law firm, the end users are highly qualified legal professionals whose time is expensive, and who can be reluctant to use their time specifying or evaluating computer systems.

Part 3 – The Politics of Survival: Keeping Usability on the Political Map

Once you have proved the case for funding and have permanent resources and a remit to improve usability within your organization, you will need to make plans, instigate policies for implementing usability and devise strategies for dealing with the inevitable political setbacks.

Flexibility does not just apply to your methodology, but to your whole approach to usability in industry, as Maggie Williams points out. Her chapter discusses the frustrations of providing usability consultancy to a major project where key elements such as budget, project specification, delivery dates or personnel change suddenly or unexpectedly. This seems to be a remarkably common experience and Maggie shows how important it is to anticipate change at all stages of a project and minimize its impact. Careful planning, maintaining close relationships, good quality documentation and a wide range of assessment strategies all contribute towards a flexible, effective approach that can work even in the most difficult circumstances.

In both their chapters, Cathy Thomas of the National Physical Laboratory (NPL) and Nichole Simpson look at how usability consultants can help you survive and ensure that the usability department remains clearly visible on the corporate map. Their messages are equally relevant to external and internal people who act as usability consultants. Cathy talks about how NPL methods can be used cost effectively in industry by choosing those most appropriate for a given organization or project. She stresses the importance of building a relationship with a development team which is a point Nichole reiterates: no project appreciates "seagull" consultants – the kind that fly in, drop their message and fly off again! Cathy also cautions against consultants working in isolation and then producing a series of recommendations that are never implemented. Building a relationship with a team is hard work, and Nichole points out that usability consultants should expect setbacks as well as "wins".

Part 4 – The Politics of Expansion: How to Work Effectively on an International, Multi-Cultural Level

When usability takes off within a company it often expands to other parts of the organization nationally and internationally. Whilst this should be considered as a huge achievement on the part of the original sponsors and champions, it brings its own problems for usability professionals. Organizations all have their own culture. This can vary even between departments and sites. Once you cross national boundaries, cultural differences increase exponentially.

As a rare species it is an exciting experience for a usability professional to discover colleagues within their own organization with similar ideas. Usability people often assume that their professional backgrounds and interests mean that they will inevitably agree on fundamental issues and work in similar ways. However, this may disguise the differences that are bound to exist. Ingrid Towey makes an interesting observation about cultural differences. In her case study of the internationalization of the US and UK usability departments at GlaxoWellcome she explains that methods for doing usability work had evolved on either side of the Atlantic and that both sides assumed that theirs was the right way. As the methodologies only existed as folklore in the heads of the US and UK practitioners it was only when starting to work as an international team that the different approaches became apparent. This forced both sets of usability workers to re-evaluate their methods and together they developed and documented common – and better – working practices.

Joanna Bawa's chapter discusses how comparative usability testing was established at PC Magazine UK and subsequently transferred to other parts of the organization around the world. She talks about the practical and political challenges associated with introducing and developing a new idea across organizational and national boundaries, even when everyone involved wants the same thing. Often, however, the effort can yield surprising results – she goes on to describe how international labs can produce truly cross-cultural results, where the final data is greater than the sum of the individual elements. Tom Stewart encountered similar issues when trying to introduce standards within a European organization where developers and users were divided between offices in Germany and The Netherlands. He points out that while standards aid consistency, they may prevent systems being suitable for any one individual user and that incorporating standards and style guides into an international organization's development processes is complex.

Tom also refers to the problems associated with different cultures and management styles in an international organization. Susan Dray's chapter has a similar theme. Her case study looks at the lessons learned from an international usability testing exercise that took place in Zurich and Tokyo and explores how everything from the administration to the testing process itself needed a different approach. Understanding of the Japanese and European cultures was key to making this exercise successful.

Has usability taken off more quickly and more extensively in the US than in the UK? This is an interesting question. Pat Dorazio challenges us to examine whether this is true – she feels that sometimes organizations say the right things but are actually paying lip service to the ideal of usability without instigating procedures to make it happen. However, she examines why US organizations appear to be more receptive to usability and discusses ways organizations can foster that and capitalize on it.

Seven Golden Rules for Managing the Politics of Usability

The case histories described in the four sections of the book provide a wealth of material about managing the politics of usability. Summarized here are the key findings and lessons learned.

1. Gain Sponsorship and Support from Senior Management

You need the sponsorship of senior managers in both IT and the business to provide funding, and you also need their support for your ventures whether they involve making changes to working practices or building a usability lab. Spend time persuading managers and the other "movers and shakers" within your organization. Show them videos from usability testing sessions, pass on testimonials about improvements in projects on which you have worked, illustrate the cost savings that usability has brought about, publish the benefits of usability engineering in the company magazine.

2. Educate Your Users, Keep Them on Your Side

Most users do not need to be told about the frustrations of using badly designed software. They naturally understand about usability when the concepts are put to them. They may not realize that it is legitimate to complain or that there are usability professionals around with a raft of techniques to help with design and analysis. Educate them. The world is becoming more consumer conscious in the 1990s. It is fashionable to ask people what they want – and it makes good business sense. Encourage your users to be more demanding – once users start refusing to put up with poor usability, there is much more pressure on IT providers to take action. The alternative is at best damage to their reputation and at worst, finding that users look elsewhere for their IT solutions.

3. Exploit Your Communication and Inter-Personal Skills

When you meet development teams or individuals who are enthusiastic and supportive, providing usability consultancy will be easy. But apathy, resistance or hostility are more normal so be prepared for them. Plan to spend a good part of any meeting building a good relationship with your clients and selling the benefits of what you do. If you are working with a team, respect their priorities, use their skills and give them time to accept you. Use good communication skills. Reports, presentations and documents should adhere to good usability principles: clear layout, relevant graphics, readable fonts, lack of jargon etc.!

4. Push for Usability to Be "Institutionalized"

The first stage in introducing usability into your organization is to gain support for the idea. However, it cannot stop here. Usability takes more than enthusiasm – it must have assigned resource. As Glaxo found out, having enthusiasts "doing usability in their coffee breaks" was not enough. It was not until a specified place on the map was assigned, in this case with the Applications Development department, that real progress could be made.

You also need commitment to changes in the applications development process. Without this you end up in the "too little, too late" school of usability. Plan usability activities into projects. Project managers hate surprises but if an activity has been planned in, it will usually happen. It is also best to use structured and consistent methods that emphasize early design rather than late evaluation. Institutionalizing usability is necessary to its success. However, changes in culture take time. The existence of a usability group or a lab or the drawing up of a new systems development life cycle document will not result in changes overnight.

5. Be Flexible!

In the ideal world you would pick the most effective and rigorous methods and techniques and apply them consistently across the projects on which you worked. But the industrial world is not ideal. Large organizations are constantly reorganizing and reprioritizing. IT projects start out with a plan and external factors cause it to change. Personal preference means that one manager will agree to usability testing while another is prepared to resource a Style Guide instead. Even on a day-to-day basis, users who have promised to help, change their plans or react in unexpected ways.

If you go in as a usability professional armed with a rigid methodology and insist that usability work needs to be done in a certain way, you run the risk of being told that there is no time or money to do it at all. Part of the solution to this problem is to spend time building a relationship with sponsors and colleagues and selling the benefits of usability engineering. But you also have to be flexible and responsive to the inevitable changes. Choose methods and techniques that suit the culture of your organization and adapt them for new situations. Jakob Nielsen's ideas on discount usability engineering are relevant here. He suggests you should aim to have some usability engineering performed with "good results", recognizing that you cannot always use the "best" method and achieve "perfect" results.

In Joanna Bawa's chapter on comparative usability testing she makes the point that it is necessary to quantify usability in order to make useful comparisons between products. However, she cautions against applying statistics over-zealously when "softer" qualitative data can often be more revealing. With both methods and data, you need to tread a fine line between using approaches which are too simplistic and therefore potentially misleading, and approaches which allow you to gain useful, concrete information quickly and efficiently. John Friend and Dermot Browne highlight the need to apply structured methods sensibly and to base the effort spent on usability and choice of techniques on the size of the project and its business benefits.

6. Capitalize on the Benefits of Multi-Disciplinary and International Usability Teams

Usability teams work best if they are multi-disciplinary. As many of our authors point out, a blend of psychology, computer science, graphic design and usability skills works well, combined with excellent interpersonal and communication skills. It is hard to find all this in one person so build a team with these elements. This may be harder for the team manager who has to match skills to tasks, get the team to gel together and respect each other's strengths and provide career development opportunities for individuals. It may still be desirable to buy in required skills for specific tasks so that these skills can be transferred to team members.

International usability teams add another dimension. Cultural differences mean that usability professionals working for the same company may have different working practices or a different focus. You need to expose these and agree on best practice. International working means extra time is needed for preparation and communication. Sometimes technology can help (email, video conference) – sometimes you need to meet and team build face to face to forge a good working relationship. Rather than thinking of the "other" culture as "wrong", try to build on each other's strengths.

7. Become Part of the Usability Community: Share Skills and Experience

As a usability professional you will often be working alone or in small departments. Usability in industry is still relatively new and we are learning from our mistakes. Part of the reason for writing this book is to help us share our experiences and gain support and ideas from each other. Do join a local or national professional association – actively seek out colleagues working in similar industries and see how they have dealt with similar problems. The wheel is simple, efficient and usable – let's not all try to reinvent it!

Usability in Industry: How Does the Future Look?

What of the future? Will usability in industry survive? The chapters in this book are upfront in highlighting the problems that exist but the overall message is hopeful. Usability engineering is becoming more mature as it becomes more widespread. It is standard practice in most IT industries and spreading throughout non-IT organizations. It is becoming fully integrated with the systems development life cycle. Furthermore, there are developments in the worlds of work and leisure that will offer new opportunities for usability professionals, as long as we are prepared to grab them!

One area noticeably absent from this book is a discussion of the political and usability issues presented by the rise of the World Wide Web. This is by no means an oversight – it simply became clear to us that the Web is now so huge it would be impossible to do it justice within the confines of this book. It is equally clear, however, that the Web has brought information and communication on an unprecedented scale to the desktops of a new and expanding user population. As long as the Web remains a novelty many people will use it, regardless of its ease of use – or lack thereof – but we are quickly reaching the point where people are saturated with information and will only visit Web sites if the process is easy and the site is well designed.

The other noticeable trend of relevance to usability professionals is the rate at which technology is becoming more closely integrated into our everyday lives. As corporate and consumer needs merge, we begin to deal with technology for banking, shopping, home management, education, leisure and communication. Intuitive user interfaces will be essential if such products are to be successful, and a greater need than ever for research into design and usability testing which retains the human user as the centre of product development, rather than as an incidental factor.

Within the organization, it is apparent that the days of one-to-one standalone applications are over. With over 80 percent of corporate PCs now connected, most applications are at least multi-user, networked or Internet ready. This raises important questions of group working, work flow and co-operative group productivity that usability professionals are ideally positioned to address; and also brings us into direct contact with economists, sociologists, planners and corporate strategists as we all wrestle with the problems of human satisfaction and productivity in today's work place.

Finally, we should all be aware that there is a continuing shift of emphasis from the product as technological marvel to the product as user tool. As it infiltrates their lives, people become less intimidated by technology and more likely to demand better usability. This trend started in the design of games and leisure software, it will impact on the development of business software too. It seems that usability will become ever more important in the development of computer software, and other technologies that we use on a daily basis. Usability engineering in industry will therefore become critical, but the politics will not go away. We cannot rely on technological changes to force the issue.

So how will we deal with the politics of usability? Some remarkably consistent themes have come through in this book and the lessons learned seem to apply across the board. Where there are differences, they tend to relate to the differences between the organizations themselves. Will your culture adopt a new idea if there is documented cost-benefit analysis, or because its competitors are doing so, or because it wants to be seen as innovative? Is the organization impressed by visible "quick wins" or will it prefer slower, proven methods? Is it structured and hierarchical (in which case it will probably be open to the idea of a permanent usability group)? Or is it "flatter" and more dynamic? If so you may be better off working as a virtual group pulling in resource as needed. Be aware of how your organization works – ultimately, usability in industry can only be a success if it is based on the culture and business goals of the specific organization, and if it provides information which is genuinely helpful, informative and – ah – usable!

LT, JB
October 1997

Part 1

The Politics of Funding:
Justifying Your Existence

1. *Making a Business Case for Usability and Beyond - the Fight for Survival*

How to Prove You Will Impact the Bottom Line

Chris Nodder

ABSTRACT

This chapter begins with a discussion of the components required to produce a business case that will justify the formal creation of a usability team. It then gives consideration to the changes that such a team will face, and how to be prepared for and find mechanisms for justifying these changes to budget holders.

A compelling business case is not something put together just once to sanction the formation of a usability function. Instead, due mainly to the dynamic political nature of organizations, it will be continually revisited and revised. Additional business cases will need to be made for expansion, new facilities, and even to justify the continued existence of your team.

Throughout this chapter there are pointers to the main areas where care is needed when setting up a usability function, to help ensure the support and the data to justify your existence to a wide range of people. These hints should help usability start-ups anticipate and thus minimize the impact of political machinations upon the team's ability to deliver quality usability advice. Where appropriate, I draw on my experiences first as a founder member and then as the manager of the NatWest usability team. Through examples, I show what the successes were, what lessons were learnt and how, with hindsight, the team could have dealt better with some of the problems we faced when working with project teams and management.

The Organization

NatWest Bank is one of the main "High Street" (retail) banks in the United Kingdom, as well as having all the functions associated with corporate and international banking and financial market trading. It employs over 60,000 people, and has around 3000 staff working in information technology.

Usability Services in NatWest Bank started formally in December 1994. A large investment was made in staff, premises, equipment and training, based on a joint business case with another team which was charged with promoting innovation within the organization. The usability team works mainly with projects that have a technology component, but also with business units on documentation and process design issues. The breadth of the business means that Usability Services have been involved in products ranging from videoconferencing solutions which help sell insurance products, to call centre management, to interactive Internet banking applications. Geographically, the Usability Services team is based in central London, although members can work at any NatWest location. Organizationally, Usability Services currently lives in the Information Technology department of the retail banking function. Their primary "client" is the retail bank, although they retain a remit to work for all areas of the organization. Projects pay for usability involvement from their development budget.

Although the team has experienced peaks and troughs in workload, there has typically been sufficient demand to keep five full-time usability professionals busy. These team members have come from backgrounds in psychology, human factors, ergonomics, systems development, training, business analysis and branch banking. This mix has allowed each person to contribute unique skills and learn from each other's experiences.

Starting a Usability Function

Although this chapter is primarily concerned with business cases for usability, the usability story does not start with a business case. Instead, it starts with an individual or team's recognition that there would be a benefit to the organization in "doing usability". This recognition needs to become action, however informally, before the information needed for a business case can be gathered. It may appear paradoxical to perform usability evaluations in order to justify expenditure on usability evaluations, but this is probably the most effective way of producing a persuasive argument.

The initial setup of Usability Services at NatWest relied in part on data gathered from team members' previous jobs. In at least one case, a former job role encompassed research into new methods and technologies, but these resources would have been available to other people within NatWest. People in other organizations can engineer similar opportunities for themselves.

Finding a Flagship Project

A business case is more than a piece of paper. The idea that several competing requests for money get compared purely on their technical merits is naïve. What often makes the difference is personal recommendations to the decision makers from people that they trust. For this reason, a usability start-up needs supporters who are influential in the organization and who can serve as "champions" for the cause.

Before you have formally announced your intention to start a usability function, note that there are three types of project manager with whom you may have to work. Enthusiasts are those project managers who believe that "usability" is a definable and desirable product attribute, or who are prior converts. Cynics need to be convinced that usability will have a positive impact on their bottom line. Panickers are those who realize something is wrong just before they are due to deliver their project.

Panickers do not make good champions. Even if a "usability fix" could be implemented with the minimum of fuss, remember that the further through the life cycle, the more it costs to fix problems, and your aim is to show that usability saves money. Cynics are likely to want rigorous justification for using your services and will seek to show there is none – their projects will not be very good proving grounds for you. Instead, the ideal project to choose is one run by a senior manager with at least some understanding of the "point" of usability, who will allow you to contribute early in the project life cycle. Use this time to introduce usability practices to the developers, run evaluative sessions and produce measurable changes that save money. This will leave the project team singing your praises, as well as giving you hard evidence which you can use as data in the business case.

You will also need grass roots support. Although it may not be something to put in the business case, having the commitment from other teams who want to work with you (such as the helpdesk, market research, technical writers) will add credibility to your case. Getting this commitment is something that you can do whilst approaching these areas for data on cost savings.

Gathering Evidence of Cost Savings for Your Business Case

The aim of a business case is to show that a usability function will reduce time and cost whilst improving quality and customer satisfaction. Time and cost savings are typically tangible. Quality and satisfaction (cost avoidance) are often less quantifiable, so you will need to find ways of measuring them (or the lack of them currently). Organizations will put much more faith in data they can understand, and that tends to be data from inside the organization, or from a close competitor. The data can be broadly split into two types, historical and evaluative.

Gathering Historical Information

Historical information exists in each department of the company. Often this data can be used to identify areas where usability can produce cost savings. Although information from published literature will not be seen in the same light as organization-based statistics, there are many examples of where time or money has been saved that you can attempt to transpose into your company's terms. A good example can be found in Bias and Mayhew's book, *Cost Justifying Usability* [1]. Before you meet with teams whose data you want, use the literature to give you an idea of where costs can be saved. This will enable you to ask the right questions.

Areas within the organization that can provide relevant historical information include:

Helpdesk
- How many calls are there per week for the five most important products?
- What are the top five questions asked? Could these have been prevented through better consideration of tasks, users, environment?
- What anecdotal evidence do helpdesk staff have about product support to which you could apply costs?
- What is the average duration of calls, the cost of staffing the helpdesk, the number of staff?
- How large a reduction in calls would it take to enable a reduction in staff numbers? (This obviously has to be handled sensitively).

Technical Authors
- How long does it take to write documentation (number of days × staff)?
- How much rework do they have because of functional changes?
- How much time and money could they have saved if the product had required less explanation?
- What is the "worst" application they have had to write documentation for?
- How long does it take to train users before they are proficient?
- Which parts of the system do users not understand? Why?

Development Teams
- Can they estimate the time wasted through changes to requirements and speci-fications? Note that this needs careful application in a usability business case.
- What is the cost of a poorly informed development decision? What interface-related issues caused extra work (i.e. lost time, additional cost)?
- For projects which are using bought-in software, what is the cost of choosing the wrong software package? Would user-based evaluation have led to less customization and documentation problems?
- What horror stories can they tell along the lines of "if only we'd known how our users worked...", or "the staff just don't seem to understand this product..."?

Market Research / Customer Service
- For customer-facing systems, how many complaints have there been, what is the nature of complaints, what could have been done to reduce them?
- How many improvements have users been asking for to the product?
- How is this product perceived against its competitors?

Wherever possible, interpret these figures by showing where cost could have been avoided, and where time could have been saved. Where the data is more descriptive than measurable, use it to indicate areas for quality improvement.

Usability is a novel concept to many managers and budget holders. The business case will therefore need to prove benefits in terms to which they can relate, but also using methods where they cannot say "area x does that already". When you ask teams for their statistics, try to gain insights into what they have previously done to overcome user issues, and how well this worked. Whilst you never want to criticize another part of the organization (remember you want supporters, not enemies), it is useful to know what has been tried already, and where it fell short.

Gathering Evaluative Information

Evaluative information is provided by studies of people working with systems. Obviously at this stage, it would be difficult to build and staff a usability lab or run large-scale longitudinal evaluations of a product's usability, but the type of data that you need can be gathered with a much lower-tech approach. By building an informal usability function you are in a position to gather pertinent metrics about products and projects which have salience for the people who will be responsible for agreeing your budget.

This relies upon you having some knowledge of human factors principles. If you have none, work with your supporters to use the project's budget to bring in a contractor or consultant on a short-term basis from whom you can learn whilst performing the evaluative work (see also Chapter 2, Selling Usability Services). Alternatively, there are books such as Nielsen's *Usability Engineering* [2] which describe methods for usability evaluation on a tight budget.

Evaluative information can be gained from end users within the organization. Only do this with the co-operation of the designers of the products being measured and explore relevant issues:

- Per task, per day, per location, how much time could be saved through improving system design? To measure this, take a function that has been identified as sub optimal, and produce a prototype redesign from the users' perspective. Use a stopwatch to measure the time savings for a group of representative users, and then extrapolate the results to the organization as a whole.
- How satisfied are users? How satisfied could they be? Being able to graphically chart satisfaction on scales that management can identify with is easy with a questionnaire such as SUMI [3]. You could just show low satisfaction now, or better still show the increase in satisfaction after usability involvement.

Data from evaluative studies can mainly be described as a potential cost or time saving. Wherever possible, seek the endorsement of managers on the development team in estimating savings, as this will make them harder for others to refute.

Even if it is not a part of the evaluation methodology, consider video recording these evaluations. Not only does this allow business case sponsors to understand better how you intend to work, but it provides data about user problems which is much harder to ignore. Such video footage requires careful control. It would be wise to have someone present who is able to properly interpret the video every time it is shown, to prevent management from blaming users for the faults of the system.

> ### Making Use of Others' Statistics
>
> One of the main data sources for the initial Usability Services business case at NatWest was provided at no cost to the usability team. A large project decided to take its application to an outside company to run a laboratory evaluation. The prospective manager of Usability Services attended as an observer.
>
> Savings made through implementing recommendations from the evaluation paid for the use of the external lab. On the other hand, the charges for the lab were so high it was calculated that if NatWest ran more than three such evaluations in a year, it would be cheaper to bring the function in-house. This formed a central strand to the Usability Services' business case.
>
> Attendance at the external evaluation also provided crucial information on how another company had implemented a usability function. NatWest's lab environment was initially designed with reference to this external setup. Criticisms of the external lab's evaluation methodology by project team members also led to Usability Services seeking a more robust solution for in-house use.

It can be easy to get carried away with figures. Remember that usability is not the comprehensive answer to all the problems of system design. Put the figures you have collected into terms that equate to viable cost savings, given your projected team size. Your team will not be able to impact every project. Choose figures that relate to important projects in the organization. Also remember that not all of the team's time will be spent saving money for the organization. NatWest Usability Services aims for 70 percent utilization on project work. The rest of the time is needed for promotional work, skills development, research, maintenance of equipment and procedures, and administration. This 30 percent non-chargeable time needs to be built into your estimates for cost recovery.

Estimating the Costs Associated with Setup and Maintenance of a Lab and Team

Savings from usability are only relative to the cost of performing usability. If you are operating as a cost centre (not charging projects for your time), then the savings to the project are greater. If you can operate successfully as a profit centre (or at least try to break even) through charging projects for your time then you can prove that people are prepared to pay for your services. As the cost to the organization is the same in both situations, the decision on whether to recover costs from projects directly will depend upon your company's culture.

Profit or Cost Centre Mentality?

NatWest Usability Services currently has a foot in both camps. Projects in the area to which we report can use the service "for free" (actually just for their generic staff rate). Projects in the rest of the organization have to pay a fully absorbed rate (about double the generic resource rate). A full 60 percent of business comes from teams paying the full rate, because using the in-house team is still cheaper for these projects than going to external consultants.

Strangely, putting in requests for small sums of money seems to take almost as much justification as requests for large sums. For this reason, consider everything that you will require through the year and put it into the same business case. That way, when the time comes to attend a conference, to train a staff member or to upgrade a computer application, you can refer back to the initial business case rather than having to justify the expense each time.

Staff Issues

For the business case, the main justifications (other than team size) will be on how staff are to be recruited and how they are to be trained.

- Will staff come from within the organization, or be recruited from outside? If external staff are to be used, will this be on a contract or permanent basis? This will depend to a large degree upon the way in which staff budgets are decided within your organization – for instance, how easy it is to obtain contract staff and what the company policy is regarding recruitment.
- New team members may need basic training in usability methodology, statistics, and also in areas which are indirectly related to usability, such as presentation skills.
- In order for the usability team to be able to offer sensible services and have their results taken seriously by project managers, at least some team members will need a background which includes applied research and use of statistics. Speedy, pragmatic application of scientific theory is the key.
- Remember that the team can cross-train. Individuals with certain areas of expertise can bring other team members up to speed.
- Conferences are excellent places to pick up tips and build networks. In the business case these may come under a catch-all phrase about "attending professional events". Examples would be the British Computer Society Human Computer Interaction conference (BCS-HCI) in the UK (quite academic), the American Computing Machinery Computer Human Interaction conference (ACM CHI) (quite academic) and the Usability Professionals Association (UPA) (more practical) in the USA [4].

It is also important to consider the model you will use when interacting with project teams. Usability staff can either be used as "consultants" or "team members". Usability Services at NatWest work as consultants. This hides a great deal of the real cost of tests since much of the legwork is done by project team members. Working more closely with a team requires deeper and more continual involvement, thus limiting the number of different projects in which usability staff can get involved. The "consultant" label gives power and status to the individual, allowing them to be taken seriously by more senior team members than if they were working as a seconded peer. The downside to the consultant model is that it is more difficult to build rapport and thus gain the teams' trust (see also Chapter 9, Cultivating an Effective Client Relationship to Promote a User-Centred Culture). This can lead to missing out on key discussions. It also makes benefit tracking harder because this requires the co-operation of the team after your formal involvement may have finished. Having to balance several projects at once also makes cost tracking harder.

Accommodation

This is likely to be your second largest cost after staff. Your location and environment can work for you or against you. Although it is possible to make do with a conventional office environment, you are likely to be working with people external to the organization. Your work may be used for marketing purposes. As a public face of the organization, you need a suitable level of comfort and an environment which enhances your professional image. Justification for expenditure over and above the level for office accommodation falls into three main areas:

- Consider your tasks. Moving bulky or heavy items of equipment around means that access to a loading bay and goods lift is useful. NatWest Usability Services took delivery of an ATM (cash machine) which had to be hand-winched up in the goods lift and installed on an inch thick steel plate to spread the load on our suspended floor. Ground floor locations may reduce the requirement to get security clearance for visitors. Access to serviceable toilets and refreshments will be essential.
- Consider your users. You will have representatives of the business and IT sides of the organization coming together for planning meetings and to observe evaluations. You will also want space to greet and "hold" participants, and space for administration.
- Consider your environment. You want people to feel comfortable, but impressed. NatWest Usability Services had a kitchen and so could offer fresh coffee in china mugs. That in itself was a novelty. We would buy biscuits for meetings and evaluations, and bring in sandwiches over lunch times so people could stay and watch. We were intentionally slightly less formal than the rest of the organization, whilst maintaining a professional image.

Equipment

Our first usability test as a team at NatWest used begged and borrowed equipment (see below). Had we needed to continue using this level of equipment, not only would we have got frustrated with the technical limitations, but video logging would have been impossible, and there would have been no way to edit sessions to provide highlight tapes.

Labs on No Budget

Usability equipment need not be expensive. Although we had specified quite high-end evaluation equipment, when we came to do our first in-house usability test, the control room of our lab still looked like some large metal bird had decided to use it as a nesting box.

Some quick scheduling got us three adjoining rooms in another building, one of which had a television and video unit. Some very creative use of the telephone system and several metres of cables purchased from a local electrical store, coupled with the team manager's home video camera, gave us an instant lab. We had a control room/viewer suite, evaluation room and greeting area. Total cost of the additional technology that needed to be purchased was around £30. This all passed through on an expenses claim.

Ensure that the equipment you specify in your business case is modular, multipurpose, high quality, rugged, standards-based and easily maintainable. Modular means both portable and able to work with other units. High quality means at least SVHS standard throughout. Stick with this, even if it means buying only one camera rather than two, or less ancillary gear. Having invested in such high quality equipment, if there is even the vaguest indication that you may be doing on-site evaluations, order flight cases for each item or set of items, and an extra one for all the cables. Flight cases are expensive, but not in comparison to broken SVHS video recorders.

Consider also that:

- High value equipment needs insurance.
- High precision equipment needs maintenance. Consider the relative cost of a planned maintenance contract over calling in technicians when things go wrong. This will depend upon the technical competence you have within the team.
- You may have to replicate the organization's systems in your lab. Often, this equipment can be borrowed for the duration of an evaluation, but ensure that the infrastructure to support it (ISDN telephone lines, strange network configurations etc) exists within your plans.
- Transport costs for performing off-site labs may include van rental to move the lab equipment. If performing international evaluations, these costs will rise dramatically.
- Hardware depreciates over time. It may be wise to lessen the starting cost impact in your business case by spreading equipment costs over three or five years.

A Moveable Feast?

NatWest initially specified a large, fixed usability laboratory with built-in equipment. This was based upon our experiences from using an external company's lab. As we got involved earlier in the development life cycle, we discovered that it was frequently necessary to take the lab to the system rather than vice versa. We ended up buying more equipment – basically a second lab – just to use in the field. Had we thought about this from the beginning, we would have made everything much more portable.

When the usability team moved locations, we left our custom-built studio desk behind. Now all the monitors sit on common office desks and the VCRs and other electronics are bolted on to a plain yet functional industry standard rack. If something breaks, it can be swapped quickly. If it is needed for an on-site evaluation, it is just placed in a flight case and then into the back of a car. If a non-standard setup is required (for instance to evaluate co-operative work environments) then rewiring is simplified.

This does not mean that the fixed lab was a wasted investment. As well as using it for many very successful evaluations, it serves as an excellent showcase for our craft. When conducting lab tours, we always leave the control room until last. People love to play with the mixing desk, and are suitably impressed with the bank of monitors and rows of flashing lights. Frustrating as it may be, this is probably the most concrete image that people can take with them of the work we do.

Unusual Consumables

Consider the products that you will require on a regular basis which you are unlikely to find in the company's stationery store:

- The usability team will get through a lot of SVHS video cassettes. This may not be a common stationery request.
- People coming to observe trials will wander off with paper and pens – these may as well have your section name and telephone number printed on them.
- User rewards are the bribe which you use to get participants in your trials. This can range from chocolate to software and need not be cash. Something vaguely usability-related which can be customized (for instance, keyboard wrist rests) also serves as promotional material.

Whether to put these items in the business case or not will depend upon the structure of your organization. If you know that you will be able to pass them through on normal expenses forms and stationery orders, leave them out of the business case. It is unlikely that the business case sponsors will consider these items.

Other Tools You May Need

The usability team will require non-standard software. A good statistical package, a video logging tool and a contact management database are all important.

You may want to buy professional, normalized questionnaires (e.g. user satisfaction ratings such as SUMI [3]). The cost may be per pack of questionnaires, or an annual licensing fee.

Brochures, posters, flyers, promotional videos and other marketing material are vital tools. Avoid the temptation to order in bulk as a way of saving money – when you move location, change personnel or update your methods, you will be left with several forests worth of scrap paper.

What to Leave Out

This is a long list of things to put into a business case. Think about things that can be left out, for instance, PC costs and some accommodation costs would have existed anyway, especially when using existing staff. Training costs may be offset against an annual training allowance set aside for each staff member. Although a business case may turn into skilful manipulations of the truth in order to get sanction for what you see as an essential service to the organization, do not deceive yourself. Do not overstate cost savings through usability. Do not underestimate the outlay required to get the ball rolling.

Thinking about Where Usability "Fits" in the Organization

If there is a choice, consider to which function usability would most naturally report. You will work with many different areas inside and external to the company, and in most instances you will want to be seen as neutral. Reporting to a person too high up the management structure may mean you do not get the day-to-day support you require, even if you do get the annual budget you requested. Reporting in too low may prevent you from getting the coverage and promotion you desire, even if you are close to the people with whom you will work.

A supportive manager who supports the usability cause is probably more important than one with seniority who ignores the team's efforts. Keeping such a manager informed of what is happening allows them to evangelize on behalf of usability, but watch for fine distinctions between interest and interference; versus indifference and leaving you to get on with things. Managers who show interest, of whatever kind, can be powerful allies.

Your organization may see the IT department anywhere on a continuum from necessary evil through to vital support. You will be working closely with developers, so reporting to the same management team as them may give you credibility in their eyes. On the other hand, it is often the non-IT departments that hold the budgets for work, and in this situation you will need to gain favour with them. NatWest Usability Services has lived in so many different areas of the organization since its inception that the distinction had ceased to matter on a day-to-day basis.

The Physical Setting of Your Usability Function
May Be Determined by Politics

When NatWest Usability Services started, there was a deep division between the "business" and "IT" functions. A decision was made that neutral territory would be the best place to bring developers and business sponsors together. Space was found on the ground floor of a prestigious central location, easily accessible to both groups – unfortunately neither group had reason to be there other than when their product was being evaluated. Thus, enthusiasm was low and the team acquired an "ivory tower" image.

A restructuring meant that suddenly business and IT teams were cohabiting, and after some initial teething troubles they started actually working together. Usability Services' neutral location became a burden. This led to the usability team relocating to the same building as the combined development teams. The new office and lab area are smaller and more spartan, but more in keeping with the type of environment in which our client areas work. These days, brochures are actually taken from wall racks, and people will pop in "just to see what is happening".

Presenting the Case

There is plenty of literature on how to do this properly. Read books on presentation skills. Study business cases that made it through, and emulate their better points. They may be business cases for much more technical items, but if you can reproduce the format then at least the layout, if not the content, will be familiar to your sponsors.

In the run-up to the presentation, ensure you know who all the necessary decision makers are, and that they know about your case. Feel free to give them information about what your team plans to do, but do not pester them. Pestering people is making them work faster than the organization lets them. This is a bad move, as you have then drawn attention to yourself and therefore brought your actions under closer scrutiny than they deserve. It also brands you as a nuisance rather than a team player.

Reasons Why Decision-makers May Not Be Persuaded by a Business Case

- They do not know what you do: "I haven't heard of them, so they can't be important." Make sure that your supporters have contacted every stakeholder. If the supporters cannot do so, maybe you can.
- They do not "get" the idea behind usability: "Users don't know what is good for them, we're the experts so we have to design the products for them." Unfortunately there is no quick response to such attitudes, so do not waste time

trying. Just smile and talk to their direct reports, one of whom is likely to replace the dinosaur sometime soon.

- An example project that you use in your business case is their "baby" – the project which they fought for and nurtured through its early months – and you are ripping it to pieces, embarrassing them along the way. It is always important to emphasize the good points that arise from an evaluation alongside the issues. Also, emphasizing the fact that usability professionals work with a development team to prevent issues arising rather than being the quality police at the end of the project is important. There are times when usability evaluations can prevent the team from costly rework, thus saving the project manager time and money.
- They are openly antagonistic. Is this their problem or yours? Maybe it is just a personality clash, in which case another proponent of usability may be able to talk to them. Maybe they have a vested interest in preventing usability, in which case you need to understand their concern and either work with them or make sure their gripe is laughably petty in the eyes of your sponsors.

Before the date, rehearse, rehearse, rehearse. Practise in front of your senior manager and tailor your message to other business case sponsors. In the meeting, ensure that you really get across what usability means to the organization. Do not leave it up to the business case sponsors to form their own opinions. Use two or three key messages that say how usability will improve the company. Be aware of their comprehension level and adjust your presentation accordingly.

That Is Just the Beginning...

The business case *promises* cost savings, but does not *prove* them. Next you have to find ways of measuring your success (and managing your failures) so that your track record speaks for you.

People and policies within the organization change with alarming frequency. NatWest Usability Services' management structure has changed at least five times in three years. During that time there have been three separate in-house development methodologies and two major departmental reorganizations. Being ready with up-to-date statistics to paste into a marketing brochure or a presentation to your new senior manager will save you time when you least have any. Take this advice from someone who was not prepared.

Measure and Monitor

- Use a profit centre mentality. Even if you are a free resource, track your costs as if you were receiving a notional sum per team member per day. This will help you focus on the value of your input to the projects on which you work.
- Always be in a position to give status reports to your managers and to the project teams with whom you work. Sudden changes in organizational direction or structure can cause people to re-evaluate the need for your involvement. Rapid response with statistics which prove your worth to the team, including

quotes from team members, major recommendations and cost savings to date, will head these threats off before they become serious problems.

- Track from a personal perspective too. Performance reviews for usability professionals are unlikely to be measurable on normal scales. You will need all the data you can get to prove you have done well.
- Under promise, over deliver. This is a great way of ensuring good feedback from projects. Make written proposals for the work that you will carry out, and then ask for satisfaction ratings against these proposals.
- Track the company's products in the marketplace. Build relationships with marketing and market research teams. Cut out newspaper articles, trade reviews. Show where your involvement made a difference.
- Measurement is an overhead for your team. Get projects to measure and track results of changes due to usability evaluation is difficult, as they will not have a structure for doing so. You have to make them see how having this data benefits themselves as well as helping you.

Promote Awareness and Build Demand

If projects can use you as a free resource today, just wait until the next organizational reshuffle. How many of your current clients would continue to make use of you if they had to pay? How can you ensure their repeat business? The answer is to market yourselves to them. It is also important to keep awareness of your services high amongst your direct managers and in the organization as a whole. Line managers are useful as evangelists to their peers – a group of people you may have more trouble gaining access to.

- Keep a list of projects that you want to be involved in, and target them specifically. At the same time use a scatter-gun approach through newsletters. Remember the newsletter is still a business case, just with a different focus.
- Carry out short-term, unprofitable work in areas where you have identified a need to gain entry and long-term commitment.
- Give open invitation seminars/presentations on usability findings in conjunction with the project team. Making it entertaining can draw lunchtime audiences.
- Human factors training courses offered to employees by members of the team are good for grassroots support – people attending the course will evangelize to their teams.
- Build people's confidence in your ability as a team – a background in or an understanding of development team practices helps. Speak the client's language.
- Show how professional you are – having a recognized methodology helps (NatWest Usability Services used the National Physical Laboratory's MUSiC methodology [5]), but remember this is real life, not academia. Do *not* rest on academic laurels. Letters after your name tend not to mean much to development project leaders. Capacity to reduce their development costs and timescales do.

- Encourage people to phone or email the team with usability questions. These are often the tip of a large usability iceberg, which can lead to major involvement.
- When developers and team leaders come to you with work requests, work with them on a day-to-day level, but also get them to introduce you to the project sponsor at an opportune time. This is the person who will promote your services more widely.
- Keep track of who you work with in some form of contact management database. If your contact moves on, get them to introduce you to their successor. Now you have two client areas for the price of one.
- NatWest Usability Services aims for a mix of 60 percent repeat business, 40 percent new. Getting repeat business means keeping track of where your clients are in their development cycle and chasing them at points where you perceive benefit in your involvement.
- Keep a library of the edited highlight tapes that you have produced for your projects. Use the tapes to show potential clients how users can really suffer, and how usability helped.

Selling Yourself

NatWest Usability Services made a professional quality video to sell its services to a wider audience. Usability staff asked the project managers on three well known, high priority projects which had received input from usability to appear in the video. Each of them was given an idea of what to say, then they ad-libbed in front of the camera. The result was a set of short, sincere soundbites from people who were easily identified as NatWest staff. Only one of the three came from a technical background, the other two were from the business side of the development process.

The video paid for itself very quickly. It has also proved useful when shown to the long procession of senior managers who have inherited responsibility for Usability Services. There is a noticeable lightening of their mood when they begin to understand the services that we offer and see that there are people in the business who actually want to use this strange group.

Take Stock

Monitor where you are heading in comparison with your goals. NatWest Usability Services started with an "evaluation" focus rather than "engineering" or "solution delivery". At that time, we were definitely better equipped to test than to provide design assistance. However, there were problems gaining entry early in the product life cycle as the organization's perception of testing was at the end of a waterfall development life cycle. The team got themselves training in "softer" usability skills (contextual inquiry, running focus groups) and changed marketing direction in order to gain earlier involvement and thus show greater cost savings.

We also re-evaluated the MUSiC methodology [5] that we had bought in from the National Physical Laboratory in order to reduce quotes to projects from 30–40 days involvement for a three-day evaluation down to 10–15 days for a two-day evaluation without a noticeable drop in the number or quality of usability issues found. We managed this saving by taking a more pragmatic approach to understanding the project's background, and through developing better relationships with projects, such that participants could take on some of the preparatory tasks themselves, under our guidance. This is something that will only come after time spent working with and gaining feedback from project areas.

We used a consultant model for our project involvement, but some of the more innovative design projects that we have been involved in have needed more frequent and in-depth attention. Creative sessions are not limited to weekly team meetings. Project members want more frequent access to a usability specialist, and more frequent tests. This has led to changes in charging and working structures for some staff members. The team has learned to be more flexible in the length, depth and type of involvement they offer.

Pragmatic Management: "Slipping Things Through"

When NatWest Usability Services moved location, the initial business case for a lab facility and separate office space was turned down. We realized that we still needed to move closer to the developers upon whom we depended, and so re-scoped our plans to move just the team into the building where the developers were mainly based, relying on portable equipment for our evaluations.

Ironically, the office space that we were offered was in the location we had previously identified as ideal for the lab. Rather than building a new business case, we just worked with the influential people in the move (property management and accommodation representatives) to ensure that the office space included a large storage room and a meeting room, with a venetian blind hiding a one-way mirror between the two. Miraculously the lab equipment appeared in the "store" room, and the cameras and microphones found themselves set up in the meeting room.

By not formally informing the management structure of our plans, management could formally ignore them whilst afterwards being able to praise us, and accept praise themselves, for moving the lab and team across on such a tight budget.

Making a Business Case for Usability: Lessons Learned

When preparing a business case:

- Get influential supporters, but remember that influence is not necessarily linked to status. Use your supporters' projects to gather data and sneak in some evaluative work to gain examples from within the organization before you prepare your business case.

- Build statistical evidence by finding information from other areas of the organization which show how money could be saved through better design, and strengthen this by knowing how much your team and their tools will cost.
- Find a home – a physical location as well as a political haven!
- Stick to a few key benefits (let the document do the rest).

Once established, keep moving:

- Measure your performance through satisfaction questionnaires and by gleaning information from project teams on how much time/money you are saving them.
- Promote your services through tours and publicity.
- Take stock at regular intervals to see whether you are achieving your goals.

Resources / References

[1] R.G. Bias and D.J. Mayhew (eds.) (1993) Cost-Justifying Usability, Academic Press, Boston, MA.
[2] J. Nielsen (1993) Usability Engineering, Academic Press, Cambridge, MA.
[3] M. Porteous, J. Kirakowski and M. Corbett (1993) The SUMI User Handbook, Human Factors Research Group, University College, Cork.
[4] Web sites for conferences and associations: information on the British Computer Society Human Computer Interaction Conference (BCS-HCI) is at http://www.bcs.org.uk; information on the American Computing Machinery Computer Human Interaction Conference (ACM CHI) is at http://www.acm.org/sigchi; information about the Usability Professionals Association (UPA) and their conference is at http://www.upassoc.org.
[5] Esprit MUSiC Project led by the National Physical Laboratory. R. Rengger, M. Macleod, R. Bowden, A. Drynan and M. Blayney (1993) MUSiC Performance Measurement Handbook, V2, NPL, DITC, Teddington, UK.

2. *Selling Usability Services*

Dermot Browne

ABSTRACT

This chapter discusses the issue of how to sell usability services. While selling is often considered a dirty word it is a necessary activity for usability professionals, be they salaried or self-employed, who believe in the value of their work. This chapter is aimed at both the usability professional and the potential recipients of usability services. The best consultancy assignments are those where each party understands the motives and limitations of the other and where business is conducted in an open and responsive manner. The earliest of meetings between consultant and client set the standard for their subsequent relations and this is why these meetings are so important. This chapter discusses these first meetings and provides a perspective on how a usability consultant should aim to influence these meetings towards a productive conclusion.

Introduction

It is widely acknowledged that usability is a determinant of application development success. There appears to be a growing realization that achieving usability, in the widest sense, is a major factor in determining competitiveness. It is not only about whether an organization achieves usability, but also how quickly it can deliver usability engineered tools and business applications compared with its major competitors, that determines business performance.

There is inevitably a shortage of relevant skills and awareness of how to make the most of new practices and technologies during the early years of their introduction. This is certainly true of modern interactive technologies and, specifically, the usability engineering of such technology. For many years academics and a few industrialists have waxed lyrical about the need for more usable IT. However there have been and still are very few usability practitioners given the amount of work that needs to be done. Nonetheless, it is not always obvious that usability needs to be on the business agenda.

Senior management in organizations, are at the end of the day the people who make things happen. If these business people remain oblivious or unconcerned for usability and its importance then usability engineering will remain largely unpractised. Therefore awareness must be raised among these individuals; the case for usability must be made and made unequivocally. It is relatively recently that the "green screen character-based interface" has been superseded by the graphical user interface (GUI) as the choice for bespoke and packaged developments. This is an important trend because the issue of usability was comparatively straight-forward prior to the emergence of the GUI. This is something of a paradox given that the prime purpose of this technology is to facilitate usability, and yet the rich design space offered by GUIs makes it easier for developers to deliver applications that under-perform in terms of usability.

GUI development is now the rule rather than the exception. Microsoft reputedly involved 10,000 users in 30 rounds of usability testing during the development of Windows 95. Business users have come to appreciate the potential of GUIs and are making demands of developers in ways never previously experienced. As a conse-quence developers are having to take a much more user-centric approach and are judged by the usability of their deliverables. Working with users instead of for users and having one's success judged in terms of usability means that develop-ment teams must change their practices. This is a long awaited and positive trend.

Selling usability has always been a Sisyphean task, but although demand is growing there is still a marketing and selling job to be done. Budgets and demand-ing timescales mean that usability practices must be justified. Potential sponsors need to be sold. They need to appreciate what they will get for their money before they buy into usability practices. They will not divert funds from existing practices unless they have faith in the ability of the consultant to deliver and can see the business sense. This chapter addresses this issue of selling and buying usability consultancy and considers whether it should come from an internal or external source. It is not about how to deceive a cheque book holder but about how to create a client-consultant relationship that is rewarding for both parties.

It could be argued that usability practices should be an internal resource in organizations. In some circumstances having permanent staff specializing in this discipline may well be both practical and desirable. For instance, many of the larger Corporations in the United States do retain specialist Human Factors groups to support software development projects. Wiklund provides descriptions of Human Factors groups operating in many organizations including Ameritech, American Airlines and Kodak [1]. It can often be difficult, however, for an organi-zation, particularly a small to medium-sized one to justify a Human Factors group. Budgets for such groups may be centrally provided and justified or in some circumstances the existence of such groups can be dependent on their selling services to other groups. Whichever of these is the case the continued existence of such groups is inevitably dependent on their impact and perceived value.

For many organizations a more cost-effective option is to obtain the services of Human Factors professionals as and when required. This is important from a Human Factors perspective as it means that to provide consultancy in this area means it has to be seen as a specialism and not something that any IT professional could undertake. There is a broader view too – why should organizations concern themselves with usability, what price can be put on usability and how is it best understood as a project issue?

The First Meeting

This section provides a discussion of the issues that arise once consultant and potential client begin to talk. What follows assumes that the usability professional is ethical and wants to sell useful services and not simply use "usability" as a banner to generate revenues.

Marketing

Marketing is the identification of a need and matching that need with a service or product and creating an opportunity for buyer and seller to meet and do business. To quote Hugh Davidson:

> "The oldest profession in the world used classic marketing techniques: it identified and satisfied a need; it created a market where buyer and seller could meet, in the form of a brothel; and it turned a handsome profit on the operation.
>
> Buying a present for your spouse is also a marketing operation. You try to establish what would please him or her through knowledge of tastes, observation of needs and subtle questioning. Then you sift through this mass of data and select an item which you believe would be most liked and which you can afford." [2]

For many IT consultants and consultancies the issue of direct marketing is over once a meeting has been achieved with a client. Often the IT consultant has been invited to a meeting because the client knows that they need a team of C++ programmers, or they need a new IT strategy, or a colleague recommended them. The IT consultant in this circumstance is largely acting in the role of salesperson; pointing out how reliable, cost-effective, flexible and so forth their services are compared with those of potential unnamed competitors. At this point, the client's main question is:

"So What Can You Do for Me?"

This is a very difficult question. If the consultant aims to answer this question too soon they will probably be shown the door. In the early stages of a meeting this question is best left unanswered or at least responded to with another question or battery of questions. However, all too often the immediate response is "we do usability engineering". Think about this for a moment and try and put yourself in the client's shoes. Do you think this is likely to be met with a favourable reaction? Do they even know what usability engineering is? Human Factors practitioners are supposed to be good at seeing problems from other persons' perspectives yet all too often we fail to market ourselves.

An important rule of selling usability services, and most services, has to be "understand the context in which you are marketing". For example, you are unlikely to be successful in selling task analysis services into a project that believes it has completed the most comprehensive requirements analysis in living memory.

So what does the usability professional need to know? The following discussion offers a flavour of the facts that can be influential. You want to find out why the client has even deigned to speak with you; what pressures this person is working under; are you talking to the most appropriate person; and what relevant areas do they have responsibility for.

Why Are You Having This Meeting?

A basic piece of information you need is why you are talking to this client. Assuming that you have never worked for this client then a lot can be learned from understanding why you have been granted a meeting. The person may have heard good things about you or your company, may have searched for a particular type of service and stumbled across some of your marketing material, or you may have requested the meeting. During one meeting it became apparent that the client had called the meeting following a meeting with another consultant who had spoken about a structured approach to user interface design. This fact was highly influential on the meeting, especially given that most clients at the time were disenchanted with structured approaches. If you know what aspect of your marketing material, or which phrase, or which facet of a previous encounter has opened the door for this meeting, this can help you direct the meeting.

What Pressures Is This Person Working Under?

If the meeting is to lead to a successful conclusion then you will probably be talking to someone of influence: a manager. Over recent years middle and senior management have come under increased pressure to perform. Focus on what is important and what pressures they are under. For instance, there is often an uneasy tension between speed and quality of delivery on projects. If this is understood then it should make it easier to pitch usability services. Where speed of delivery is paramount then the issue of whether usability services will slow progress will need to be addressed head on.

Who Are You Talking to and What Is Their Hidden Agenda?

Meetings may take place where you are not talking to the most appropriate person or people. It is not untypical to be in a situation of promoting your services to an IT Director or Programme Manager, when in fact you should be talking to a Business Manager or end-user representative. You may be having the meeting because of pressure that has been brought to bear by the business, yet the business is not represented. You may be being used simply as a pawn in other people's games. You may be posed a series of questions by the IT Director such as: "are you trying to say that my staff cannot design user interfaces?", and "what benefits did you achieve in your last assignment?" or "how well do you know our business?". Good homework can help you to answer some of these questions but it may be the case that you are being used by the IT Director to show the Marketing Director that user concerns are unfounded and that pleas from Marketing to spend more on usability cannot be justified.

What Responsibilities Does Your Contact Have?

Insights can be gained from a knowledge of the responsibilities that a person has. For instance, the motivations and drives of a person responsible for the quality of a system are often very different to those of a Programme Manager. If you understand what motivates your contact you can more accurately pitch the importance of usability and what it can achieve. To market usability you must talk in terms that are both familiar and important to the other party. A Quality Manager may want to be reassured that usability is an issue that can be quantified and planned for, whereas a Programme Manager is more likely to be interested in how usability services will impact a project plan. This is not to say that you would sell a different set of services – it is just a matter of how you market those services.

Marketing: The Broader Context

So you think you have understood the situation; but have you? You understand the motivations of the individuals you are talking to, but what about the context in which you might be asked to operate? To sell your services successfully, you need to know the context of the project under discussion. Important factors include: the skills available, existing development practices, available resources and, of course, politics.

The Skills Available

The team you may be asked to work with may have a little or a lot of knowledge of usability. Given that you may be asked to assess their work, your dealings with them will need to be conducted appropriately. This relates to one of the basic skills of consultancy and is treated in more detail in Nichole Simpson's chapter in this volume. However, suffice to say that in your negotiations and marketing of your services it is prudent to understand as best you can the skills of the team members with whom you might be working. Your counterpart may expect you to investigate this area as evidence that you are not going to steamroll the team and that you can demonstrate tact and diplomacy. There is always a risk in introducing new faces to a team and your counterpart will often want evidence that this risk is small.

Existing Development Practices

Working practices are also an important aspect of the situation you may be entering. For instance, some organizations now practise Rapid Application Development (RAD) while for others structured development approaches are ingrained and accepted. Whichever is the case, usability services must blend in. For instance, where RAD is practised it is unlikely that traditional task analytic methods will be acceptable or indeed that full-scale documentation will be tolerated. However, it should not be forgotten that current practices may have been imposed and may not be receiving the full support of your potential sponsor. You may be wise to keep quiet or even be mildly sceptical of certain practices.

Available Resources

To work effectively, usability professionals need resources. Chief amongst these is access to users but others such as space and hands-on access to prototypes are also required. Lack of resources is a potential obstacle to being able to deliver an assignment and therefore should be discussed even during the earliest negotiations for feasibility. A particularly pertinent example is where an organization has its own usability laboratory. This may be very useful to you during an assignment but can also be a political minefield. Your sponsor may have a negative attitude to this facility because it has been paid for from his/her budget and yet it has received little, if any, use. It may be that this can be turned to advantage by pointing out how valuable this resource will be during the assignment even to the extent of using it for demonstrations and for political advantage during development.

Inevitably the most critical resource will be prospective users. Usability professionals understand the importance of user involvement, but project sponsors, to this day, may not. Users are still often seen as the enemy and kept as far away from projects as possible. If you can appreciate the prevailing climate then you will be better able to address the issue of user involvement.

Politics

In most circumstances there will be influences from past projects. Good and bad precedents will have been set. Again if these influences can be understood then potential pitfalls can be avoided and successes may be built on. For instance, the last project might have been seen as a huge success by all concerned except the users. This might still be being felt in terms of the costs associated with help desk support, requests for greater accountability, moves towards the business servicing its own IT requirements and so forth. In such a circumstance there may be a great opportunity to sell usability services. However, you will not know this unless you ask the right questions and understand the situation.

What about the Project?

So now you know a great deal. Surely now you can start selling your services? Almost – but we still do not know:

- how large or complex the project is;
- how large or diverse the user population is;
- what stage the project has reached;
- how important usability is;
- what the delivery timescale is;
- what the business wants from the project.

Project Size and Complexity

How much work will you have to do? You may not need to know about network architectures, communications protocols and the like, but you will need to know the extent of the interface design to which you may contribute. Projects vary in the amount of usability work that is required. Some may only amount to designing a single screen while others may require the development of tens or hundreds of screens. The complexity of individual screens varies enormously. While there is no recognized method for establishing the complexity of a design, the consultant must gain some appreciation of the scale of the problem. The difference between re-designing the interface of an automatic teller machine in order to add an extra function compared with designing a multi-lingual messaging system for an international conference is enormous.

User Population

How could a usability consultant ever forget their users? It is not simply the number of users that is important, it is also the variety of user roles and experience, and availability of users. It is important to know whether the users are going to be available to you. For instance, an assignment might be to provide a user interface design to enable neurosurgeons to obtain expert advice while performing an operation. Another might be to design an interface for use by the general public and another might be a design for a captive audience of clerical staff employed by the company directly. Each of these poses different problems in terms of resources that will be required and likely delivery timescales.

Project Status

It will also be important to appreciate the stage the project has reached. Usability consultants generally want to be involved in projects from the outset. However, this often does not occur and the consultant's impact is severely restricted. It might be too late to perform a complete task analysis or any analysis whatsoever. It may even be too late to contribute to the design. There is no point trying to market services that a project would be unable to accommodate. The limitations of your assignment should be made clear to all concerned.

How Much of an Issue Is Usability?

It is easy to assume that usability must always be of the highest quality – this is a mistake often made by usability consultants. The bottom line is that a system needs to be as usable as can be cost-justified. To be extreme, there is no point in suggesting a spend of £100,000 on usability activities when the estimated value of the project will only be £100,000. Usability activities must be commensurate with the amount of value they will provide to the business. Again this is not an exact science but estimates should be guided by an appreciation of the value of usability to the overall project. Some good insights can be had from an understanding of why the project is being performed, what the prospective users expect from the project and what competitors are offering. For instance, you might ask about the existing system (manual or automated) and why it is being replaced. Of course the prospective size of the user population and how much time they can be expected to spend in training and having hands-on experience of the system will also indicate the importance of usability to the overall success of the project.

When Must it Be Delivered?

The project will have deadlines and these may well be imposed on your input. The development team may be awaiting interface designs. The go-live date for the system may be cast in stone. Whatever the situation, there is no point in trying to market services of a scale that is not feasible.

Identifying the Need for Usability

So now we know the situation, it must be the right time to start selling. Wrong. As Davidson's definition stated:

> "Marketing is the identification of a need and matching that need with a service or product and creating an opportunity for buyer and seller to meet and do business."

And we still do not know what the **need** is. For there to be a need there has to be a problem or an issue. Sometimes, with respect to usability, the problem can be straightforward, such as: "our development approach requires us to perform a usability analysis and we don't have the resources", or "we've demonstrated the prototype to the users and they say it is worse than the existing system". Far more frequent are those occasions where the problem is not couched in such obvious usability speak.

Defining the Problem in Business Terms

For years, academics and usability professionals have been shouting that systems are just not usable enough. But what does this mean? Where is the problem in that statement? The problem needs to be couched in terms that have meaning for the receiver of the message. This is where the crux of most failed usability sales resides. The problem is not sufficiently well understood at the outset. Sometimes there may be no problem. When there is a small user community, or a simple system, or an obvious design then there may be no usability issue. Any sensible person, with no specialist expertise, could design a usable solution to a simple problem.

Where is the will to make a system usable? Who cares if a system is not user friendly, not intuitive, or not easy to use? Tell a project or programme manager that you can make a system easy to use and they will say "so what?". To a business, what matters is that the system makes the business more effective. The things that matter to most businesses are the same things that matter to their shareholders. That is, facets of the business that contribute to the profitability of the business. The simple point is that if a usability consultant wants to make a sale then it is best to stop talking about ease of use or friendliness and talk about the needs of the business. Of course to do this, you first need to know what the needs of the business actually are. Therefore you have to ask questions such as "What does the business expect to achieve through the current project?" A few of the many possible answers are:

- reduce reconciliation costs – it may wish to make fewer mistakes so that the costs associated with rectifying mistakes are reduced;
- increase efficiency – it may wish to create more products using less effort, or create the same volume of product at a cheaper cost;
- shorten delivery times – it may wish to get products to market more quickly;
- reduce training costs – it may wish to reduce training costs associated with the existing system or anticipated for the new.

These are just a few of the types of business needs that may be encountered. Once the business need(s) has been identified it begins to make sense to talk about usability. The fact is, and this is often forgotten, that business benefits will not be achieved through the introduction of a new system unless the usability of that system has been assured.

For a system to deliver the benefits expected of it, it must demonstrate certain qualities to a required standard. Quality is achieved at a price and that price must be commensurate with the benefits to be achieved (the subject of making a business case to justify the adoption of user-centred practices is well addressed by Bias and Mayhew [3]; see also Chapter 1, Making a Business Case). The point is that usability must be seen as an enabler to achieving business benefits.

Relationship between Business Benefits and Technology

If a business wants to be more productive then it must enable its staff to be more productive and this means giving them better support including more usable tools. If a business wants to reduce mistakes one way of achieving this is to introduce more usable systems. This begs the question "what is usability?" The phrases "ease of use", "user friendly", and "intuitive" are often bandied about as descriptions for usable systems. However, this is problematic as these are neither measurable qualities nor qualities that businesses care about. A usability consultant's progress and ultimate success cannot be gauged against a measure as ill-defined as "friendliness". What is required are reliable and valid measures such as the length of time it takes a user to complete standard tasks, or the length of time new staff have to spend in training before they meet a predetermined level of performance. Such measures can in turn be used to assess the effect of these improvements for the business. For instance, if 1000 users will, as a result of usability engineering activities, be able to save one hour on training, and each person's time is worth £20 an hour, then the benefit is a £20,000 saving. Such figures are of interest to business. In most sales situations the consultant is best advised to forget friendliness and concentrate on business.

Gaining an understanding of the business objectives of a project is essential in order to set objectives and priorities for a usability assignment. By way of example Table 2.1 suggests some of the activities that will be important given particular business objectives.

Table 2.1 Impact of business objectives on usability activities

Business objective	User-centric activities implied
Efficiency improvements	Analysis of business processes Job design Task allocation
Error reduction	Critical incident analysis Task design Screen and forms design
Reduced training costs	Training needs analysis User documentation production Analysis of existing systems

There is no formula for planning user-centred design activities. Rather the usability consultant must be driven by the needs of the business in determining the most appropriate approach to take. And this approach must also be tempered by the prevailing situational factors as discussed earlier.

Matching the Usability Service to the Buyer

If you have obtained the contextual information discussed previously and understand what is required as well as the business drivers, then you are well placed to make a proposal of consultancy services. However, even at the stage where you know the situation and the problem faced by the potential buyer there is still an amount of marketing to be done. To use Davidson's quote one last time:

> "Marketing is the identification of a need and matching that need with a service or product and creating an opportunity for buyer and seller to meet and do business."

We still have to match the usability service to the needs of the potential buyer. For instance, there will be no value in offering a full usability service incorporating a full task analysis, design and usability engineering into a project where user input is not feasible and the project must deliver in two weeks' time. At such a stage of a project the best you could probably hope for would be to conduct an expert evaluation and offer a guiding hand. As with any consulting assignment it is important that you are clear about what you are offering and what it is practical to expect to achieve.

In matching your offering to the needs of the project and the business it is incumbent on you to be realistic regarding what is practical and achievable. Attaining this match is one of the greatest skills of a consultant. Some basic rules apply. When any or a number of the following are true then the case for usability services is greatest:

- a large prospective user population;
- a complex system, in terms of variety and volume of dialogues;
- a marked business need for a highly usable system because of, e.g., a discerning user population;

- a project in its infancy;
- a positive attitude to user involvement;
- high-level involvement and commitment from the business.

Lessons Learned

This chapter has described some of the main determinants of successful usability services selling from the author's experience. It is no easy task. From our experiences, key lessons are:

- Successful selling requires a diverse range of skills, and in particular, good marketing capabilities.
- Understand the context into which you are selling including the motivations of your potential sponsor and the particulars of the project in question.
- Comprehend the business objectives for the project and accurately match your services to the requirements.

Good, ethical consultancy is about matching your services to the needs of the business paying for those services. If this match can be defined and assignments can be delivered as proposed and intended, with clearly beneficial results, then there is every possibility that a rewarding client-consultant relationship will result.

References

[1] M.E. Wiklund (ed.) (1994) *Usability in Practice: How Companies Develop User-Friendly Products*, Academic Press, Boston, MA.
[2] H. Davidson (1972) *Offensive Marketing*, Penguin, Harmondsworth.
[3] R.G. Bias and D.J. Mayhew (eds.) (1993) *Cost-Justifying Usability*, Academic Press, Boston, MA.

Part 2

*The Politics of Set Up: What to Do with the
Money once You Have Got it*

3. *Overcoming Inertia within a Large Organization*

How to Overcome Resistance to Usability

Tasnim Kaderbhai

ABSTRACT

Introducing usability to an organization is a political issue. This chapter provides a case study of how a large pharmaceutical company tried to introduce usability to its IT division. It describes the attempts made by a newly formed "Usability Group" to raise awareness, influence management and IT staff and change working practices, and identifies where opposition or resistance was encountered. It concludes by summarizing which initiatives were most effective in breaking down the inertia, highlighting the need for usability to become "institutionalized".

Introduction

Many organizations have tried to get on the "usability bandwagon", but once on board do not seem to move anywhere. This chapter examines some of the factors to which this inertia can be attributed and why, even where organizations have usability enthusiasts and experts, usability is not placed high on the agenda. Many Human Computer Interaction (HCI) methodologies, tools and techniques have been proposed by academics for use during project development. Unfortunately, their uptake has been slow in organizations, and the systems being produced today often do not include usability as part of the project development life cycle.

Managers are aware that the quality of end-user computing can play a critical role in the operation of organizations. In the "big picture" they can also affect the organization's ability to respond to competitive demands. The reason often given for not considering usability is the difficulty in making a business case for it (see Chapter 1, Making a Business Case for Usability). The pressure to reduce development time and to make cost-benefit justifications also seem to be contributing problems. Although this may be true, the usability issue is not just a matter of designing usable systems, but of user awareness, developer commitment, technical infrastructure and organizational support. All these factors have a big role to play in reducing inertia.

Usability can be described as a value-adding process, but what does this mean in terms of actual benefits to the business? It is hard to answer this question categorically. Managers often want proof that addressing usability issues will produce quantifiable business returns, for example, by reducing costs or increasing profits. However, some of the more common types of usability benefits are often seen as "soft", for example, increasing user productivity by reducing errors, reducing training and support requirements. Other examples include increased user confidence and greater organizational flexibility since users can deploy their skills on different applications.

This chapter is based on research into HCI within organizations and on findings from a company which has taken the first steps in trying to make usability an issue. The case study is based in the IT division of the pharmaceutical company, Glaxo R&D UK. (The research for this chapter was carried out in 1996. The company is now GlaxoWellcome R&D – see Chapter 10 for details of how usability evolved and became international within the corporation.) The main theme addressed by this chapter is an exploration of how the notion of usability grew within the organization. It covers the following areas:

- Identifying the main organizational factors faced by the Usability Group in trying to promote usability issues within the company and making it a part of systems development.
- Finding out the attitudes of developers in the IT Division and also how successfully usability ideas filtered out into the Division.
- Investigating the degree of management awareness, encouragement and support of activities directed at improving the usability of computer systems in the organization.

Usability in Industry

Usability can still be regarded as an innovative idea within most organizations even though research, and indeed practice, have been in existence for several years. As with any innovation, it has to be compatible with the organization and the people within the organization. Any company that is going to adopt the practice of usability must be prepared to support its IT developers. This does not just mean financial support, but also encouragement to practise usability and learn more about it.

In many companies, usability has been the concern of a few human factors specialists, or has been taken up by a "usability champion". This has led to methods for improving usability to be supply-pushed by "experts", rather than demand-pulled by developers and end users. Until this balance shifts, usability in organizations will change but slowly however favourable other organizational factors may be. If there is no interest amongst users, developers and management, all usability speak will fall on deaf ears. So, no matter how much company support there is for usability, until it is demand-pulled by the other stakeholders in the organization, it will be performed half-heartedly and the benefits will not emerge.

The Case Study

The Usability Group at Glaxo R&D, UK (Glaxo) consisted at the time of 12 members of the IT division who had some interest in or knowledge of usability. They were given the backing of a senior manager willing to give this group of enthusiasts a chance. At the time of the case study, the Usability Group had been in existence for over a year and had made various efforts to promote the usability issue to users, developers and managers.

The main reason for the formation of the Usability Group was that usability issues were recognized as becoming more important, especially with the increase in GUI development. The Usability Group's main objective was to make the organization's computer systems more usable and the following goals were set at the Group's inception:

- to learn about all aspects of usability;
- to become a centre of expertise;
- to promote the concept of usability;
- to build usability into the design cycle.

I carried out my research in two out of the four departments in the IT Division. From now on these will be referred to as Department X and Department Y. Department X supported the research side of the business and was more flexible and open to innovative ideas because of this. Department Y supported a side of the business that had strict regulations to adhere to and was therefore less willing to innovate.

It was very encouraging to hear support for usability from the manager of Department X. His understanding of usability was that "usability depends on a whole variety of things. It is the totality of the service that we provide to our users, not just the interface design, but also how we provide support". One Usability Group member commented that, at the start: "we did not know what we were letting ourselves in for. We just thought it was a good idea." However, it takes far more effort to make usability an issue than just the formation of a usability group keen to address the problems!

How Usability Was Promoted

Usability Lecture

A usability lecture was used to launch the usability awareness campaign and was attended by over 80 employees from throughout the company. A usability expert from the Open University explained that usable information technology means productive information technology. He referred to case studies where the redesign of user interfaces had significantly reduced transaction times, error rates, and time spent on training. The lecture helped raise usability awareness throughout the organization and especially to the IT division.

Usability in Practice Workshop

The usability workshops were attended by a total of 37 people, mainly from the IT division. The purpose was to educate developers and managers on how to make usability work in practice. It tried to provide practical ideas about how to "do" usability and most developers thought these were workable within the project development life cycle.

The Benefits of Usability as Seen by the Organization

At the start of the case study I interviewed many members of the organization about what they considered to be the main benefits of "doing usability". One senior manager said, "the main business benefit is to produce systems that users want to use. In the past, systems have been produced that users have had to use." A Usability Group member said the main benefit is that "users will like it". These answers were representative of everyone interviewed. They showed that the organization placed great importance on the user, and an understanding that if the users were happy, it would be advantageous to the business. In the long term it could ultimately mean better productivity through reduced support and maintenance. However, no one placed any emphasis on possible financial savings.

Organizational Factors Affecting Attitudes towards Usability

There are many organizational factors that can affect usability within organizations. Early research indicated that those listed below would be of possible relevance to Glaxo:

- cost-benefit justification;
- time constraints;
- management support;
- attitudes of developers;
- user proximity;
- political issues regarding the usability group;
- usability – supply-pushed versus demand-pulled.

I investigated the extent to which each of these factors was playing its part in the uptake of usability at Glaxo by means of a survey of IT developers and through interviews with senior IT management. In the survey, developers were asked to state their attitudes on a scale of strongly agree, agree, unsure, disagree and strongly disagree, for a variety of statements. An overwhelming majority disagreed with the statement "*no one has complained about usability in the past, so why is there a need to start now?*". It was encouraging to get such results as this indicated that although the take-up of usability within the organization was slow, there was support for it. In general, the developers favoured bringing usability issues into the organization. (Statements presented for comment in the survey are italicized in the following sections.)

Cost–Benefit Justifications

The interviews and survey both echoed the same view – that usability benefits cannot be measured in monetary terms, but in terms of user satisfaction. The manager of Department X said that by having a usable system you could achieve monetary savings in maintenance and support. However, the case study showed that even those already "sold" on the benefits of usability recognized that although financial benefits could be gained, these were not readily quantifiable.

In contrast, the manager of Department Y said that he felt a cost–benefit analysis was necessary. He was very much in favour of having a set of measures to aid the justification of resources, but appreciated the subjective nature of these measures. How do you measure if an application is 50 percent easier to use? An interesting remark made by a Usability Group member was that people who are so caught up in making cost-benefit justifications should ask themselves why corporations such as Microsoft are investing huge amounts in making their products more usable.

The group of developers surveyed were asked whether they felt "*managers allowed extra time and resources for usability work*". Interestingly, the developers working for the manager who was less sold on usability benefits (Department Y) said they were unsure about resource/management commitment. Developers in Department X were much more confident that resource was available from their manager.

At Glaxo, the IT Division's function is to support the business. Projects were not rigorously cost justified as they were developed for internal use and not for competition on the open market. There was an understanding that the financial benefits are difficult to quantify, but this was not really an obstacle to usability because the "soft" benefits such as increased use of the system and user satisfaction were given more priority.

Time Constraints

Everyone interviewed made no hesitation in saying that time was a major factor preventing the uptake of usability. The manager of Department X gave an example, where in a project chosen to promote usability, an estimate was made that it would take 12 months to complete. However, the users of the system wanted it delivered in three months, so many things had to be omitted. Usability testing and task analysis were reduced and also some functionality was postponed for later versions. "We are trying to work usability into the shorter timescales, but this requires commitment".

The manager of Department Y considered time constraints to be "a different way of expressing costs", but at Glaxo there did seem to be a distinction between time and cost. Although one does imply the other, since IT projects were generally not cost justified in detail within the company, time was a major factor that needed to be treated separately.

A Usability Group member said that estimated development times might be slightly longer if usability activities had to be included. He felt "a certain amount of trust must exist between developers and users, so they can understand that an extended development time will ensure better systems". Another member of the Group reaffirmed this by stating "people perceive that usability will prolong the process". Whilst this may not be true, the perception can be overcome if users are educated that time spent on usability will benefit them and that if time needs to be added to the development cycle in its early stages, this will save time and improve quality further down the line.

One developer wrote in the survey "usability should not take 'extra' time, it should be part of the process". This showed that the importance of usability was recognized and that the perception of it adding to development times was not held by all developers. It was also noted by a member of the Usability Group that "training for developers is a further time constraint, but there has been no resistance to this". For Glaxo, having to spend extra time on usability was not of itself the biggest problem. More specifically, those interviewed said that the business demanded new systems "yesterday", without necessarily understanding arguments about process and quality. Nevertheless, there was commitment from developers to include usability as standard in systems development, so the users' perceptions of spending "extra time" could eventually be conquered.

So, developers were saying, "usability is being fitted into coffee breaks", because there was no time allowance for it. On the other side of the coin, during the interviews with management, it was established that cost was not the bottom line, and that more importance lay with delivering systems users wanted, and were "happy" to use. Consequently, there was an inherent conflict, which needed to be resolved for progress to be made.

Management Support

From the findings presented so far, it was evident that there was a great deal of support for usability by the manager of department X. However, he admitted there was still a lack of support from the managers who reported to him. "Within the IT Division there is an awareness that usability is something we ought to do, but some people think by designing a pretty screen, they have solved the problem." The other manager admitted that he was ambivalent about usability, saying, "there is no question it is a good thing", but it was something he was still not sure about, and he was "not flogging the issue". He could only commit to usability after reassurance that interest in the subject was not just a passing phase. Usability needed to be placed higher on the agenda to change this attitude. Still, there was some support by the other managers as witnessed by the fact that all the departments in the IT Division provided representatives for the Usability Group.

The different degrees of management support could partly be explained by the nature of the business that each department supported. There was a great deal of difference in the work that was done, and the ways in which it was completed. The majority of Department Y's developments adhered to strict regulations, monitored by external bodies. In contrast, Department X was less regulated and had a more flexible approach to the introduction of new methods and techniques.

The developers' survey showed that they were unsure or disagreed that "*managers are generally supportive of making systems more usable*" in Department Y. On the other hand, Department X's manager was exploring what training courses were available to help developers with making their systems more usable. He was looking at how to build usability concepts into the development life cycle. His support was again apparent in the fact that he expressed a willingness for the company's Quality Assurance group to audit the usability of their systems.

These findings strongly suggested that for usability to be taken up by developers, there needed to be clear management support for it. During the interviews, a member of the Usability Group said, "I respond to what I perceive my manager's agenda to be". It appeared that management support was essential if usability was going to take off within the organization.

Attitudes of Developers

The majority of developers agreed that they were "*enthusiastic about making their systems more usable*", that they had always tried to ensure systems were usable and that "*there was nothing new about usability*". This was a very positive finding, which might have been attributable to the usability initiative. However, some said that although they wanted to, they were "*not sure how to practise usability*".

The majority of developers disagreed that "*most usability issues are just common sense – there is no need for special training*". It was important to be aware that this feeling existed because any attempt at training developers would be resented by those who believed it was just common sense. In fact one developer did write that "usability is common sense" and that "the Usability Group is not needed!".

Another point worth emphasizing was that nearly all the developers surveyed said they would welcome "*the idea of user-participation as part of the development process*". So, this again was another positive finding for the organization. A Usability Group member who had been practising usability, said "in my experience users actually enjoy being included as part of the development process".

It is often said that developers think they understand users, and that users themselves do not really know what is best for them. Nearly half of the developers disagreed with the statement that "*users don't know what is best for them in terms of interface design*". This was an interesting result when compared to responses for having user-participation. Surely if users were going to participate in design, developers had to be prepared to believe to a large extent that the user did know what was best. One of the managers commented, "the IT Division does not realize the extent to which it does not understand what the business really wants – it is much further away from it than it believes". This highlighted a communication problem and the fact that in certain situations, developers did not understand the users' needs.

The developers were asked to define what usability meant to them. They tended to use "usability", "ease of use" and "intuitiveness" synonymously. Nevertheless, the fact they made some attempt at answering showed that they had taken time to think about usability, even though some definitions were vague. Overall there was a good understanding that usability issues are not just concerned with interface design. A selection of responses to the question: "*What does usability mean?*" follows.

Usability means...

- "...Systems which are designed to be largely intuitive to use, allowing the user to carry out their most commonly used procedures with as few keystrokes as possible. The system fits in with the user's work practices easily."
- "...Task-oriented design giving rise to ease of use. Usable systems should require lower training effort and should appear to be 'natural' to the user."
- "...A system which is intuitive to use, and the functions should be consistent throughout the system. The system should be designed around the way the user works so that it becomes a useful tool that is part of their work."
- "...Designed and implemented with ease of use in mind. The ease of use should be for all functionality and should include ease of support."
- "...Someone from a non-computing background being able to operate a computer system with minimal training and plenty of obvious help messages/ advice / suggestions on what to do next."

Of course, the attitudes of developers do affect the uptake of usability, but at Glaxo much progress had been made to raise awareness. Developers were enthusiastic about bringing usability into the design process, even though some felt they did not know how to. But the notion of usability was slowly filtering throughout the IT Division.

User Proximity

Another factor that can slow down the uptake of usability in organizations is difficulty gaining access to end-users. The Department managers expressed the view that geographical separation was a hindrance for any process. This was questioned in the survey by the statement "*I don't have time to consult users because they are located in a different building*". The majority of developers did not feel that proximity was a reason for not consulting users, but approximately half agreed with the statement "*it would help to be situated with the users because they would be more accessible*". A Usability Group member felt that if developers were closer to users, they would better appreciate how they struggle with systems that developers consider easy to use. But the majority did not echo this as a concern.

Another Usability Group member noted that close proximity to the user was not always possible, especially when customers are located worldwide. In these situations, he said, "I would have to make decisions on the users' behalf".

However, in the majority of cases, developers would have access to the users who are located in the UK. Hence, not being able to access users was not an organizational obstacle for Glaxo.

Political Conflicts between Developers and Usability People

In a meeting of the Usability Group, members felt that their presence on a project team might be seen as an intrusion when they were called in to give HCI expertise. This was tackled in the survey by asking developers to state their opinion on the statement "*I see usability experts as intruders into our development teams*". It emerged that over three-quarters of developers did not consider this a problem. The sentiment of the Usability Group being regarded as the "usability police" did not seem to exist (although the phrase had been bandied about).

A further political issue was the fact that developers might be reluctant to hear criticisms about their work from usability experts, and so not ask for advice or help. The statement "*I am wary of consulting the Usability Group for help because they may be critical of my work*" was put to developers. Over three-quarters disagreed or strongly disagreed with this statement. For the majority of developers, the fact that experts might be critical of their efforts was not a reason to prevent them consulting the Usability Group.

Almost all developers agreed or strongly agreed that they would welcome ideas for improving usability from someone who is already on their development team. This suggested that the formation of a Usability Group made up of people working on different projects was a good idea. This way the central core of expertise could be distributed around the IT Division on different projects, although the number of people in the Group would have had to increase for there to be representation in each project team. So, at Glaxo there were no real organizational politics preventing usability.

Usability: Supply-pushed versus Demand-pulled

The question of whether usability was being pushed into the organization, rather than being demand-pulled, had not been considered before by the Department managers or members of the Usability Group. There was unanimous agreement that users were not explicitly asking for better HCI in the systems, but "it comes more subtly, through constructive criticisms and comments about improvements". The fact that users were not insisting on usable systems was because of their lack of understanding about HCI, rather than the fact they were not demanding it. A department manager said the organization tended to visualize the implementation of a new computer system to replace an existing one as doing the same process but with a different tool. The business did not understand what it meant to change the processes around that tool. The fact that usability was not demand driven made it very hard to force it through.

Developers disagreed that there were "*no incentives to make systems more usable*". This showed there was realization of the benefits to having more usable systems, for the users in terms of ease of use, and for developers in terms of ease of support. But these were just assumptions; there could have been some hidden agenda.

A few developers agreed that there were "*no incentives to make systems more usable*". There seemed to be a contradiction here in the fact that the majority of developers answered that they were enthusiastic about making systems more usable. Their enthusiasm must certainly have been motivated by something, whether it was by having more satisfied users, or something on another level such as promotion prospects by making an important issue of usability. Management and the Usability Group were aware that the supply push for usability was probably stronger than the demand pull, but this was "not considered to be a negative aspect". As one of the Department managers commented, "users of technology do not realize the effort it takes to make systems more usable, and don't ask for it until it is too late".

This balance of supply and demand needed to shift towards greater demand for usability from users, to change the minds of developers and managers who believed there was no such demand. Glaxo operated very much by demand pull, especially in those functions that support the business, like IT. In short, if there were a lack of demand, there would be no incentives for managers and developers to put usability higher on the agenda.

The Inertia of Usability at Glaxo

The case study undertaken at Glaxo highlighted the impact of some of the organizational factors that can affect the uptake of usability in a specific company. There are many factors that can account for the inertia of usability. However, it was clear from the case study that there were a few dominant factors in this case. These were: the lack of management support across the IT Division; the pressures of time; and a lack of demand for better systems by the end users. In the survey, one developer wrote "what is important is that usability input is timely and of sufficient quality and in tune with other design objectives of the system. It is not *more* important, but it is *as* important." It is vital for all usability enthusiasts to keep this in perspective.

The Crux of the Problem

The situation at Glaxo could be represented by a "vicious circle" which existed between the main organizational factors preventing usability (see Figure 3.1).

Nielsen advocates a five-point plan for management to increase usability within their organizations [1]:

1. Recognize the need for usability in the organization.
2. Make it clear that usability has management support.
3. Devote specific resources to usability engineering.
4. Integrate systematic usability engineering activities into various stages of the development life cycle.
5. Make sure that all user interfaces are subjected to user testing.

By mapping the achievements of Glaxo against Nielsen's plan, it can be seen that the company did appear to have made significant progress since the formation of the Usability Group. The need for usability was recognized amongst management, developers and users, although not always explicitly. Awareness and enthusiasm were high, but whether point 2 of the plan had been accomplished was still debatable. Usability had more management support in some departments than in others. It appeared that this balance could change if managers who were still cautious about usability were shown the benefits of usability in actual projects.

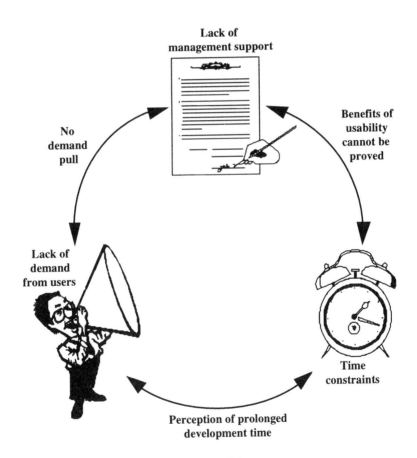

Figure 3.1

The matter of devoting resources to usability was most obvious in Department X. The fact that so much time was devoted to it, and that people were being encouraged to go on HCI courses, showed this. Resource was also made available to fund the usability lecture, workshop and the procurement of HCI books. According to the five-point plan, integrating systematic usability activities into various stages of the development life cycle was the next stage. This was where significant progress needed to be made.

As a better understanding of usability was gained, the organization needed to consider how usability could be put into practice. This was not an easy task, particularly in a complicated environment like the one at Glaxo, with its variety of hardware and software, and range of users with differing needs and skills. So, what was the next stage?

Progression of the Usability Initiative

The Usability Group put forward the following recommendations for progressing usability within the organization:

- The Usability Group to act as a pressure group and network for those interested in HCI.
- Management recognition of the need to invest in usability.
- Changes to the development cycle: usability metrics specified up front; more analysis of users and tasks; prototyping; usability testing; use of design standards and guidelines.
- Usability testing for vendor software.
- Analysis of support calls to identify recurring usability problems.
- One "Usability Champion" on each new project, gaining support and expertise from a central core.
- Each IT department to identify local priorities and take suitable action.

In my report on the progress of usability within the company, I noted the value of these recommendations but also pointed out omissions and a "recipe for action".

The Recipe for Action

The list above showed there was already acknowledgement that the level of management support needed to increase, but there was no mention of the need to educate users. Being a user-led organization, this was a significant point that had been omitted.

There was HCI interest at all levels, but in such a large organization change takes time. There could be no HCI revolution. One of the major opposing factors to the implementation of usability in any organization is the attitude of developers. The Usability Group's awareness campaign seemed to have paid off, as proved by the fact that there was a large amount of usability enthusiasm among developers. The organization needed to exploit this. I recommended that developers be given just-in-time training on usability engineering techniques and changes to the development life cycle. More experimentation needed to be done to find out what suited the organization. Developers needed to spend more time visiting users and observing their work.

The Usability Group organized a visit to IBM's Usability Laboratory for its members and a few managers. During the interviews, the Usability Group members said this was an overwhelming success and helped usability "sell itself". I recommended that the Group could video usability testing of IT's own software. Once managers saw how users struggled with some of the systems, the amount of support for usability would increase.

There was also a suggestion that usability testing be part of the selection criteria for vendor software. I endorsed this as I felt that it would be seen as public recognition that usability was just as important as functionality, and for software applications such as word processors, possibly even more so.

Although analysis of support calls to identify recurring usability problems was an admirable goal, I felt that this was not so urgent at the early stages in the initiative. During the interviews a comment was made that it would be easier to include usability as part of new systems development, rather than in the modification of existing systems. During the interviews, many usability practitioners stressed the importance of considering usability at the inception stage of a system, rather than adding it as an afterthought. In the case of Glaxo there was still the need to prove the benefits of usability, and starting on new projects seemed like a better way to proceed. It would also be seen as less "political" than seeming to criticize existing software. Another possibility was to improve an existing system by usability engineering to show managers the distinction between "before" and "after".

The Usability Group needed more opportunities to implement its expertise. The "usability champion" idea seemed like a good one. Knowledge would filter through the development team and be carried forward to other projects. Soon all projects would have a "usability champion" on the team. The "champions" would also be in a good position to identify local priorities. For example, in a long development project, an HCI methodology would need careful selection to ensure it was compatible with the working practices of that department. It has been suggested that, "to be effective and influential human factors must be institutionalized i.e. built into the whole policies, practices and infrastructure of an organization" [2]. Glaxo were right to try methods to institutionalize usability and include these in the IT strategy. I felt they also needed to convince the users and more actively demonstrate the benefits of usability activities.

Lessons Learned

- When introducing usability to an organization, the kinds of resistance encountered will be relative to the organizational culture.
- At Glaxo R&D UK key organizational factors were: perceived time constraints, senior management support and user demand. These factors became a vicious circle, i.e. one caused/prevented the other.

- Once an organization is "usability aware" there are many actions that may be taken to overcome the inertia of usability. Principally, usability needs to become institutionalized.

References

[1] J. Nielsen (1993) *Usability Engineering*, Academic Press Inc.
[2] L. Damodaran (1991) "Towards A Human Factors Strategy For Information Technology Systems" in B. Shackel and S. Richardson (eds.) *Human Factors for Informatics Usability*, Cambridge University Press, Cambridge.

4. Integrating Usability into Systems Development

How to Avoid Reinventing the Wheel by Using Existing Systems and Resources

Alison Crerar and David Benyon

ABSTRACT

This chapter is aimed at project managers and software developers who are new to the concept of user-centred design and may be unsure of what resources are required and what impact such efforts will have. Of course, if an organization is thinking of adopting a user-centred approach to systems development, it must expect to invest. However, this investment does not mean that each organization has to reinvent the wheel. There are many principles, guidelines and standards which can be easily and cheaply adopted. There are consultants, educationalists and experts ready to provide expertise and advice. There will often be "in-house" resources in the form of quality assurance functions, active and interested end users or system designers who are ready to take on usability issues.

The chapter begins by examining the concept of usability, its emphasis on tasks and on user characteristics and its insistence on the context of use, or environment, as being an important design consideration. Standards, design principles and style guides are then discussed. The next section offers pointers to usability in practice, giving examples of how to formulate a problem statement incorporating usability factors from the outset, what to include in the initial requirements analysis and examples of usability metrics that can be included in the acceptance criteria. We advocate an iterative approach to software development, based on prototyping and continuous evaluation to replace the traditional waterfall. Next, we provide an overview of usability tools, resources and existing centres of expertise: appealing to tried and tested methods and enlisting the expertise of those with a track record is by far the best route to success. To help organizations quickly locate sources of interest we have created a WWW site to support this chapter [1].

Introduction

Many fine words have been spoken about the notion of "usability", but it can be an elusive concept to pin down. Usability engineering is about making systems easy to learn and use, efficient and effective, safe, functional and enjoyable. There is a misconception that user-centred design is somehow soft, woolly and at odds with the engineering approach to software development. This is not so. It does, however, make developing software more challenging by widening the scope of the analysis to include factors that the traditional software engineering life cycle tends to neglect. Far from relaxing development requirements, embracing usability imposes additional performance criteria that can be specified in quantitative terms. Moreover, a range of usability evaluation methods that yield data of various sorts and quantities has been developed. This data can be used diagnostically during development to enhance the ongoing design process.

One of the main aims of this chapter is to identify for newcomers some of the key sources of information and expertise available to them. However, it is important to stress that user-centred design is a philosophy which should permeate the whole software development enterprise. One cannot produce systems in the machine-orientated mould and then somehow bolt on a bit of usability testing to magic away the problems. Even if external consultants are to provide the usability evaluation, the development team must share a user-centred mindset if the project is to be a success. What does this mean? Put simply, it means believing usability to be as important as functionality. It means thinking about tasks as done by people, rather than functions as supported by machines. It means caring about the quality of experience that users have (if only for commercial advantage!), instead of just whether the system fulfils its functional specification. Fulfilling a functional specification is a fairly straightforward business – it means satisfying what the system should do, any old how. For example, a functional requirement might be:

The system will permit the following operations on records – add, view, edit, delete.

Contrast this with a user-centred amplification of that same requirement:

The system will be targeted at hotel receptionists taking bookings over the telephone and will allow part-time workers, who are novice computer users, to add, view, edit or delete bookings confidently in an environment subject to interruptions.

Now we have shifted our focus from the machine to the human operator. This short problem statement conjures up the work environment; we see a busy receptionist dealing with telephone enquiries about bookings he or she may not have originally taken. The usability challenge is to the forefront and the record handling recedes, as it should, to the background.

Difficulties experienced by users in mastering everyday appliances are well known, the video recorder being one of the most commonly cited offenders. Think of your telephone answering machine or microwave oven. Do they have functions you do not know how to use? These are instances of dedicated technologies with limited and related sets of features. The computer, on the other hand, is a general purpose machine used for all manner of business, leisure, education and communication activities. This very generality means that appropriate interfaces need to be designed to mediate between the machine and its users. Functionality and interface are semi-independent, while there is a necessary relationship between the two (if functional feature A exists it must be accessible via some interface component), there will always be a large number of possible interface designs for any functional specification. Getting the interface right depends on a detailed understanding of the target users, the tasks they will be performing and the work environment.

People differ in characteristics such as age, education, physical and cognitive abilities, job function, computer experience, cultural background, anxieties, enthusiasms and personality. Sometimes systems will be developed for relatively homogenous user groups whereas at other times the intended users will be very diverse. There may be discretionary users to deal with (those who do not have to use the system) or infrequent users who will forget the details of how the system works. Increasingly, personnel are working on short contracts and learning time must be kept to a minimum if they are to be productive. The proliferation of telephone call centres giving customers a "one-stop-shop" means that operators must be able to deal with any and every enquiry efficiently. The work may be routine or exceptional. In some systems speed of response may be critical at all times, while in others there may be peaks and troughs of transactions to cater for, or the need to support detailed interactive design work. Systems will need to operate in a variety of environments; noisy, cold, wet, dirty, stressful, and so on. The organizational environment may be supportive or not, people may be concerned about the effect on their work practices and job content, worried about de-skilling, shifts in power, or centralization. Support for users may be poor.

To achieve optimum usability, the system development team has to achieve a "harmony" between these different facets of the overall system. Figure 4.1 provides a useful aide memoire, "CUTE", summarizing the four main aspects to be considered when approaching a new system. Shading has been used to highlight those factors often neglected in traditional systems analysis.

Constraints	Users
Time-scale, equipment, budget, standards or styles, technical performance criteria, development personnel, user training requirements, legal requirements relating to usability or accessibility.	Physical and cognitive needs, domain expertise, education, usage profile, cultural background, computer experience, attitude, work methods.
Environment	**Tasks**
Physical aspects of the context of use including environmental conditions, siting, response needs, criticality, health and safety issues, desk bound or mobile, job stresses, ergonomic issues.	Functional specification. User-centred analysis of tasks, their components, sequences and typical scenarios. Context of work including work pattern, work group dynamics.

Figure 4.1: Four main headings to consider when approaching a new system from a user-centred perspective.

We will return to the "CUTE" grid shown in Figure 4.1 to derive some preliminary requirements for the hotel reception problem. However, before delving further into specific usability examples, it is important to note that there are a number of issues that are common to all systems with which an organization might be involved.

Standards, Design Principles and Style Guides

Irrespective of the application domain, there are common criteria to be met by all interactive systems. These requirements range from mandatory, where there is a legal obligation to comply, to highly recommended where the principle derives from research on human capabilities and behaviour. Any organization involved in software development has three "codes of practice" to consider: national and international standards, general HCI design principles and in-house or proprietary style guides. We give a brief introduction to each of these below. It should be noted that the ordering is not accidental: standards are the most important, these can be enforceable; design principles make for generally usable systems and cut across matters of individual style; finally adherence to style guides is important for consistency and "look and feel". The logical ordering is thus to consider them in the order presented below, always making sure that subsequent decisions do not contradict previous principles. Admittedly this can sometimes be difficult where guidelines appear to conflict, or where it is hard to find a design that respects a number of criteria simultaneously.

Standards

There are a number of national and international standards bodies responsible for formulating design policies. Compliance with these standards is useful both for marketing, as an external sign of quality, for satisfying regulators and ultimately for avoiding litigation. It would be misleading to give the impression that adopting standards is straightforward. Standards covering interface issues are still evolving and using them requires a good deal of interpretation. What standards do provide is a set of very useful checklists for the design team and therefore a way of encouraging them to make their systems user centred.

Standards tend to fall into two groups, those concerned with ergonomics and matters of accessibility and those concerned with design. Further information and contact addresses can be found in our WWW site [1] (see also Chapter 12: Standards and Style Guides).

Design Principles

Universal design principles apply to all interactive systems and all user groups, with rare exceptions (for example when compound disabilities demand unique solutions). Design principles have generally emerged from psychological research on human visual perception, attention, memory, information processing and motor skills. Resulting guidelines concern memory load, task sequencing, task closure, display organization, use of colour combinations, menu structures, preference for selection (point-and-click) over generation (command line and type-in styles) and so forth. When implementing guidelines within an industrial context, be aware of possible cultural variations among users that would impact on appropriate use of colour, icons, metaphors, terminology, etc. There are many accessible sources of guidance, but one of the best known and most comprehensive is the text by Schneiderman [2].

Guidelines vary considerably in specificity from very general exhortations to good practice, such as "*reduce short-term memory load*" or "*all actions should be reversible*" to much finer-grained directions such as "*in menu-based interaction, where users make frequent selection and the list of options does not change over time, use letter identifiers paired to each option*" [3]. It can therefore be daunting for the novice designer. Bridging the gap between a general guideline and its effective realization within an industrial context calls for creativity – as in all good design work. Skill and intuition take time to develop, which is why seeking help from external HCI experts (or employing human factors people on the design team!) is something we strongly advocate.

An alternative type of guideline can be found in the form of aesthetic principles; this approach tackles the problem of producing pleasing and easy-to-use interfaces from a graphic design angle. Rather than deriving from mainstream cognitive psychology, they appeal to senses of form, balance and texture in an artistic way, offering advice on such things as depth cues, texture changes, overlapping and perspective. In this category Marcus [4] is a key source.

When applying guidelines or design principles within the context of an organization or specific IT project, the overall aim is to support the users' tasks in the most effective way. This means understanding the application domain and its task in detail and understanding the users' characteristics (skills, knowledge, work patterns, roles, preferences).

Style Guides

Style guides may be in-house, that is, developed by an organization for its own use, or proprietary, which means developed – typically by a large manufacturer such as IBM or Microsoft – to support a particular development environment or operating system. Most interfaces today are GUIs. In-house style guides dictate the uses of and placement of widgets, the use of colour, fonts and the like, to ensure that all products across the organization have a common "look and feel" – that they conform to the corporate standard. Proprietary style guides aim to do this more generally, so that a high degree of consistency is achieved by all developers working within the same development environment. The benefit of this uniformity is that users can transfer their learning from one package to the next. Within organizations this provides benefit by helping reduce the costs of training and support.

You may be familiar with suites of software by major manufacturers, where interface consistency has been achieved across a range of applications. The functionality typically differs little between the leading office packages, but usability counts for a lot and customer loyalty is often built on "look and feel", and of course on disinclination to purchase from a competitor if it means mastering new conventions. Application style guides (e.g. Microsoft, Macintosh, OSF/Motif) are useful for industrial designers. You can also use an application style guide as a basis for designing your own corporate style guide, adding company specific detail and specifying preferred options where several are available. References to proprietary style guides and to further reading can be found on our WWW site.

Knowledge of HCI design standards and guidelines has many benefits for an organization and should inform all of the phases of system development. When working with guidelines is second nature it does not just help the design process, it makes specifying usability criteria at the requirements definition stage much easier to do and feeds naturally into evaluation activities by suggesting possible performance metrics. An important consideration in design is making the software accessible to users with special needs. Designing for "extra-ordinary" users can enhance the usability for all.

Approaching a New System

Having taken on board any statutory requirements and working within any prescribed style guides, development teams can begin to elicit requirements for a new system and to sketch early designs. In the next section we will present a revised system development model showing how various usability related techniques fit into the development process. But first, to make the shift of emphasis implied by user-centred design more explicit, some examples of problem formulation, requirements capture and usability evaluation criteria may be helpful.

Problem Formulation

A useful checklist for helping define user-centred design objectives is:

(a) identify the **human activity** that the proposed interactive system will support;
(b) identify the people, or **users**, who will perform the activity;
(c) set the **levels of support** that the system will provide, otherwise known as the system's **usability**;
(d) select the basic **form of the solution** to the design problem.

Using this checklist we have generated two example problem statements below, which contain all the components needed to begin requirements capture. The examples use the checklist identifiers in parentheses so that you can marry them up easily.

Design a walk-up-and-use (c) multi-media kiosk (d) for dispensing advice and information (a) for out-patients attending an oncology clinic (b).

Design an interactive music editing package (d) that will allow composers (b) to create, edit, save and print their work (a) in a musically intuitive way (c).

Requirements Capture

Let us return to the hotel reception problem mentioned in the introduction to this chapter. The machine-centred view presented in the first problem statement might result in a standard database approach, paying attention to rooms and their attributes, charging structures, security and backup, but not seeing the context of work, the users' characteristics or the work patterns as within the scope of the analysis. Whereas the user-centred problem statement below begs fuller treatment:

> *The system will be targeted at hotel receptionists taking bookings over the telephone and will allow part-time workers, who are novice computer users, to add, view, edit or delete bookings confidently in an environment subject to interruptions.*

Using the CUTE grid (Figure 4.1) as a framework, we can think fully round the problem, seeing it not primarily as a record handling problem, but as one of service provision where the comfort of the receptionist and the satisfaction of the customers are the goals.

The emphasis in requirements gathering would be to look at the needs of these two groups, the receptionists **and** the customers; they are both users of the system. Indeed one might think of the customer on the telephone as the user and the receptionist as an intermediary, after all, 99 times out of 100 the customer will initiate the transaction! The system boundary must be drawn broadly. Solving the whole problem will mean designing a system which helps to handle the communication between receptionist and customer within the context of the other interruptions (clients at the desk, internal phone, query from colleague). The elements of the final system may not all be contained in the software (telephone queuing system, doubling up personnel at peak times). Smooth working may be assisted by a change of current hardware (hands-free phone or head-mounted mouth piece), but inevitably success will depend on understanding more about the nature of the incoming enquiries (frequency of enquiry types, ordering of query components, peaks and troughs, tolerable wait times).

User-centred design certainly entails immersion in the intended working environment and a detailed understanding of the day-to-day realities. "Field work" is the generic term for a range of observational techniques and their associated analysis methods. An excellent practical source on field work case studies, written by software practitioners, is Wixon and Ramey [3]. The relationship built up in the early stages of an investigation builds a foundation for involving users in offering input, feedback and prototype evaluation as design gets underway.

Usability Evaluation Criteria

Usability criteria or usability metrics are measures of performance by which the success of a new system can be gauged. It is important to specify these at the requirements stage, firstly, so that designers can work towards them, and secondly, so that evaluation processes can confirm whether or not they have been met. Usability criteria can relate to both quantitative and qualitative outcomes. The following list provides examples of commonly used usability criteria; the acronym FLUMES makes it easy to recall. Remember the evaluation results must be obtained from target users, not from developers!

- **Flexibility** – degree to which users can re-organize working and customize the interface;
- **Learnability** – time and effort needed to learning the system;
- **User satisfaction**;
- **Memorability** – re-learning or retention;
- **Errors** – rate, type and recoverability;
- **Speed** – of performance or productivity.

Thinking back to the hotel reception problem, we can readily see that a successful outcome would necessitate meeting usability targets for the last five criteria in the above list, possibly also the first one.

A User-Centred Model of Software Development

Unlike the traditional "waterfall" view of systems development (a neatly compartmentalized analyse-specify-design-test-deliver model), designing for usability requires an iterative approach. The waterfall model may work well for tried and tested applications (perhaps a new payroll system), but may not work when innovative systems are proposed (for example a new hand-held communications device). This is because analysts cannot truly understand user requirements until some design work has been completed; moreover, with new products, users cannot foresee or suggest what they will need until they have used a prototype. This may sound like a hacker's licence and can make IT project managers nervous, but a prototyping approach does not necessarily mean loss of control. Project planning and monitoring are not forfeited. Appropriate timescales, milestones and deliverables need to be set for every project and traditional milestones such as "requirements specification completed" can be replaced by alternative milestones such as "first prototype implemented", "evaluation of first prototype completed" and so on.

The main difference between the user-centred and "waterfall" models of development is that the user-centred approach puts evaluation (involving users) at the heart of the development process and accepts evolutionary prototyping as being an inevitable and healthy consequence. In industry this has the consequence that IT developers must often spend more time working with users and that user managers must be prepared to release staff time to work with development teams. Chapter 6, which looks at the use of a structured user interface design methodology within a law firm, highlights the problems of gaining access to users – in this case busy legal professionals who charged for their time by the hour.

In Figure 4.2 we try to capture this paradigm by enclosing the interface design process within an "evaluation bubble", and annotating each major phase of development with examples of the evaluation and analysis techniques that might be appropriate. This is a simplification concentrating on rapid prototyping of the interface rather than on the whole of system development. We cannot describe each of the evaluation techniques here, but there are many HCI texts that do this and the WWW site [1] provides further information. The main thing to be aware of is the range of techniques available, the fluidity of the design process and the continuous role of usability evaluation. You then need to consider the political context in which you are working to help decide which techniques will work best in your organization.

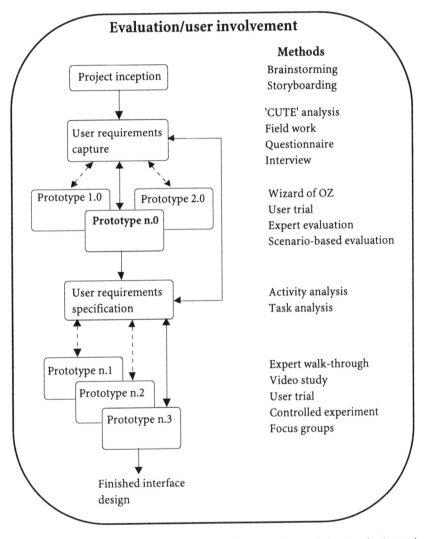

Figure 4.2: Model of user-centred interface design, showing some of the analysis and evaluation methods applicable at each stage

Tools, Resources and Centres of Expertise

An organization new to usability concepts has three main resourcing options to consider:

- train existing staff;
- recruit staff with HCI skills;
- use external usability consultants.

The likelihood is that for any medium to large company a mix of the three will produce the best results. When training existing staff, bear in mind that you may already have in-house resources in the form of quality assurance functions, active and interested end users or system developers who are keen to take on usability issues. Universities with strong HCI research groups are very useful contacts: they will offer courses, produce employable graduates, have qualified staff who can act as consultants and perhaps provide opportunities for research collaboration. Developing a reciprocal relationship with such a department can have many bene-fits. Academics are always keen to have "real world" case studies to teach from and to find industrial partners for research projects, and in turn universities have valuable resources: libraries, usability labs, TV studios and lots of students (potential system evaluators) which a company can arrange to use. Looking at your local university's WWW site is a good way to find out if the expertise you want is close at hand.

In the previous section we named some usability evaluation techniques (see Figure 4.2). Many of these were generic rather than specific, for example, "field work" is something that can be done in a variety of ways, drawing on techniques used in anthropological research. Deciding which method or combination of methods to use can be daunting. Luckily there are a range of off-the-shelf tools and systematized techniques that can be used without having to reinvent the wheel; there are also examples in other chapters in this book of both formal and informal evaluation techniques with indications of how easily they may be applied in industry.

Below we give a short list of key contacts and resources. Our WWW site [1] provides additional information.

Useful Organizations

http://info.lut.ac.uk/research/husat/inuse/
Network of 13 European usability support centres providing information, advice and tools. Many useful links from this site too.

http://www.upassoc.org/index.html
Usability Professionals Association (USA) – articles and a list of usability consul-tants.

http://kmi.open.ac.uk/~simonb/bcs-hci/hci-grp.html#business
The British Computer Society's HCI Group.

Usability Tools

http://www.npl.co.uk/npl/sections/us/index.html
National Physical Laboratory's Usability Services site, contains information of four integrated usability products: DRUM – for video analysis; UCA – for context analysis; MUSiC – for measuring usability performance; and SUMI – a validated usability questionnaire with scoring and report generating software.

Standards and Style Guides

http://www.sirim.my/clinks_sb/others.html
A site providing links to all the major standards organizations including those mentioned in the chapter.

http://www.system-concepts.com/stds/status.html
The current status of ISO 9241 "Ergonomics requirements for office work with visual display terminals".

http://128.205.200.128/graph_based/.software/
Designing with disabled users in mind can improve the usability for all.

Universities Offering HCI Courses and Expertise

http://www.cis.ohio-state.edu/~perlman/educhi.html
This survey is by no means comprehensive but provides a starting point.

Relevant Forums and Mailing Lists

http://www.io.tudelft.nl/uidesign/netsites.html

Summary

Several things are happening in technology and in business that make fore-fronting software usability imperative. Software functionality is expanding, the user base is growing, work patterns are changing, user expectations are rising and businesses themselves are coming round to customer-centred missions in the form of service-based philosophies. PC interfaces are no longer required to support only individuals, but increasingly to support groups of people working co-operatively, though they may be physically miles apart. In this climate the job to be done is clearly what matters and the supporting software must facilitate, not hinder.

In this chapter we have explained the concept of usability and the characteristics of user-centred design. We have given some practical guidance about approaching new systems from this perspective and an overview of some of the evaluation methods that can be employed. The main point to note is that gearing up for usability does not mean reinventing the wheel. There are many sources of information and advice available. The WWW sites included here are a good start.

Lessons Learned

- Usability is as important as functionality when successfully designing usable systems in industry;
- User-centred design must permeate the whole software development process;
- Including usability criteria in initial requirements definitions provides the basis for objective evaluation throughout the development process;
- Don't reinvent the wheel. There are many resources and techniques available off the shelf and universities can often supply HCI expertise very cost-effectively.

Acknowledgements

The authors are grateful to Catriona Macaulay for researching resources for this chapter and for creating the WWW site to support it.

References

[1] http://www.dcs.napier.ac.uk/hci/usability.
[2] B. Schneiderman (1992) *Designing the User Interface: Strategies for Effective Human-Computer Interaction*, 2nd edn, Addison-Wesley, Reading MA.
[3] D. Wixon and J. Ramey (eds) (1996) *Field Methods Casebook for Software Design*, Wiley, New York.
[4] A. Marcus (1992) *Graphic Design for Electronic Documents and User Interfaces*, ACM Press, New York.

5. A Structured Approach to User Interface Design

Let the Clients See the Benefits, Not the Methodology

Dermot Browne and John Friend

ABSTRACT

The belief that user-centred design practices are central to the successful delivery of information technology is widespread. But this view is rarely justified in terms of successful applications of these practices in industry. This chapter helps redress the imbalance by reporting experiences from a project that applied a structured and user-centred approach to the design of an interactive computer system within an international law firm and some of the lessons learned.

Introduction: The Organization

Linklaters & Paines are an international law firm – the second largest of those based in the City of London. The firm has over 1800 staff including more than 700 legal professionals. As a business sector, the legal profession has in general been slow in its uptake of information technology. Much of legal business is still paper based and lawyers remain reluctant users of information technology. In the early 1990s Linklaters & Paines began an IT strategy based on the use of NEXTSTEP user interface technology, and a mix of bespoke and packaged software running in a physical three tier client-server environment. The objectives of this strategy included reducing IT costs and, importantly, providing better support to legal professionals up to and into the 21st century.

User Population

The potential IT user community of a law firm is divided into legal professionals and support staff. Professionals range from trainee solicitors to senior lawyers respected for their work in highly specialized areas such as mergers, take-overs, and trademarks. Support staff range from junior secretaries to group secretaries and personal assistants. The applications typical of a law firm can be divided into those for running the business – such as accounting and billing systems, office automation including electronic mail and document management – and legal specific, such as know-how systems. Each of these applications can be used such that all computer interaction is conducted by support staff.

IT Strategy

Linklaters & Paines's IT strategy includes the objective of deploying IT to legal professionals, that is, putting a workstation on each professional's desk where previously there was only an infrequently used dumb terminal that primarily supported electronic mail. Linklaters & Paines selected NeXT technology as its development and deployment environment. The NEXTSTEP operating system, which is highly regarded for its usability, is available on many manufacturers' hardware.

The ACCESS System: Its Success Would Depend on Usability

The first bespoke application to be developed as part of their strategy has become known as ACCESS. This application is enquiry only, providing information on most aspects of engagements conducted by legal professionals on behalf of clients. The legal community refers to such engagements as "Matters".

ACCESS was developed to replace a system developed in the 1970s that provided a character-based user interface. The original system was provided on a "walk up and use" basis – a number of terminals were sited at selected locations about Linklaters & Paines's offices. Any employee with a valid password could use one of these terminals on demand to display information about matters. For instance, users could identify a matter using parameters such as a client identifier or a matter's unique nine-digit code. Having identified the appropriate matter the user could then enquire about details like the amount of time booked to the matter, its billing history and expenses incurred.

This application was chosen as one of the first to be replaced by a NEXTSTEP application for a number of reasons. It was notoriously difficult to use as judged by interviews with users – professional staff preferred to ask their secretaries to obtain the required information and in turn, secretaries tended to make enquiries by phone and maintain ad hoc records of matter details rather than use the system. While it was certainly a valuable system, it could not be considered as business critical. If the system were unavailable, legal business could still be conducted. It was believed that making matter information more accessible would improve the process of billing. Legal professionals would issue bills in a more timely fashion if the information required for this activity were more freely available.

Very early on it was acknowledged that the success of the development would depend on the usability of the finished system. If the objective of making the matter information more accessible were to be achieved then the system to support this would have to be usable as measured in terms of the following:

- required training;
- speed of accessing data;
- user satisfaction;
- low error rates.

Given the importance of and emphasis on usability, Linklaters & Paines decided to adopt a structured approach to the design of the user interface of ACCESS. A number of consultancies were invited to tender for this design work and emphasize their approach to user interface design. The selected approach was STUDIO™ (STUDIO™ is a registered trademark of KPMG developed by Dermot Browne) [1]. This structured method was probably the first that addressed the user interface design cycle – from project proposal through to prototype development and evaluation – to be placed in the public domain.

STUDIO: A Structured Method for Ensuring Usability

STUDIO has five stages. The first is "project proposing" during which justifications for using GUI technology and employing a structured approach to design are made. This is followed by "user requirements analysis", which delivers models that provide a basis for making design decisions. Usability criteria are established during these first two stages. These criteria provide measurable objectives for the design and are used as controls for project activities. The next stage is "task synthesis" during which designs are produced and documented. "Usability engineering" is then performed using prototyping and impact analysis to finalize a design that meets the usability criteria. Finally, the design is developed into the full system.

STUDIO is designed to be adapted to project circumstances. Individual steps can be applied in isolation and particular stages adapted as required. In this way STUDIO can be applied to both small and large projects. Having said this, it is recommended that design activities are not undertaken until appropriate user requirements analyses are completed. For the development of ACCESS the analysis, design and evaluation stages of STUDIO were applied.

Task Analysis and Usability Criteria

Analysis was performed largely through interviews with a sample of both legal professionals and support staff. This provided a set of task models and usability criteria. The usability criteria generated were that users:

- be able to conduct an enquiry in less than 1 minute (on average);
- interact with an error rate of less than 1 in 100 attempts;
- judge the design as a "four" using a five point semantic differential scale labelled difficult to use (1) and easy to use (5);
- require no more than one hour of training in order to demonstrate the above levels of performance.

Design

Design included the documenting of a style guide specific to the requirements of Linklaters & Paines. Design was performed by generating many alternative outline designs. By reflecting on the task models and usability criteria a particular outline design was selected for elaboration. This design was then detailed on paper in accordance with the style guide. Figures 5.1 and 5.2 provide a snapshot of the design (without data for reasons of anonymity). In essence the design is composed of two windows. One window (Figure 5.1) is primarily used for searching. Towards the top of this window there are three action buttons that enable users to decide whether to search by clients, matters or responsible principal. Depending on the selection, various combinations of input fields are made available (white backgrounds) for the input of search terms. The results of searches are presented towards the bottom of this window. The user can then select from these search results. The details of the matter selected by the user are presented in the second window (Figure 5.2). Various views of these details can be selected by invoking one of the action buttons displayed towards the top of this window.

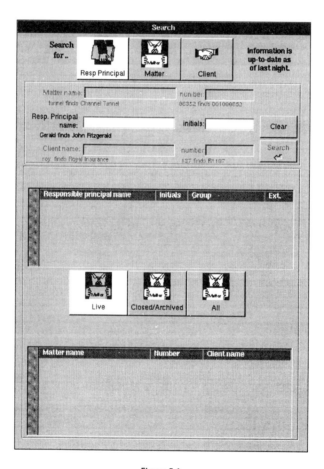

Figure 5.1

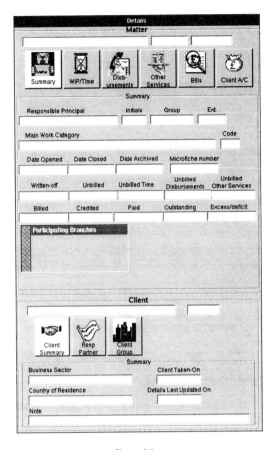

Figure 5.2

The design was again reviewed in the light of the task models and usability criteria, resulting in a number of modifications. The design itself was documented as screen dumps justified by task models, usability criteria and design principles. STUDIO suggests that the behaviour of a design be documented using Statecharts [2]. Given the productivity of the Interface Builder environment (supplied with NEXTSTEP) it was decided that the design should not be specified rigorously.

Prototype

The design was then put into development as an evolutionary prototype. The first prototype was used to provide demonstrations to the business: the prospective end users. Such demonstrations were not intended to and could not replace the need for usability engineering of the designs. However they did serve at least two important purposes. Firstly, they continued the process of user involvement and demonstrated to the business that their requirements and feedback were important and were being utilized. Additionally they helped to identify omissions or oversights in the design at an early and cost-effective stage of the development. For instance, it was identified that it was desirable to display the telephone extension numbers of staff listed in the search window. This enabled users to then contact those people, if desired, without having to check a separate application or telephone directory.

Once completed the design was submitted to a design audit as provided in STUDIO. This again identified required changes to the design, which were implemented. Having completed the development of the prototype it was ready for evaluation.

Pilot Evaluation

Prior to performing a full evaluation, a pilot was conducted. Two users participated in this. They were required to complete questionnaires and perform tasks with the prototype in the same manner as described below. The value of this pilot was that it acted as a test of the evaluation procedures, and importantly, the design itself. Any major design flaws could be identified and resolved prior to embarking on the evaluation proper – even a single major design flaw might undermine the findings from the main evaluation. And some serious design problems were identified. For example, the first prototype design included a flexible search facility. Users could type a search parameter into any of the search fields and use the asterisk (*) character as a wild card. Prompts underneath the search fields made this mechanism explicit; or so we thought.

The pilot evaluation revealed that users did not understand this use of wild cards and therefore a design change was required. To this end it was decided that wild cards would be added automatically to all user input to the search fields. The re-design resulted in an asterisk being placed at the beginning and end of all input strings and used to replace all separators (i.e. spaces, periods, slashes) input by the user. (These asterisks were not displayed but simply used in executing a search.) Only following this and other modifications was the prototype submitted to a full evaluation.

The Full Evaluation

Eight potential users participated in the evaluation – four secretaries and four legal professionals. Each participant was asked to first complete a questionnaire designed to assess their opinions of the existing matter enquiry system. The only training users received was of the order of ten minutes explanation of the design, for example, how to perform a search and read the data presented. They were then asked to work through a booklet of enquiries using the prototype. For instance, one question asked of them was to "Ascertain how many matters Linklaters & Paines were conducting on behalf of United Airways". Participants recorded their answers in the booklet and then moved on immediately to the next question. While performing these tasks, evaluators observed the users' interactions to identify any problems and also noted timings to ascertain how productive users were with the prototype.

After an hour the hands-on interaction was brought to a graceful and grateful conclusion. Next, the users were requested to complete a second questionnaire to gauge their subjective impressions of the prototype. The evaluation was completed with a de-briefing of users in order to manage their expectations of how the results of the session would be used and when they could expect the system to be rolled out. The timings, observations (including notes of errors made), and questionnaire results enabled the evaluation to determine whether the design was likely to meet the usability criteria as well as where design modifications were necessary.

The evaluations provided encouraging results. All of the usability criteria were achieved or surpassed. A number of minor issues were identified but these were primarily of a presentational nature in terms of labelling and relative positioning of fields. Given the trivial nature of these changes it was felt unnecessary to repeat the evaluations.

The Benefits of Using a Structured Design Methodology in Industry

The adoption of a user interface design approach (STUDIO) provided structure to design activities and was found to be beneficial for a number of reasons. Primarily it enabled design activities to be planned with confidence and ensured that important activities were not overlooked.

Among the highlights of applying STUDIO were the value of setting usability criteria, performing task modelling, and conducting a pilot evaluation. The usability criteria enabled the project to assess the design as it developed and enabled the prototyping activity to be managed. Prototyping is necessarily an iterative process but in the absence of criteria there is no basis for knowing when to break the evaluate–modify–evaluate cycle and decide that a design is acceptable. The main value of this is that planned iterations can be foregone once the criteria have been met or, alternatively, more resources can be made available for re-design and re-evaluation if a design is found to be not as usable as required.

The task modelling performed was found to be invaluable. It provided a basis for designing a user interface that would match the users' task flow. The modelling captured the required sequencing, selection, iteration and parallelism inherent in their tasks. This knowledge enabled the power of the NEXTSTEP environment to be deployed to best effect by creating a dialogue structure that was appropriate, facilitating parallel activities through appropriate window management and employing suitable controls to facilitate highly repetitive and iterative tasks. In addition the analysis enabled the design team to understand the frequency of task execution and therefore to know where to concentrate design effort.

Given the team's analysis and design efforts, evaluation was approached confidently in the belief that users would experience few problems and the usability criteria would be met. The pilot evaluation was useful as it demonstrated that the team's confidence was misplaced so the pilot prevented us from engaging prematurely in a full-scale evaluation.

Following the evaluations, the design and its specification were finalized and the project progressed to the development stage. The NEXTSTEP environment is fully object-oriented. While the development team were experienced object-oriented developers, no specific object-oriented development method was applied. The development and subsequent implementation and roll out progressed to a successful conclusion and the team considered that the application of STUDIO had been worthwhile and that the approach should be adopted on subsequent developments. The development team also felt that subsequent application developments would benefit from a more structured approach to software design and development.

As a consequence a subsequent project adopted the Objectory [3] method. This was helpful for the documenting of software design requirements and building robustness into the software. However the integration of STUDIO and Objectory was less straightforward. For example, Objectory suggests the production of "use cases" very early in the analysis phase of projects, but experience showed that use cases impose user interface design decisions. The sequence of task execution is often made explicit in use cases without sufficient consideration being given to the implications of such decisions. In addition use cases assume that the scope of the work is fixed at an unrealistically early stage. As a result of these experiences Linklaters & Paines decided that use cases and the later stages of Objectory should not be used until the user interface design has been completed through the application of STUDIO.

Lessons Learned

The lessons Linklaters & Paines learned about using a structured methodology in industry are:

- To deliver the highly interactive and highly usable applications demanded by a discerning user population, a structured approach to user interface design should be applied.
- A structured approach must facilitate user involvement and provide opportunities for testing the adequacy of a design as it develops.
- Only when a user interface design has been produced and evaluated is it appropriate to begin performing object-oriented analysis and design activities.

References

[1] D.P. Browne, (1994) *STUDIO: Structured User Interface Design for Interaction Optimization*, Prentice Hall.
[2] D. Harel (1987) "Statecharts: A Visual Formalism for Complex Systems", *Science of Computer Programming*, vol. 8, pp. 231-74.
[3] I.M. Jacobson, P. Christerson, P. Jonsson and G. Overgaard (1992) *Object-Oriented Software Engineering: A Use Case Driven Approach*, Addison-Wesley.

6. *Making Usability Part of the Culture*

How to Use "Change Management" Techniques and a Flexible Approach to Integrate Usability into the Corporate Culture

Janet Saunders and Alan Arnfeld

ABSTRACT

In order to be really successful, usability needs to become part of the everyday culture of the organization. This chapter describes how the recently established Usability Group at Thames Water is introducing a usability culture. Initially usability techniques were piloted in connection with a new software development project, and focused on establishing a usability lab. We show how usability has been incorporated into both in-house development and purchase of off-the-shelf packages, illustrating the need to understand the time and budget constraints of projects.

Making project managers responsible for usability was an important principle of these changes. In particular we focus on the need to employ "change management" techniques to ensure that the way "usability culture" is introduced fits with the existing organizational culture and methodologies. We adopted an approach based on the idea of "giving usability away"; using communication to spread usability messages and co-operation with developers and project managers to evolve methodology alongside them. Finally we describe some examples of how we are keeping the culture growing and the results of some of the changes.

Introduction

Introducing a "usability culture" into a large organization represents a significant effort in terms of "change management" – the challenge of applying an overall approach across differing product development methods that will be appropriate to the time and budget considerations of a wide range of projects.

Usability specialists have at their disposal a variety of methods for analysing user goals and business objectives, designing for ease of use, and testing that products are effective, efficient and satisfying to use. Applied in an ad hoc fashion these techniques will yield moderate results, but it is widely acknowledged that in order to be really successful, "usability engineering" techniques must become part of the culture of the whole product development cycle[1].

Some of the major system suppliers, for example Rank Xerox, Microsoft, IBM, BT and Philips [2] and major system procurers such as the UK Ministry of Defence and the US Department of Defence [3], adopt this "usability culture" approach, while several "user" organizations such as Glaxo R&D (UK), the Department of Employment and NatWest Bank, have also implemented significant changes. For the majority of large corporations, however, building this "culture of usability" is only just beginning. In the majority of IT projects it is left up to individual project managers and developers to apply their own ideas and methods to ensure usability – hence luck often plays a big part in the outcome.

This chapter describes how the recently established Usability Group at Thames Water is introducing a "usability culture" into the organization. Developing a usability culture is a non-trivial task, ensuring that key system design guidelines are followed [4], but at the same time managing the opportunities and dangers of internal organizational politics. The goal of the Usability Group at Thames is to enhance the performance of the company's business processes by ensuring that design solutions capitalize on user strengths and reduce the impact of user weaknesses. For this, usability is applied in its broadest sense, addressing human factors that are known to affect mental and physical task performance: organizational factors, group working factors, physical environment and the user interface with work equipment. Usability has a role throughout the product development cycle, from project scoping and requirements specification to implementation.

However, making this happen across an organization entails more than just gaining acceptance that a problem exists and convincing people that usability methods can solve the problem cost-effectively – it requires spreading this message throughout the organization so that all projects take account of usability. It is important that this is achieved through voluntary "buy-in" by management rather than coercion through senior management directives, as the methods will be much more effective if applied willingly and thus begin to "sell themselves". For this reason, getting usability into the everyday culture of the organization is crucial, and it is this process which forms the main focus of this chapter.

Thames Water

Thames Water serves 7 million direct water supply customers, and over 11 million sewerage customers. It has 371 sewage treatment works, 99 water treatment works, 22 supply reservoirs, 356 service reservoirs and over 7000 employees. It is a major user of IT, using software supplied by third parties as well as produced and maintained by its own in-house IT department. Usability methods began to be formally introduced within Thames Water (TW) in 1995 when an increased awareness of usability issues coincided with a major project to develop a new mainframe based system with a Graphical User Interface (GUI) front-end. This new system was a radical step for Thames Water which, like many other large corporations, manages the majority of their large databases through "old style" legacy mainframe systems, with menu-based or command-driven interfaces, notoriously difficult for users to learn and prone to user error.

As a first step, and to establish a benchmark, an analysis was undertaken of the usability of existing systems across the company, using the Software Usability Measurement Inventory (SUMI) [5] (see also Chapter 8, Consultants with Clout). This measures subjective user satisfaction against calibrated scores developed from analyses of a wide range of software products. A score of 50 is regarded as acceptable, with 60 and above representing "state-of-the-art". Out of nine systems tested, only two reached the score of 50 and there was clearly room for improvement. The SUMI analysis helped to convince senior management that placing particular emphasis on usability in the new GUI interface would improve the performance and job satisfaction of TW staff and reduce errors – leading to crucial benefits in cost saving and customer service.

A Usability Group was therefore established, with the new GUI project (known as QE2) as its first assignment. The usability team employed a methodology known as MUSiC, which emphasizes the importance of understanding the context in which systems are used [6]. For this, a usability laboratory was established and considerable success was achieved by running scenario-based tests using sample users and prototype systems, and feeding design issues back to the design team.

Through the QE2 project many users and software developers gained an increased awareness of usability issues, such as ease of learning, use of familiar terminology, ease of navigation and consistency between windows. Usability had proved its worth, but to apply a usability approach across all of TW software projects presented challenges. Involving other members of the department through lab tours was an important step in developing awareness of the benefits of usability. However, although visitors agreed that usability was a good thing, the effect of lab tours was to focus their understanding solely on the "testing" aspects of usability.

This has provided particular change management issues as the Usability Group sought to develop its services beyond the testing role. One negative lesson from the QE2 project was that developers had learned that applying usability methods is not without cost in time and resource, and the usability team had to take this on board as a challenge for future projects. The Usability Group at TW is small, around three people plus contract support, and it would be impossible for them to provide extensive support to all projects. Employing a change management approach to develop a "usability culture" across the company, was seen as a way of getting maximum benefit from scarce usability skills.

"Stopping the Rot": Working with Established Teams, Attitudes and Practices

It was seen as essential to get usability into all development projects, not simply those employing "new methods" like QE2, but also changes to legacy software and maintenance of existing systems. In addition, desktop applications were set to multiply in the wake of company-wide introduction of PCs and the migration to Windows 95 with Lotus Notes as an email and shared database tool. Some of these applications were being developed in-house, while other programs were in operation to purchase off-the-shelf software packages. It was important to ensure that usability issues were considered in both development and purchase of new applications, often in the contexts of minimal allocations of budget and timescale.

Working with Project Pressures

The project manager's role is frequently one of performing a delicate balancing act between meeting user requirements, incorporating rapidly changing technical possibilities and working round technical constraints, while delivering completed projects on time without over-spending on budget. The pressure is always on to reduce the "cycle-time" of development. In this scenario, emphasizing that products have good usability is inevitably seen as raising user expectations, together with raising time and budget costs.

Ironically a further problem has been created by the appeal of "user-centred design" (UCD) as an objective, without adequate education in the software community about what UCD actually involves, with the result that it has been frequently misapplied. Projects may simply have a user representative on the development team, who soon becomes too technically involved to provide good feedback, while too many projects try to be "user-led" asking users for requirements and feedback on designs, ignoring the problem that users are not trained as analysts or designers and are not skilled in software ergonomics. Once a product is in use, however, users can quickly discover problems in using software and the situation then easily deteriorates into one of apportioning blame. How often we hear of projects where developers complain that "the users changed the requirements". Bad experiences like this will mean that "usability" may not be a popular subject for some people in your organization.

Working with Developer Attitudes

Developer attitudes in general have to be taken into consideration. Many will want to focus on the technical part of their job and will consider that usability relates solely to the interface and is something that can be tidied up at the end of the project. Legacy programmers may have learned to their cost that getting the interface design and task flow wrong can lead to costly re-work, but newer tools and methods which separate the underlying technology from the interface appearance can encourage the view that usability is an add-on feature. Education of developers about usability's role and the need to focus on the user task is an important part of any strategy. In particular, from previous experience in organizations, the usability team at TW felt it was essential to emphasize a partnership approach with developers to avoid being seen as the "usability police".

Working with Diverse Methodologies

Software development methodologies come in many different flavours. At Thames an overarching process had been established to cover variations according to size and type of project. Two basic models were in existence: one broadly following a "waterfall" approach in which projects move through discrete phases of development, from inception, requirements specification, design, build and test; the other, still evolving, a methodology adopting a "rapid application development" (RAD) model, based on iterative steps and prototyping. In addition, special projects might be set up using a new tool with its own methods, in which case only the "terms of reference" part of the established methodology was used. With a multitude of software development methodologies to choose from, the last thing project managers and systems designers needed was an extra tier of "usability" phases. In addition, tying-in usability methods too closely to one software methodology invariably means that when the method is superseded, so too will your usability processes be. The challenge at TW was to introduce usability techniques into the traditional development methodology, at the same time as enabling the RAD model to take advantage of usability without compromising the time-saving benefits of its iterative approach. It was crucial to provide a set of options which could be used flexibly without losing value, particularly if usability was not to be ignored by any new methodologies that were adopted.

Beginnings of a Usability Culture

Work begun in the summer of 1996 to overhaul project development cycles was integrated into this effort. The goal was to establish a minimum set of usability standards and checkpoints in all development cycles, but the team was also determined to integrate usability across the board, and not merely impose a new level of "usability work" – which would have met with opposition from project managers, concerned to keep cycle times to a minimum. The established TW design methodology was based on a large set of process documents, together with skeleton documents, checklists and checkpoint documents for sign-off. All this documentation was reviewed and amendments were made to key documents to ensure that usability was considered at every appropriate stage, including management sign-off. Emphasis was placed throughout on integration with existing practice, rather than creating extra stages of work.

An essential factor in applying usability methods is to begin early in development. Close attention to the user task in the early stages of gathering requirements and initial specifications can avoid the costly pitfalls of only discovering severe usability problems through testing later in development. The amended documents emphasized this – for example, the Terms of Reference document required at the start of a project included a new paragraph describing the usability goals of the project and what usability techniques would be used. Attention was drawn in the skeleton document to the possibility of testing paper prototypes, and testing early screen designs.

Responsibility for usability and for involving the Usability Group, was left with the project team. This approach was important in fostering "buy-in" from project managers to the idea of seeing usability as part of their process and working with the Usability Group, rather than viewing usability as a "test" administered by the "usability police" which projects had to pass.

The key usability techniques were identified as follows:

- **Assign usability analyst to project** – intended for use in larger projects, or projects with major impact on users.
- **Define usability work in set-up documents** – critical to getting project teams thinking about usability from day one.
- **Set usability targets in the quality plan** – this ensured that usability was included in the QA process.
- **Carry out usability context analysis** – analysis of the context of the user task prior to scenario testing, and recommended for any large projects involving significant new design.
- **Use GUI guidelines** – the use of style guides and guidelines for screen design can be of help in ensuring consistency.
- **HCI and design consultancy** – consisting of more in-depth involvement of usability team in design.
- **Expert evaluation** – applying usability heuristics to assess interface designs.
- **Usability testing** – scenario-based testing of prototypes.
- **Training needs analysis and advice** – to assist the design and implementation process.

Any manager setting up a new IT project would find pointers in the process documentation to what techniques were appropriate at different stages of development, indicating whether these were optional, recommended, or mandatory, according to the project size (i.e. person days and budget) or impact on users. This provided flexibility to the project team and focused their attention on getting the maximum cost-benefits from usability techniques by applying them as early as possible.

As an additional means of gathering feedback, the Usability Group was added to the list of people to receive reports from post-implementation reviews, to assess the impact of usability methods and the team's involvement.

Applying Usability Techniques to Package Selection

The major challenge to applying usability in the package selection process is that although several products may need to be evaluated, budgets for the selection process are generally much smaller than for development projects. For example, an early project undertaken by the group allowed ten days for evaluating four products, with users available to take part in usability tests. The lab tests proved invaluable for giving users real hands-on experience and demonstrating potential problems with the packages, which had not emerged from supplier demonstrations, and the cost of making a wrong choice was avoided. However, several problems with usability lab tests for this kind of project have emerged:

- some packages being evaluated may be prototypes, for demonstration purposes, and are not easily adapted to the testing conditions;
- in designing scenarios, time must be spent ensuring that the packages can be used with suitable data;

- users need training time on new packages, in which the supplier must be involved;
- it is difficult to remove the influence of the supplier;
- it is very difficult to ensure that you are comparing "like with like".

Although the cost of making a wrong choice of package is considerable, the problems inherent in these kinds of evaluations can prove costly in analyst and lab time, and this may be hard to justify for package selection. (For a discussion of comparative usability evaluation see Chapter 11.)

In the light of these experiences the usability team at TW has adopted a trimmed-down evaluation method. This consists of encouraging project teams to pre-select a short-list of only two or three packages; carrying out user tests on the "favourite" package only, with a small number of users (perhaps only two) and a short scenario. All packages in the short-list are then subjected to "expert evaluation" by two usability analysts aided by a checklist. This approach has proved to be very cost-effective – it can be adjusted to fit even tiny budgets, but still shows up most of the major usability problems that will be encountered. This streamlined approach has allowed usability to have a presence in projects where it would otherwise have been considered an expensive – and thus expendable – luxury.

For package selection projects where no usability time could be allocated, the team felt we could nevertheless offer help and advice to project managers. The group has produced a checklist of ten basic usability checkpoints, written simply without jargon (with a qualifier that this cannot replace the greater benefit of expert evaluation or testing), which has been very well-received. Getting involved in package selection even in this small way provides an opportunity for the usability team to demonstrate their knowledge and "leaves the door open" for future work such as contributing to any package customization which might follow.

Cultural Sensitivity

With a set of usability methods for both in-house development and package selection ready to be integrated into projects, careful consideration was given to winning support for the changes and ensuring that project teams really "bought into" the goal of making usability part of everyday life. The usability team needed to be aware of "cultural" factors in the Thames Water organization and work within these for maximum effect. It is not an uncommon experience in organizations to have the ground move beneath your feet, and while the groundwork of setting up usability processes had been taking place, changes occurred in the Thames Water IT structure which had to be taken into account. (For a discussion of change management see Chapter 7.)

Reviewing the Group Strategy

During the last few months of 1996 the organization and staffing of the Usability Group was radically changed. While still remaining, importantly, within the IT division of Thames Water, it was moved to reside within a new permanent group called "Development Services", which was established to provide a home for specialists in usability, geographical information systems and architecture, to provide support to projects throughout Thames Water. This was an important milestone in establishing the Usability Group with some degree of stability. Furthermore, with comprehensive changes of permanent staff, including the appointment of a group leader with responsibility for usability strategy as well as projects, the group was ready to reorganize, looking ahead for the next five years.

This presented a golden opportunity to widen the objectives of the Usability Group and to clarify what services it could offer, not merely as a general portfolio, but very specifically directed towards the needs of Thames Water. Meetings were held with all senior staff within the IT department and area managers to provide a clear model of future IT strategy within the department. This enabled the Usability Group to develop a one-page brochure of "Usability Services". Managers' time is always squeezed, so the brochure was not a flashy document but a simple black and white text-based document designed to allow usability staff to give quick five-minute presentations to busy managers.

The brochure contained the following key messages:

- statement of the goal of Usability Services;
- business benefits;
- how these would be achieved;
- example services.

Growing the Culture by Giving Usability Away

One of the major outcomes of the meetings with senior management was the desire to "give usability away" to developers across the department. With the limited resource of a small group of usability professionals, helping developers to become more self-sufficient in applying usability techniques was seen as the key to improving standards of usability in development projects. This was quite a revolutionary goal, which to succeed in the long-term required far more than simply providing usability training, which could all too easily be forgotten when developers were faced with the trade-off between design and technical choices.

The group considered a wide range of ad hoc approaches to "giving usability away", such as reinforcing training by fostering a usability culture among developers through such strategies as letters to key personnel, newspaper reports, regular briefings etc. It was decided, however, to adopt an approach based on Badiru's "Triple C" model, a proven methodology based upon project management and psychological principles [7]. This approach is structured around three phases – communication, co-operation and co-ordination – in which communication facilitates transfer of knowledge, attitudes and skills, and co-operation between personnel fosters acceptance of these new concepts within normal working practice. These two phases form a prerequisite to a third phase in which the new skills can be co-ordinated across IT personnel onto projects as part of everyday activity. The Usability Group does not see this as a one-off activity, but envisages a continuous cycle of giving skills away and co-ordinating their application, such that as developers become self-sufficient in one area of usability, the transfer of other skills can be put into operation.

At the time of writing we have been using the Triple C model with TW usability for about seven months, with emphasis predominantly on the communication and co-operation aspects. The co-ordination phase will come fully into operation when developer awareness and training has progressed further, and so the sections below are based on our experiences with the first two phases and challenges we expect to meet in the co-ordination phase.

Communication: Selling the Message

In practice the communication activity spirals out from the core group within the IT department to the company as a whole. The initial focus has been on communicating with all functional groups and individuals within the IT department, particularly key people who can exert influence across the organization.

To begin the communication, individual presentations for managers and team talks were given, and are continually offered to explain key usability messages. Individual presentations were based on the five-minute presentation noted earlier in this chapter, consisting of a statement of the goals of usability services, the business benefits, how these would be achieved (including training) and example services. The team presentation extended this, with a greater emphasis on our aim of "giving usability away" to developers, by providing training and support (which was enthusiastically received), discussions of how we could work together in partnership to improve the usability of business processes and systems, and some indication of what would be expected from developers, for example access to users, test prototypes etc.

It is essential to continually sell and resell the usability messages within the IT department. In addition, we have also discovered considerable demand for our services in projects outside the IT department, for example in research and technology, and engineering. These opportunities have developed as a result of our communication activities, such as:

- Thames Water has an IT departmental magazine called "Connections" which is distributed around the company quarterly. We have begun a series of regular articles and adverts explaining how to optimize product usability. The first article introduced the Usability Group's one-day "Systems Healthcheck", which has proved to be very popular.
- The IT department, in connection with our work on package selection outlined earlier, has produced a "Buyers Guide" that will be distributed internationally.
- Publicizing the Thames Water Usability Group's activities to the outside world is viewed as beneficial. Publications in professional magazines and books such as this one, add credibility to the Usability Group's standing, which contributes towards achieving our aim of "giving usability away" within the company.

Not all communication activities should necessarily come directly from the Usability Group. Messages have even more power and directness when they come from senior IT management personnel. While they may not have detailed knowledge and experience of usability tools and techniques, these people can "say the right things" at meetings and to their teams, quickly breaking down some of the barriers to usability. We see these managers as "champions of usability", and the importance of their contribution to spreading the word can be indicated by recent examples.

Thames Water is involved in many projects with local schools. One has involved an IT specialist providing a series of talks to a local school. Her senior manager suggested usability should be an important part of explaining what IT in industry is all about. At school the children were taught about usability and carried out some exercises. Some children were then able to visit TW Headquarters which included a tour of the usability lab and participation in a usability trial, in which they had great fun pretending to deal with library customer enquiries. This kind of activity raises the profile of usability within the company as well as in the outside world.

Within TW we are constantly reviewing our development methodologies and in addition to those mentioned earlier in this chapter, a new methodology to support "three-tier architecture" is being developed. The senior manager in leading this project has listed usability as one of the three key drivers and benefits, which has been a key selling point to the Board and to the company as a whole.

Co-operation: Encouraging Staff Involvement

From our experience elsewhere, it is rarely sufficient merely to inform key IT staff about usability. For the strategy to be successful, co-operation has to be explicitly sought and the usability strategy has to incorporate developers' needs as well. The justification of the usability objective must be explained to all groups concerned, including IT staff, managers, clients and suppliers. Merely giving a nod to the usability effort may not be an indication of full co-operation, and so in seeking the co-operation of IT staff, explicit statements must be made about roles and responsibilities and co-operative work.

Leading by example rather than merely stating that co-operation is required is essential. The changes required within the company to bring about a usability culture are quite radical and one must manage expectations carefully and take things step by step. For example, within TW, the Usability Group has a five-year plan for "giving usability away" across the company – we do not expect change to happen overnight.

A good example of how the Usability Group is fostering co-operation is demonstrated by a project connected with the introduction of Lotus Notes. As the use of Lotus Notes spreads across the company it is expected that a large number of bespoke applications will be produced. A design database has been jointly produced by the Usability Group, other members of the IT department and engineering. These guidelines from different sources merge seamlessly and what was particularly nice about this project was that some of the usability guidelines were suggested by other contributors, that is, not usability staff, which is exactly what we want to see across the company.

Within projects it is essential that the usability team is flexible about the degree of involvement it takes. Some project managers have a very clear idea of the support they need while others are unsure and require advice. Rather than acting as the "usability police" we aim to provide varying levels of support. Obviously as part of the long-term training and awareness programmes within the company we expect greater demands to be placed upon the group in the future but it is important not to push project managers and IT developers too hard, otherwise one risks creating resentment and severe barriers to future development of our services.

Co-ordination: Sustaining the Usability Process

As we have previously explained, co-ordination is, to date, the area of least practical experience for the Thames Water usability team. Two levels to the co-ordination process have been identified, and the challenges they present are described below.

The first involves co-ordination of usability staff across multiple projects. The major challenges here are in locating all the projects requiring support and scheduling work across these projects. Scheduling work often presents difficulties because there will be many unknown variables when projects are outside the control of the Usability Group. There are no easy answers to this and it is important to be aware of the problem and try to keep on top of scheduling by regular review. For locating projects and co-ordinating them, the key is to ensure that all project steering groups and managers are regularly informed of what the Usability Group can do, and to ensure that the usability team actively elicit what projects are likely to occur in the future.

We have yet to tackle the issue of co-ordinating the usability activities of IT developers, once they are trained. It is anticipated that training will be a continuous activity with a general awareness briefing followed by specific training programmes such as usability testing. It will be important for these people to maintain contact both with the usability specialist and with each other. Some options for formalizing contact include: setting up a usability discussion database; an annual or bi-annual usability conference forum where everyone can share ideas on how usability techniques worked in particular situations, with problems and solutions proposed; and developer secondments to the usability group.

It is important to note that "Triple C" is a continuous process, and that levels of its development will vary in different parts of the organization. This is not seen as a problem, because experience learned in one area can be transferred to another.

Growing the Culture: Gaining Commitment to Change

Within most IT organizations there will be various individuals, or committees responsible for overall technical strategy, including technical direction and development methodology – it is important that these people are won over in implementing any usability strategy, because they can provide the route to spreading the change throughout the organization. Within Thames Water in-house development methodologies are guided and monitored by a steering group comprising representatives from across the internal IT departments. Winning over senior managers in this group at an early stage, provided invaluable assistance in persuading the whole group that usability integration was going to be of major benefit, and the resulting commitment of the steering group has helped considerably in ensuring that usability becomes integrated in practice. This group was also responsible for approving the adoption of new technologies in development, such as rapid application development and object-oriented methods. It was important to ensure that usability was not seen as competing with these methodologies, but in a complementary – and essential – role.

Having gained the methodology steering group's approval and commitment to the proposed changes to development methodologies, the next step was to communicate the changes to the development community. Specifically this meant providing the information to project managers in a format which would yield results, rather than just a cursory glance. Project managers needed to understand the changes without having to read all the amended documents. Reassurance that this was not "just more work" was important.

Publicizing the Changes

Project managers and software developers are familiar with a publication format known as a "reference card", in which information is summarized on a small three column folding card. It was decided to publish a "Handy Guide" to usability in the Thames Water development cycles in this format. The card's first page provided contact information and outlined the key points of the changes, while the inside fold was headed "Making Usability Part of the Process", and described in more detail how the various usability techniques could be applied through the life of the project. The central three pages of the card opened out to present a tabular guide to usability activities and their applicability to the different product development cycles, indicating mandatory, recommended or optional methods.

The style of the card was concise and helpful, and was tested by internal review within the Usability Group, and by a member of the methodology steering group. At this stage some inconsistencies between development terminology in different cycles were ironed out. The card was professionally printed and sent to every project manager. Publication coincided with an article about usability services in one of the company's internal magazines.

Keeping the Culture Growing: Early Results

The goals of establishing and maintaining a usability culture can be summarized:

- Improved customer orientation of processes: improved usability, process quality, user performance, customer satisfaction.
- Reduced costs of system development through reduced re-work and faster user training.
- Reduced through-life costs: reduced training and "skill fade", reduced staff turnover and absenteeism.

- Increased staff flexibility – through improved inter-operability between software processes.
- Marketing edge for products competing in the marketplace.

Early feedback from projects already undertaken by the team indicates that significant benefits can be expected from the "usability culture" approach at Thames Water: the new systems are less prone to user error, and are well-accepted by users; developers and users have indicated an increased faith in the product development process; and managers are beginning to appreciate the benefits of "fire safety" rather than "fire-fighting" to get more usability into products.

In the past, usability staff have had to be very proactive in identifying projects which would benefit from usability. Making project managers responsible for usability and giving them a structured set of techniques which can be applied inside product development cycles has led to many requests for advice on choosing usability methods from managers scoping new projects – three occurred within a week of distributing the handy guide! Getting involved at the start of projects is a key part of the TW Usability Group strategy – so getting the communication out to project managers seems to have paid off. It will no doubt remain a constant challenge to explain to cost-conscious project managers that they must spend time on usability early on to reap through-life benefits – keeping the communication channels open plays a part here. Wherever possible expert evaluation and use of guidelines are recommended as less time-consuming than lab-based prototype testing, but on projects of major impact, lab-testing is imperative.

Various activities are ongoing to maintain a high awareness of usability and to support the usability culture. As new methodologies are introduced into the company, the Usability Group is being fully involved in joint development projects, co-operating with software teams to ensure that usability is integrated into any new methods. As part of the strategy of "giving usability away", to help developers be more self-sufficient in applying usability techniques, education and training programmes are being put in place. Usability staff will remain available to provide technical support and to coach project teams wherever necessary. In this way the team hopes to be able to raise the awareness of usability methods still further and to co-ordinate usability efforts across a growing number of projects.

Making Usability a Part of the Culture: Lessons Learned

Making usability part of the organizational culture is a way of ensuring that your team can increase the awareness of usability at the same time as serving the resulting ever-growing demand for usability services. At Thames Water this is an on-going programme and we still have some way to go, but here are some of the key points from our experience so far:

- Be sensitive to the culture and methods of your organization – your methods have to fit in if they are to be successful.
- Keep an eye on changes in organizational structure and work with them to spread usability – do not just defend your corner.

- Keep strategy plans and documents advertising your services short and snappy.
- Choose a strategy based on project management concepts which will be well-accepted by other project managers.
- Make project managers responsible for usability and keep the communication channels open so that they can ask you for help. All too often the Usability Group has responsibility without authority – beware of this.
- Keep an eye on new methodologies – they may claim to include usability methods, or may exclude them altogether. Keep on top of new developments and let your development community know what new methods and tools can and cannot do.
- Do not compete with new development methods – co-operate and ensure usability is integrated.
- Be prepared to "give usability away".
- Do not forget that usability methods can help in evaluating purchased packages as well as in-house development.
- Remember that usability lab tests can be time-consuming to prepare, conduct and analyse. They will probably always take longer than you think – recommend expert evaluations where budgets are tight.
- Do not overlook the need to constantly sell, resell and explain usability to senior management, outsiders, clients, project teams and other departments.

References

[1] J. Nielsen (1993) *Usability Engineering*, Academic Press, London.
[2] J. Nielsen (1994) "Usability Laboratories", *Behaviour and Information Technology*, vol 13 nos. 1 and 2, pp. 3-8. (This volume was a special issue on usability, containing papers describing usability processes at 13 companies).
[3] H. Booher (ed.) (1990) *MANPRINT: An Approach to Systems Integration*, Van Nostrand Reinhold, New York.
[4] J. Preece (ed.) (1994) *Human Computer Interaction*, Addison Wesley, Wokingham.
[5] M. Porteous, J. Kirakowski and M. Corbett (1993) *The SUMI User Handbook*, Human Factors Research Group, University College, Cork.
[6] Based on the Esprit MUSiC Project, led by the National Physical Laboratory. R. Rengger, M. Macleod, R. Bowden, A. Drynan and M. Blayney (1993) *MUSiC Performance Measurement Handbook, V2*, NPL, DITC, Teddington, UK.
[7] A.B. Badiru (1987) "Communication, Cooperation, Co-ordination: The Triple C of Project Management", *Proceedings of the International Industrial Engineering Conference*, Spring 1987, Washington, DC, pp. 401-404.

Part 3

The Politics of Survival:
Keeping Usability on the Political Map

7. *A Change is as Good as a Test*

How to Respond to Changes in Project Structure and Still Do a Good Job

Maggie Williams

ABSTRACT

The objective of this chapter is to examine some of the changes that can affect usability input to a software project and to identify techniques for re-scoping usability work whilst keeping sight of the main goals. Typical changes to software projects involve budgets, project specification, timescales and delivery dates, personnel and internal politics. In order to do meaningful usability work within this context, the chapter recommends that usability practitioners try to limit the likelihood of change, predict possible changes and plan for contingency and find ways to respond to changes when they occur. It draws on the experience of a team of usability analysts acting as in-house consultants to a large scale bespoke project developing financial software and focuses on changes that affected the evaluation phase.

Introduction

When planning appropriate usability work for a software development project, factors such as the availability of suitable skills, time and budgetary constraints need to be taken into account. However, even judicious plans made well in advance are subject to unexpected change which can impact the scale of usability involvement as well as the type of work which may be carried out.

It is easy for usability work to be sidelined or diluted within a project as a result of changes such as reductions in timescales or budget. Understanding the types of change which can affect your plans and recognizing risk points when those changes occur are important elements in ensuring that usability remains a facet of system design, development and testing, regardless of changing circumstances. Responding to those changes once they occur requires flexibility and good communication on the part of both the usability analyst and the project team. In the following sections, I outline some of the major types of change which can affect projects, and suggest some methods of responding effectively to those changes.

The Suite Project – a Case Study

The case study in this chapter draws on the experiences of a team of five usability analysts within a large financial organization in the UK which undertakes most of its own bespoke software development. The team had a cross-organizational remit, allowing them to work for any part of the company or any of its subsidiary businesses, several of which were based in Europe. Usability work was not a compulsory part of software development in any part of the organization, and a cross-charging system was operated whereby the usability department was required to charge individual projects for all work undertaken. Payment was generally made from the development budget. As such, usability work had to deliver quantifiable benefits in the shortest possible time and fit into the project's methodology.

Usability analysts were not integrated into software development teams, and were required to work on an ad-hoc consultancy basis for several projects simultaneously. This also generated a number of potential problems, most of which were related to the level and quality of communication between the main project team and the usability department.

Many of the discussion points in this section relate to a specific programme of usability work undertaken for a major strategic project, referred to here as the Suite Project. This suite of software products would be used in a network of financial outlets by staff who were relatively inexperienced in using PC-based applications, but possessed a very high level of specialist task knowledge. The tasks involved financial processes such as opening a personal bank account, providing customers with information about financial products, monitoring overdue accounts and providing banking services to small businesses. Geographically, the software development and business analysis teams were spread over a number of different sites, none of which was located in the same building as the usability department. Access to the software's potential users was relatively unlimited, but the majority of the staff had targeted workloads which would be impacted by time spent on usability testing.

In this instance, the usability department was involved from a reasonably early point in the development life cycle. However, in the initial stages of the project the experience of the usability analysts themselves was limited and predominantly focused on running laboratory based tests. With a project of this size and scope, it was vital to respond quickly and effectively to changes in the project timescales, budgets and requirements. A high standard of usability work needed to remain a key objective for the project and the usability section needed to establish its position within the organization as a whole. Usability work on the Suite Project spanned most of its life cycle, which ran to several years. For the purposes of this chapter, I have taken examples from the development stages.

Predicting the Unpredictable – Where Do Changes Come from?

In order to respond effectively to project changes, a usability analyst must understand the types of changes that may take place and develop an ability to predict when changes might occur. It is almost inevitable that there will be changes to the delivery dates and design scope of products as a development progresses. Although it is possible, and advisable to build a level of contingency into usability plans in terms of timescales and budgetary constraints, it is difficult to plan for more extreme modifications to a project, such as alterations to the scope of the requirements, or changes in the project team.

From experience, there are several key forms of change that can affect the type of usability work that can be undertaken. The following is not intended to be an exhaustive assessment of project risks, rather it identifies a number of factors that had to be taken into consideration on developments that my colleagues and I were involved with, in particular on the Suite project.

Financial Changes

Reduction in budget is one of the most common reasons for cancelling usability work, and one of the most difficult to overcome. In the most extreme cases, loss or reduction in budget can result in an entire project being cancelled or put on hold, although it is more usual for the budget to be capped, often in mid-development. The ways in which this can manifest itself include removal of resources or shortening the time in which the project must be completed. At this point, project managers sometimes begin to question the importance of usability input altogether, particularly if usability consultants were employed on an ad hoc basis. In more favourable circumstances, the project manager will consult with usability staff to identify ways in which a more limited set of activities can be carried out.

Time spent convincing sceptical managers of the importance of usability to the core success of their project occupied many hours during the course of the Suite Project, which suffered a number of budget cuts during its development. Most of the application budget holders understood the relevance of usability and its likely impact on the project and were prepared to negotiate to identify lower cost techniques. However, in certain cases, retaining any usability input to the individual applications was a lengthy and frustrating process. Sometimes this was due to the perception that the usability analysts were not part of the project team (as mentioned earlier, usability work was paid for as an "extra" from the development budget).

Changes in the Project Specification

Changes in project requirements can also be linked to financial changes – a decision to remove non-critical functionality from an application design is a further way of reducing expenditure. However, from a usability perspective, changes in project scope affect the design of the work which is carried out, particularly if the way in which the software will be used, or the types of user who are likely to interact with it also change as a result of the revised specification.

Within a multi-function application such as the Suite Project, this type of change manifested itself in a number of ways. In one instance, two applications were merged together, and hence the range of users who would have access to the system expanded accordingly. This required considerable amendments to the way in which we approached the usability testing for this new application, to ensure that the needs of all types of user were being addressed.

Slippage in Delivery Dates

When a project's deadlines slip for whatever reason, there is usually a need to either amend the scope of the usability work which is undertaken, reschedule the entire evaluation, or establish a compromise between these two possibilities, such as testing part of the system at a later date. Slippage can cause problems in the availability of usability staff as well as requiring changes in the planning of the work. We found it preferable to assign an analyst to a project throughout its life cycle whenever possible, as this resulted in a better relationship between our department and the project team. Changes to the project timescales happened at fairly regular intervals. To help the analyst and to assure continuing quality of service to the project team, we documented our progress carefully so that new usability staff could take up the baton at short notice, if required.

Changes in Management

Attitudes towards usability varied within the organization from keen enthusiasm to suspicious murmurings of "overhead cost" and "nice to have". From discussions with other usability practitioners, I am aware that our department was not unique in experiencing this diversity, particularly in the early stages of our existence when the concept of usability as a part of systems design was not well established. And it is a theme that appears frequently in this book! When restructuring took place, either within a project or at a higher organizational level, it was not unusual to find an enthusiastic project manager replaced with a more cynical incumbent, and vice versa. The former situation often resulted in renewed discussions on the validity of usability to project success – the latter placed us in the difficult but more desirable situation of having to scope and carry out usability work on a project at short notice.

How We Learned to Cope with Changes

Dealing with the types of change outlined above required a subtle blend of technical and interpersonal skills that our usability department developed with time. Over the course of the Suite Project, we made a number of changes to the way in which we approached usability with development projects of this type. Although the large scale of this particular project was exceptional, the lessons which we learned from undertaking the work were subsequently applied to other software development projects across the organization. Again, the following pointers are not intended to be exhaustive, and many of them reflect the experiences of carrying out work as an internal consultant operating as part of a large organization.

These experiences can be grouped into three main categories:

- limiting the likelihood of change;
- predicting change before it occurs and providing contingency;
- responding to change.

Limiting the Likelihood of Change

I have yet to be involved in a software development project of any size which has not experienced some form of change to its scope, timescales or budget during at least one stage in its life cycle. Although it would be impossible to try to predict and make allowances for all of the possible changes that might occur in a software development project, certain types of change can be contained quite effectively.

Set Clear Objectives for Usability Work

Although obvious, and fundamental to any form of project work, setting precise, achievable objectives for usability work was frequently overlooked in the early projects undertaken by the usability section. Measurable goals and realistic plans must do more than merely outline what is to be achieved: they must also provide a means of encouraging a project to "buy into" usability involvement and recognize it as a critical success factor, as important as accurate functional specification.

In the case of the Suite Project, setting objectives needed to be undertaken at two levels: goals for each of the constituent applications within the suite, and higher level criteria to ensure consistency and ease of use between products and across the suite as a whole. Identifying and gaining commitment to this latter set of objectives was particularly problematic for a number of reasons:

- General communications within the Suite Project were poor. Development teams were located in a variety of different departments, and were not always in contact with one another.
- Each application had a separate project manager – there was no overall "owner" (or funding) for usability issues related to the suite as a whole.
- Attitudes towards usability varied between sub-applications. Some proactively looked for input whilst others considered evaluation work a drain on project resources.

Because of these problems, our higher level goals were generic and poorly defined, for example, we stated that, "the user interface must be consistent across the products". In retrospect, setting more precise global goals would have saved time in each of the individual developments, and would have enabled us to design and evaluate the suite as a whole from a far more scientific perspective.

In the case of the composite applications, it was possible to define much more specific aims and assign targets for the product. By setting usability-specific objectives in addition to functional requirements, it became easier to integrate our goals into the project's general success criteria, and hence become a more established part of the development process. In doing so, the likelihood of usability work being marginalized or removed from the project plan was reduced. This also enabled the usability analysts to alter the type or magnitude of an evaluation if time or resources were cut at short notice yet still to achieve the same general goals.

Understand the Nature of the Software Development Life Cycle

As the majority of the usability department's work was carried out on an ad hoc basis, gaining a general understanding of the structure of individual project life cycles was sometimes difficult. Appreciating the level of pressure with which developers and analysts are required to work is vital both to making achievable recommendations at the end of a usability project and to gauging the amount of input that can be requested from other members of the project team.

In the case of the Suite Project, achieving this understanding was particularly important, as it used a number of broadly similar but slightly different project development methodologies within the constituent products. Each application within the Suite Project had varying levels of complexity and timescales for development, as well as differing user profiles and tasks. Individual products were assigned a priority ranking related to their relevance to the business, which was reflected in their budget and the stability of their resources. This in turn dictated the amount of time and money which, if the project manager were willing, could be allocated to usability work.

Know which Tasks Are Critical

In most cases, software will have a set of core functionality which will be used frequently and by the majority of end users. Other additional functions may be used only rarely, and/or by a different type of user. For example, a large-scale accounting system may contain data entry functionality that will be used virtually every day by the majority of its users and also system administration capabilities that will be used a few times during the entire life of the product. In this instance, assigning limited usability resource without an awareness of task criticality could result in poorly designed data entry functionality that is used daily and a beautifully designed administration function that is used by a handful of people.

Focusing usability effort on features which will be frequently used, or require a high degree of accuracy from the user is likely to have the greatest impact on the system as a whole. General tenets regarding consistent interface design and navigation can be extrapolated to the less well used functionality and a less structured form of usability testing applied, if appropriate. Identifying which features are the most critical or frequently used can be derived from contextual analysis as well as by observation of current working methods and additional interviews with users. In this case, "participative evaluation" involved showing prototype, or limited functionality systems to two or more users simultaneously. Each user was given some opportunity to carry out tasks on the system, but as part of the group rather than in a laboratory situation.

Table 7.1 shows some examples of how tasks can be prioritized for inclusion in usability testing.

Table 7.1: Examples of task prioritization

Project: **Suite Project**
Product Name: **TimeManager**
User Type: **Personal Financial Advisor**

Task Name	Frequency of use	Criticality of output	Priority/type of testing	Comments
Enter customer appointment	3-5 times daily	High – date and time must be correct	High – recommend inclusion in lab test	
Create customer appointment letter	3-5 times daily	High – letter contents must include correct information	High – recommend inclusion in lab test	
Create new letter template	3-4 times yearly	Medium – templates must incorporate changes in company details	Low – recommend brief review by usability analyst	Task only required occasionally if and when company details change – assistance in creating templates also available via on-site specialists

The benefit of this type of analysis is that if the scope of an evaluation needs to be reduced (or expanded), there is an agreed set of guidelines which outline tasks should be retained as part of the work, and areas of the system which could be tested in a less stringent fashion.

Identify a Clear Set of "Rules" for Usability Testing

Any form of usability work which involves genuine users, from relatively informal focus groups to structured laboratory evaluations will attract attention from a number of different sectors of the organization. Some may wish to gather information from the participants, and others may have entirely different objectives from those of the usability evaluation. Co-ordinating contact between users and representatives from other parts of the company requires careful planning – we found balancing company politics with adherence to the goals of the usability work was one of the most consistently difficult parts of carrying out laboratory based tests. Box 7.1 shows some of the most effective ways we developed of ensuring that an evaluation stays true to its original aims.

Laboratory based testing in the later stages of the Suite Project was frequently perceived by project managers as a way of demonstrating the success of their product to senior management, rather than as a diagnostic tool for providing feedback to developers. Persuading project managers to release software at an appropriate stage for usability testing and focusing attention on the core tasks of the system, rather than the parts of the application which the project team considered to be the most impressive, often required considerable effort. Preliminary discussions with the project team to ensure that developers understand that it is the software which is being tested, and not their expertise as programmers can be as important as reassuring users that they are not, personally, being assessed.

Box 7.1: Harmonious usability testing: making sure everyone gets what they want from a laboratory evaluation without changing the nature of the test

Set a deadline for changing the evaluation plans – accepting new tasks as part of a lab-based evaluation at short notice, or agreeing to add additional questions into a focus group structure at the very last minute are sure-fire ways of limiting the effectiveness of the evaluation. The usability analyst will not be fully prepared to handle the new inclusions and will not be able to produce high quality results. Agreeing a cut-off date beyond which the structure of the evaluation cannot be altered encourages the project team to agree what they require from the testing in advance, and provides the usability analyst with time to prepare.

Agree a structure for the test day – other members of the project team, such as trainee developers or help designers may also need to talk to users in order to successfully complete their work. I have found that it is preferable to allocate additional time slots during the test days when designers and users can get together to discuss areas of development such as this, rather than attempting to gather all of the information as part of the usability test itself. Experienced training and help design staff understand their own information requirements better than a usability analyst, and holding a number of shorter, informal discussions is less intensive for users than one lengthy session. However, it is also important to structure the day in such a way that the user is not put under undue pressure, or thoroughly exhausted by constant rounds of questioning!

Brief observers and technical support staff in advance – if you want observers to do just that and nothing more, let them know in advance. In my experience, most observers are content not to encroach on an evaluation or interview session, provided they know in advance. Similarly, explaining to technical support staff about the type of help they should give users during a lab-based evaluation will reduce the likelihood of support staff bursting into an evaluation room and carrying out the tasks for the user (as the apocryphal tale has it!).

Predicting the Need for Change

Being sufficiently aware of a project's progress to be able to predict when and where in the project life cycle changes may occur requires some degree of practice and a good understanding of how a software project operates. "If we'd known x, we could have done y" was a piece of feedback which frequently passed between the usability department and the Suite Project development teams – in both directions. In the majority of cases, it related to situations that could have been avoided.

Establish a Good Working Relationship with the Project Manager

Being made aware of potential problems as early as possible is dependent on good communication between the project managers and the usability analyst. Establishing an effective means of ensuring that realistic information about project progress is relayed to the usability department is essential so that potential problems and changes to timescales can be identified as early as possible. Experience on the Suite Project highlighted the dangers of relying on management reports and "official" documentation for tracking project progress. These frequently presented a far healthier image of progress than was the true case, resulting in work having to be rescheduled or cancelled at short notice.

Ensuring that the development team as a whole understood the reasons for carrying out usability testing, and establishing a role as an extended part of the development team resulted in less fraught, and more beneficial usability input. We did not want to be regarded as the "usability police". In general, we found that agreeing a single, main point of contact within a project at the outset, and creating a good working relationship with that person was fundamental to successful and timely usability work, and also paved the way for better discussions when changes were required.

Box 7.2: Asking the right questions: how to ensure that you know how a project is really progressing

Official documentation – although not always the most up to date or accurate reflection of project activities, progress reports and management summaries ensure that you are aware of progress on an on-going basis.

Be aware of impending personnel changes – changes in a project team, particularly at a higher level may bring different attitudes towards usability, as discussed earlier. Finding out about a new manager's opinions in advance, and meeting to discuss work already in progress can help you predict possible changes in direction or emphasis.

Ask the obvious – projects often have to communicate change at a number of different levels. As our department worked with developments on an ad hoc basis, important information was not always passed on to us. In general, this was not intentional – more often than not, it was simple oversight. Asking "stupid" questions, confirming that the scope of the project remained the same, and that its priorities and required benefits still remained consistent with the original plans often unearthed vital pieces of information which had not been communicated to us and were fundamental to the success of the usability work.

Retain Control over as Much of the Usability Process as Possible

Where large scale evaluations are concerned, retaining control over as many different facets of the testing as possible reduces the risk of generating inappropriate results and allows the greatest flexibility if the need for change arises. Writing suitable scripts for a lab-based evaluation is a particularly good example of a process which can be delegated to another area of the project, such as trainee developers, or business analysts. Delegating the script writing in this way is beneficial in cases where the users of the final system possess highly specialized areas of expertise which it would not be feasible for the usability analyst to acquire in the time available. However, overall control of the script content and suitability for evaluation should remain with the usability analyst, who should be prepared to assign and adhere to strict timescales for its completion and testing.

The Suite Project contained a number of applications that were highly specialized. One early evaluation involving a data processing task generated problems of nightmarish proportions during usability testing. Most of these could have been avoided with better communication and a greater involvement with the project team. Due to the specialized nature of the application, it was agreed that the project developers would write the script for the evaluation. Lack of co-ordination between the usability analysts and the project team meant that the test scenarios were not delivered to us until the day before the evaluation. At that point, it transpired that the script lasted 20 minutes, rather than the expected hour, leaving us with long gaps in the testing schedule. This was compounded on the days of the test when the users who had been recruited did not understand some of the terminology used in the script and were unable to complete the tests as expected. In order to gain any valid data from the users and salvage the evaluation, we had to hurriedly construct a set of questions and simpler scenarios which could be worked through in conjunction with the usability analyst using a developer from the project team to gather feedback from users.

Responding to Unforeseen Change

In an ideal situation, this part of the chapter should not be necessary! However, some changes cannot be predicted, and it is generally these situations where a response is required most quickly. Flexibility in terms of methodology and approach to working with a project prove to be the greatest assets in this situation, as the above example illustrates, and many of the pointers discussed in the previous two sections, such as good communications and solid usability objectives lighten the load when this type of change is required.

Adopt a "Toolbox" Methodology

As our usability department gained experience and stability, it became possible to broaden the general range of services which could be offered to projects. By creating a "toolbox" methodology, analysts were in a position to identify techniques that could be tailored to the requirements of an individual development. This also gave us the ability to substitute techniques if changes occurred in a project, without losing sight of the application's overall usability objectives.

The underlying tenet of ensuring that whatever usability work is carried out produces appropriate, good quality results still applies, even if you suddenly have half as much time in which to produce them. In my experience, it is better to change the type of evaluation undertaken (or reduce the scope of the scheduled work), than to attempt to carry through the original plans if they are no longer achievable in the time available. There is one major caveat to this approach: certain types of activity are essential to carrying out any form of usability effectively, and these are eliminated at the risk of invalidating the results. Box 7.3 illustrates some types of activity which are fundamental to gaining a good understanding of the system regardless of the types of work which are later carried out.

Box 7.3: Essential usability work

Context analysis – understanding the skills and background of typical users, and the environment in which they work are vital to contributing effectively to a product's development. The information which is gathered during context analysis provides a basis for any evaluative or design input to the project, and also provides information for business analysts and developers.

Task analysis – understanding what a user needs to achieve using a soft - ware product, and how they go about fulfilling those goals to a reasonably low level of detail allows usability analysts to assist in structuring these tasks in a pragmatic fashion in the software development. (However, you may need to restrict task analysis to key tasks if time is short.)

Usability objectives– some of the risks (and bitter experiences) associated with not setting clear usability objectives for a project have been discussed elsewhere in this chapter, however a box on "essential usability work" would not be complete without reiterating the importance of this point.

Be Prepared to Experiment

Provided that work can be done to a sufficiently high standard, developing new techniques, or amending existing ones can allow usability practitioners to respond more effectively to change. On the Suite project, flexibility and a willingness to experiment with new techniques enabled us to find innovative ways of including usability work in projects which we would otherwise have been unable to assist. We drew on the experience of others via research, collaborative working and discussion groups and this gave us a wealth of new approaches to evaluation. We experimented with techniques from within the traditional usability domain, and also adapted them from other disciplines such as market research.

Many of the early evaluations carried out on the Suite Project required a considerable amount of resource and time to prepare and produce results which were of limited benefit. We quickly identified the need to streamline the way in which we carried out lab-based evaluations, as well as developing new techniques which would generate good, appropriate results in the minimum of time. For example, we used participative evaluation to gather diagnostic feedback on prototypes. This involved showing systems in prototype or with limited functionality to two or more users simultaneously. Each user was given some opportunity to carry out tasks on the system, but as part of the group rather than individually in the lab. We also held focus groups to gain an understanding of the way in which a current system was being used and this provided as much benefit to developers as the original larger-scale lab evaluations we had planned.

Develop some "Hands-off" Techniques

There is no substitute for true user involvement in the development of a system, preferably at regular stages throughout the life cycle of a project, and getting the most out of that user involvement is one of the prime responsibilities of the usability analyst. However, sometimes, cuts in budget or reductions in time-scale are sufficiently severe that there is no way of including formal usability input. Working on the principle that some usability is better than no usability at all, we also developed a number of quick, simple techniques which could be applied by the project team themselves. These included:

- a template of suggestions for interview questions, so that usability feedback could be gathered as part of a wider review process;
- checklists that business analysts could use to evaluate user interfaces;
- general research consultancy to enable projects involved in more unusual systems design (such as interactive television banking services) to gain an understanding of work that had already been carried out in a similar field.

Conclusion

This chapter has focused on the experiences of a usability team working as internal consultants in a large organization, and has dealt almost exclusively with usability evaluation within development projects. However, I have found many of the general points, such as the need for careful objective setting and almost neurotic planning are equally valid in smaller organizations and other situations, such as comparative testing of commercial "shrink-wrapped" software.

It is probably no coincidence that the projects where we prevailed upon to change the nature of our usability testing most frequently were those that worked with us in the very early days of the department when we had the least experience. We reduced the need to respond to unforeseen change to a minimum by finding ways of minimizing the likelihood of change. We did this through formal means, such as establishing clear quality plans for documentation, and through the use of less structured methods like fostering good informal communications between members of project teams and the usability department.

The benefits of learning from other people, both usability practitioners and researchers, as well as adapting experiences and techniques from other professions also cannot be underestimated. Without a wealth of reference materials and good external contacts, we would not have been able to develop such a flexible approach to design and evaluation and would therefore not have been able to respond as effectively to changing project needs.

Lessons Learned

- Identify the most likely sources of change in your organization and the most appropriate way of predicting when those types of change may occur.
- Reduce the risk of changes to usability requirements by understanding the internal workings of the project, by setting out clear objectives at the start of the project and by establishing good communication mechanisms.
- Predict change by ensuring that you are given realistic information about project progress, asking the right questions, understanding the company structure and predicting how organizational change will affect a project.
- Equip yourself with a range of techniques and gain experience which will allow you to alter the scope of the work you are undertaking without losing sight of your overall objectives.

References

[1] J. Nielsen (1993) *Usability Engineering*, Academic Press, London.
[2] P. Coleman, M. Salzman and D.S. Rivers (1994) "Smoke and Mirrors: Setting the Stage for a Successful Usability Test", *Behaviour and Information Technology*, vol 13, nos 1 and 2.
[3] J. Preece (ed.) (1994) *Human Computer Interaction*, Addison Wesley, Wokingham.

8. *Consultants with Clout*

How to Avoid Gathering Dust

Cathy Thomas

ABSTRACT

Organizations have problems. Often, they employ consultants to help them overcome those problems. Sometimes they even employ usability consultants. The consultant works hard to develop solutions for the organization, then the consultant moves on. But what happens to all their good (and often expensive) work? This chapter addresses the issue of ensuring that, as consultants, our recommendations are taken seriously, and are in a form that the organization can easily apply and support. Specifically, I look at how to ensure that the consultancy contract provides valid and useful output that is actually implemented – and not a report that sits on a shelf and gathers dust. I begin by discussing the extent to which consultant's recommendations are acted upon in practice – or not – and look at potential reasons why they may not be. Then, I suggest some solutions, both for the consultant and for the client organization, to ensure that findings do make the appropriate impact.

Introduction

An organization brings in consultants to deal with problems it has not encountered before, or whose solution demands resources it does not possess. Consultants are brought in, for example, to assist with management concerns, with the supply of software, and with usability issues. This chapter addresses some of the problems which may be encountered when usability consultants are hired – either individually or as part of a larger team – by a client organization.

The problems and solutions in this chapter are gained from some 13 years' experience in the ergonomics, usability and computing industries. This has included work as an independent consultant, as a member of organizations offering both internal and external consultancy, and within client organizations who employ consultants. Many of the examples here are based on the experiences of NPL Usability Services, a team of seven people who work within the National Physical Laboratory, the UK's national standards laboratory. We provide usability consultancy to clients ranging from large government departments to small software houses to sections within NPL who produce scientific software. Products we have worked on have ranged from tax forms to multimedia public access kiosks, large information systems and customer support terminals.

The definition of usability that we use incorporates the effectiveness, efficiency and satisfaction with which specific users use a product under defined conditions. This "quality of use" approach enables us to take a broad view, incorporating many factors such as business processes, software functionality and reliability.

Why Are Consultants Brought in?

There are many similarities between management consultancy and usability consultancy, indeed much usability consultancy is carried out by management consultants who list it amongst their skills. It may be a management consultant who points out that there is a problem with usability, and who then goes on to develop his or her own solutions. Alternatively, an organization which is more "mature" in usability terms may recognize a specific problem for which specialist assistance is sought.

Usability consultants are typically brought in to work on:

- style guides;
- design methodology;
- interface design;
- expert evaluation and usability inspection – that is, examination of usability-related aspects of a user interface (e.g. [1]);
- user-based evaluation – working with and observing users as they try to use a product or system;
- skill transfer, with the aim of making the organization self-sufficient.

Beyond these technical processes there are a number of "political" background reasons why usability consultants – in common with other management consultants – are brought in:

- an organization does not have the skills or resources it needs to perform certain tasks, and cannot obtain them quickly enough;
- the resources may only be needed for a finite amount of time, or there may be some unpredictability about the work that would prohibit taking on new permanent employees;
- the organization may want a broader view that can only be provided by people who have experience of similar issues across a range of situations;
- they may want an independent and objective view to "settle differences";
- they may require "external sanction" or confirmation of information that is in fact already suspected;
- an unpopular decision can be "depersonalized";
- they may just want to know what the problems are – even if they cannot do anything about them.

One example is where a large client organization was considering buying in some new scheduling software. The package under consideration would have required an extensive amount of tailoring, and was viewed unfavourably by nearly all its potential users. There were, however, political reasons (not divulged to us!) why it should be purchased. Reading between the lines, it became apparent that we were brought in essentially to add an "independent" voice to the arguments against the purchase. A usability evaluation of the product revealed significant flaws – and our findings predicted high potential costs of going ahead in terms of staff motivation and efficiency. The planned purchase was dropped.

How Consultants Work

A typical consultancy programme will begin with discussion over the details of the work – for example, the client may define approximate limits of cost, and the consultant then proposes a way of using those resources. Once a contract has been agreed, the consultant will need to spend some time becoming familiar with a product or system. The bulk of the consultant's work will then be to carry out or assist in a process – for example, writing a style guide – or to carry out work which results in design recommendations. In this chapter, I am concentrating on the type of consultancy contract which produces recommendations intended for take-up and implementation by the client organization.

The Problem...

There is a cost involved in hiring consultants. Good quality consultancy does not come cheap, both in terms of the costs paid to the consultant, and of the time costs of administering the contract. It is a shame, therefore, if recommendations are not acted upon. Company confidentiality disguises the extent of this problem, but anecdotal evidence and discussions with many organizations suggest that all too often findings and recommendations are not implemented – and this appears to be true for both management and usability consultancy.

Organizations will, of course (it is hoped), act intelligently with all information that comes to them, and will prioritize issues according to their own agendas. But if an organization has chosen to employ consultants, and has paid a great deal of money for recommendations, one would assume they would take them seriously. So why is this not always the case? Why do some reports sit on shelves and gather dust?

By looking at the issues involved, two potential reasons for poor take-up of recommendations emerge:

- the recommendations developed by the consultant may not be practical for a number of reasons, including the consultant taking an approach which is not client-centred;
- recommendations may be politically difficult for the organization to take up because, perhaps, there is a lack of resource to implement them, or even because members of the organization are suspicious of the consultant.

Practical Considerations in Consultancy Work

The Consultant's Approach Is Not Client-Centred

One problem which besets work with client organizations is the very one we are seeking to address – that of user-centred design. Not adopting a client-centred approach will result in findings that do not address real problems, and that the client does not fully understand.

Communication between the consultant and client is the key to a client-centred approach, but can sometimes be a problem – both in terms of the jargon and specialist language used, and in setting up structures for communication through-out the duration of the contract. This is often exacerbated in "third party" contracts where one consultancy organization, performing work such as software design for another organization, employs usability consultants to work for them. The usability consultant is then "shielded" from the real client and may not have a full awareness of their needs. This can also cause problems of "working for two masters" who have different goals for the contract.

We have experienced just such a problem – we were employed by a software producer to evaluate the usability of a public-access system they were writing. They were writing this for a design consultancy, who had in turn been employed by the "real" client, the manufacturer of the product being demonstrated on the public-access system. So, our findings had to (a) highlight usability fixes that would be required of the software, to enable the software producer to enhance the system, (b) demonstrate to the design consultancy that the software producer was doing an excellent job, even though our findings concentrated on identifying usability bugs, (c) demonstrate to the manufacturer that the design consultancy was doing an excellent job and (d) make sure that we were seen as doing an excellent job by the software producer, the design consultancy, the manufacturer and, of course, the end user – the general public.

Lack of client focus may also result in solutions that work only in limited circumstances. One example was where a measurement process was (quote) "time and motioned". Proposed increases in efficiency recommended calculating some figures at a different time in the process, which was fine in some cases, but in others – for example if an error had cropped up – made the new way of working much more expensive.

The Consultant May Not Fully Understand the Problem

The consultant, by definition, will not know the organization's business, or the technical project details, as well as permanent staff will. Throughout the course of projects, consultants tend to be excluded from the organization's policy and management issues – and whilst this means that they are less distracted by administrative bureaucracy, it also means less involvement in "company culture". This can potentially lead to recommendations not being appropriate to the ways of working of the client.

The Nature of the Work Is Inappropriate

The very nature of the work being carried out – that is, the methods used, and how they are applied – may be inappropriate. This is because consultancy is by nature reactive, responding to requests from clients, but often needs to be proactive in putting forward different methods which may be more appropriate. Whilst for most contracts the nature of the work itself is defined largely by the consultant, some organizations request specific activities to be carried out at a particular stage during product development. A consultant, with wider experience, may be able to suggest – but not implement – a better way.

Another cause of inappropriate results is failure to keep up with changing circumstances. Some contracts extend over many months, if not years. During this time, many facets of their subject matter will be changing. The organization's priorities may change, or the technology to be implemented may be updated. Frequent re-structuring of departments and staff is a fact of life for many people – so that the methods and approaches proposed by the consultant at the outset cease to be valid, and produce inappropriate results. We have worked on projects where even keeping up with client's addresses has proved a problem, as they move offices with each reorganization.

Political Considerations in Consultancy Work

Lack of Resource

Whilst very often the client organization appreciates that the consultant's ideas and recommendations are good in theory, in practice they may not have enough time or skilled staff to implement them. Alternatively, other problems take precedence over the usability recommendations put forward. For example, a project team may know that their software is slow and crashes frequently. They bring in usability consultants to identify potential problems. The usability consultants discover several other issues along with the speed and reliability problems – but the development team are fully stretched fixing these bugs and are unable to start on the other recommendations before release. Or perhaps only the easiest and cheapest solutions are applied, leaving other – possibly fundamental – usability problems unfixed.

Recommendations being made too late for cost-effective implementation is another common cause of poor uptake of findings. All too often, usability consultants are called in when a product is nearing completion, when it becomes apparent that usability needs to be improved. However, at a late stage in design, changes are much more costly to make and the more fundamental ones may simply be impractical.

The Company Is Not "Mature" Enough to Be Receptive to Changes Regarding Usability and Does Not Plan for Change

Change is a fact of life for all organizations, and needs to be planned for. Some are better at this than others – and since usability consultants' recommendations often put forward some element of change (for example, a software development process to include some prototyping and iteration), organizations that plan for this will be more receptive than those which are more set in their ways. Equally, organizations that are open to new ideas, and have a good understanding of and commitment to the issues around usability, will get more value from consultancy.

There Is a Decline in Enthusiasm for the Work

When the consultant leaves at the end of the contract, not only is their knowledge about the systems and processes lost, but in some cases, so is the "driving force" or the "champion" for particular issues. If that knowledge or drive is needed at a later date, for example to help implement recommendations, the consultant may no longer be pushing the ideas forward.

There may also be a decline in motivation during the contract. This is particularly a problem where staff get partially diverted to other projects. It is common for people to be keyed up and excited at the start of a contract – but then acclimatization sets in and enthusiasm diminishes. Enthusiasm (often mistaken for panic) usually returns with the approach of the end-of-contract deadline.

Hidden Agendas

There may be hidden agendas behind the employment of consultants. For example, some people, particularly those in senior posts, do not want to be seen to need training in particular issues. Employing an expert consultant is one good way to gain knowledge – and whilst the contract may be to provide recommendations, the client's hidden objectives are actually skill transfer. Equally, the consultant and consultant's organization will have an agenda which may or may not match what the client wants. A consultant may be interested in a follow-up contract of a certain type, or in skill development and experience in specific areas. Good consultants will not let their own agendas interfere with their work – but clients, as well as consultants, should always be aware of hidden (or not-so-hidden) motivations.

Some Members of the Organization May Be Suspicious of the Consultant

There are occasions where some permanent members of organizations appear suspicious or resentful of consultants. Some resent the seemingly high remuneration given to contract staff, other do not like "outsiders" dictating to them. Where these attitudes prevail, it will be difficult to persuade staff to carry out work proposed by the consultants.

There May Be Problems Demonstrating the Value of Work to the Client

The benefits of carrying out recommendations are not always clear to the client, with the result that some actions are given a lower priority than is perhaps desirable. There is often also something of a "loyalty gap" between the client and the consultant – the client organization, naturally, will be familiar with, loyal to and biased in favour of its own products. The consultant's view will be more objective – and needs to be put forward carefully!

Trained Staff Move on, or the Product Is Abandoned

All too often a partnership between a large organization and a consultant, or team of consultants, comes to a premature end because of major organizational changes. Key staff may be moved on, or a team may be disbanded. In extreme cases, development of the product which was the subject of the consultancy is halted.

Solutions ("Recommendations about Recommendations")

In the preceding section I discussed many of the pitfalls of consultancy, and detailed potential causes of less-than-satisfactory take-up of recommendations. In this section, I propose some potential solutions – those that my colleagues and I have found to be useful. Many ideas are obvious, but perhaps on a day-to-day level may not be given the weight that they deserve. Some have been found or reinforced only through practical experience. Other solutions are for hypothetical cases which have not affected us yet – but of which we need to be aware.

For the consultant, the main lesson is that we need to take our own medicine, and adopt a user-centred approach. We also need to ensure that our work is "politically appropriate". Consultancy is an art, not a technique [2].

For the organization, the importance of selecting your consultant carefully – and operating good management – is stressed.

Adopt a User-centred Approach

Keep a Constant Dialogue with the Client

It can be tempting, once the problem has been outlined by the client, to go away and get working, ready to present the client with a nicely polished report when it is ready. This may be entirely appropriate in some cases – for example, for a specialist report on a technical area, independent of its implementation in the client organization. In most cases, however, the report – nicely polished or otherwise – needs to be matched closely with the client needs, and much is to be gained by involving them (as much as their resources allow) in development of the issues, and of reports. There is of course a fine line between getting plenty of feedback, and "being a nuisance" – but I have yet to find a client who complained that they were receiving too much consultancy. Equally, it is important to get feedback, and a good understanding of the problem, from the right people. The person who commissioned the contract may not be aware of all the causes of their problems, and will not commonly be on the receiving end of the recommendations.

When final recommendations are being formulated, they need to be developed in consultation with users and the client. This issue of ownership is crucial – if clients themselves are partly responsible for the ideas, not only will the solutions be practical and appropriate, but they will be taken more seriously. So, try solutions out with users or developers, prototype them. A good technique is to have facilitated group recommendation discussions where usability staff, consultants, developers and other stakeholders "brainstorm" solutions together.

Make Sure Reports Are Usable, with Focused Recommendations

Most people are short of time. So reports should be brief, to the point, and tailored to the audience. If there is more than one audience – perhaps a software developer client who wants constructive recommendations for software redesign, but wants to look good to a client, then prepare two versions of the report – one concentrating on recommendations, another stressing good findings. If client resources are tight, provide cheap and quick solutions, detailing the more complex ones separately for potential future reference.

It is also important to speak the client's language. Each organization has its own dialect. At first, this can be somewhat confusing – but recommendations couched in this terminology, rather than a technical jargon, will have far greater impact.

Be Politically Smart

Ensure "Powerful" People Are on Board

Nothing in an organization is sustainable without the support of the managers and budget holders. One of the pitfalls of usability consultancy, particularly in software development, is that the client is often in a department which perceives extra up-front cost in implementing recommendations. Where budgets are short-term and "department-centred", the client may focus on their own immediate costs rather than on savings for other departments, or their own savings in a future accounting period – which is why commitment from someone higher up, with a broader responsibility, is important.

Use Tested and Visibly Cost-Effective Methodologies

Clients will be more accepting of findings if they see that they have been produced via an appropriate and accepted methodology. It is also vital – though often difficult – to do the work at the right stage in design. The sooner problems are found, the easier and cheaper they are to put right. But methods do not have to be "scientifically mysterious". We have successfully used a range of techniques, from formal laboratory-based evaluations, to loitering in the underwear departments of high-street stores observing (supposedly unobtrusively) users of multimedia kiosks. Clients will, however, want to see that they are getting value for money – so it is important to be able to cost-justify services and methods, whatever they are.

"Educate" the Client

Make sure that the client understands what is being done, and comprehends what will result from the consultation – both its benefits and its limitations. Make sure that their understanding of technical usability issues is adequate, and then they will be able both to define the work effectively in the first place, and to implement findings which result from the work. Also, instead of just providing a list of "do this, do that", it is important to make clear which recommendations are most important, and what the consequences of implementing each (or not) are. In most situations, there will not be resource available to work on all findings. This makes it vital that the most important, in terms of user satisfaction – effectiveness or efficiency – or whatever else is important to the client, are given highest priority.

If providing training, ensure that trainees are aware at the end of a short course of all the things that they still do not know! A little knowledge can be a dangerous thing – but can be assisted with further "mentoring" and accreditation. Of course, working closely with a usability consultant will be an education in itself.

Monitor Change

It can be difficult to keep track of how situations change throughout the contract – and to modify methods and solutions appropriately. But it is crucial if work is to be appropriate.

Fit with the Organization's Infrastructure

Another recommendation that is often easier said than done. A consultant on a two-month contract cannot hope to have the in-depth knowledge of a product and what makes an organization tick than someone who has been working there for five years will have. But by making all attempts at integrating as much as possible (including integrating with other consultants – even competitors!), and getting feedback from the "product experts", a more focused result will be achieved. Integration is not often an onerous task – and generally involves spending a little more time down the pub. This is a good way of improving relationships with other staff – and, hopefully, reducing any feelings of suspicion or even resentment that they may have.

It is also important to look beyond the initial solutions – look for things the client may have missed, and look at the politics of what lies behind their employing you.

For the Organization...

Select Your Consultant Carefully

There is a growing number of usability consultants and organizations offering services. The vast majority are well-qualified, conscientious and experienced. These people will all have an awareness of the issues discussed here. But how do you know that the consultant whom you select belongs to this "vast majority"? The easy answer is that the "usability" or "HCI" (Human-Computer Interaction) communities are still small enough for most practitioners to at least be aware of each other – so for clients with an awareness in the area, finding a recognized consultant should not be a problem. Where this is not the case, look for membership of recognized bodies – the Ergonomics Society, for example, has a code of conduct and strict application rules to its professional register. The British HCI Group is a useful source of relevant information.

It is important to look beyond the cost to the value for money. Hix and Hartson [3] quote Red Adair, the famous Texas oil-well firefighter, when someone confronted him about his costs: "If you think the experts are expensive, wait until you bring in the amateurs!".

Operate Good Management

This goes without saying, but issues such as making sure that all parties have the same understanding of goals and objectives are crucial – and not always achieved. The main management issue is to ensure that resources will be available to implement recommendations that arise from a contract. It is important to estimate, and plan for, follow-up actions – with the help of the consultant if necessary.

Integrate Consultants with the Organization

In the same way that consultants themselves need to "fit in" in order to produce good results, the organization itself will also obviously benefit and may need to make a little effort to encourage integration. Back down the pub again!

There are a number of international differences in the way consultants are used. My experience leads me to conclude, for example, that North American corporations tend to make more use of internal usability engineering teams – who will naturally be integrated into the organization's culture – than UK organizations. These specialists themselves then act as consultants within their organization. Whilst this is also the case with many of the larger companies in the UK, a large number still rely on being able to call in external assistance – so the issue of integration is of extra importance here.

Consider Carefully the Impact of Usability Problems

It can be easy for some people to dismiss usability bug fixes as "nice to haves" rather than essentials. Whilst some recommendations will undoubtedly fall into this category, it is important to assess the implications for poor usability on efficiency. Where large numbers of users carry out the same transaction, say, 40 times a day, a 30-second efficiency saving as a result of a usability bug-fix will reap huge benefits for the organization.

The Challenges...

Harder nuts to crack are changes in the client organization – such as movement of key people, abandonment of a product, or dissolution of an enthusiastic team; and decline in enthusiasm on the part of either the client or the consultant. Organizational changes are largely out of the control of the external consultant, and must be accepted pragmatically and philosophically. Occasionally a little well-directed (usually at the decision-makers) communication may support the case of the product/person/team.

If lack of enthusiasm is an issue, this can sometimes be addressed by more rigorous planning and control of deadlines and milestones. A big project meeting – preferably in an interesting location – can also revive flagging spirits and fire up new energy. However, one does need enough enthusiasm to put these measures into place.

Lessons Learned

The benefits of enhanced usability are huge, and many organizations are beginning to see usability as a crucial element to their competitiveness. To address the issues involved, organizations either set up their own usability departments, or call in usability consultants. More commonly, they do a mixture of both. Each consultancy contract is a learning experience, both for the organization and for the consultant. In the majority of cases, all goes well, and everyone is happy. The crucial elements to ensuring this success are maintaining frequent and appropriate communication, and keeping a client-centred approach. It is no use producing wonderful recommendations about how such-and-such a system needs to be enhanced to meet the needs of its users, if the recommendations themselves are on issues that are not important to the client, are couched in the jargon of HCI and not that of the client, and are themselves not user-centred.

References

[1] J. Nielsen and R.L. Mack (eds.) (1994) *Usability Inspection Methods*, John Wiley and Sons, New York.
[2] A. Young (1986) *The Manager's Handbook: The Practical Guide to Successful Management*.
[3] D. Hix and H.R. Hartson (1993) *Developing User Interfaces: Ensuring Usability Through Product and Process*, John Wiley and Sons, New York.

9. Cultivating an Effective Client Relationship to Promote a User-Centred Culture

Nichole Simpson

ABSTRACT

This chapter describes the practical issues associated with establishing a relationship with a product group for the timely, pragmatic and effective application of human factors advice and consultancy. The chapter takes the form of a site study based upon experiences gained while acting the role of internal consultant in a large telecommunications equipment provider. The role involved providing a range of human factors support to the organization's research and development establishment.

The study touches upon methodological and management issues and covers the process from initiating contact, through to the delivery of service and after-care. The information is presented in a series of stages that may be encountered in the process of setting up, delivering into and maintaining a relationship with a product group. The chapter concludes with a summary of the salient features of a successful relationship of this kind. Throughout, the emphasis is on what was learned in particular project situations, and how this may be generalized to address an issue common throughout human factors consulting – how to cultivate an effective client relationship to promote a user-centred culture.

The Organization

The organization considered is a leading telecommunications manufacturer and supplier. At the time of the consultancy described in this chapter, the organization was running its operations as two arms. Sales, manufacturing and marketing being dealt with by one part of the organization, and research and development activities being serviced by another. The R&D operations were split into three sections which dealt with the three main functions of a telecommunications network – access, transport and switching – with each section home to several product groups dealing with sustaining, new generation and visionary products. As the complexity of a network and the sophistication of its components increases, the need to effectively and responsively manage it through complex network management products becomes of paramount importance. The user interface of these products is given high profile within the organization and usability is regarded as a key issue in product success.

Human Factors within the Organization

The usability and human factors expertise are based in the UK and North America, and function as a design support group to provide market research, analysis, design and evaluation services. The UK group is approximately fifteen strong and has members with skills such as industrial design, user requirements analysis, user-interface and interaction design and usability testing. The group is centrally funded and each year takes a strategic direction which focuses it on a product or technology area. The organization has very well-defined software development methods, and a strong product approval mechanism. The user interface is seen as an area which can confer advantage in the marketplace, and effort has been expended to define a process for handling human factors input to the normal product development process.

The User Population

The users of network management and associated products are in the main very technically trained. The high degree of technical awareness of the users, and the specialist nature of their tasks does not, however, obviate the need for:

- Network equipment that demonstrates a high level of usability. Tasks such as network monitoring, fault diagnosis and dynamic reconfiguration all require special consideration at the user interface.
- Task dialogues that demonstrate the accessibility of information at the right time and in the right formats. Users are frequently required to multi-task and switch task contexts, and task dialogue structures must support this.

In addition to these requirements, the design of equipment must take into account the changing organizational structures enforced by an expanding network. Furthermore, as telecommunications equipment is deployed in more locations and environments throughout the country (for example, underground, in large buildings, in temporary locations, in rural locations), the use of portable equipment will increase, again bringing very specific user interface and usability concerns to bear.

The remainder of this chapter describes the consultancy relationship which was established and maintained with one of the technology areas (transport products) over a two-year timespan. It is divided into the following sections which deal with the different stages in the process of cultivating the relationship:

- definition and sponsorship;
- first encounters;
- getting access to users;
- delivering the results;
- follow-on work;
- maintaining control;
- developing a user-centred culture.

Definition and Sponsorship – Getting a Foot in the Door

Although the design support group could rely on a central funding structure, new issues associated with definition and sponsorship presented themselves. The group still had to advertise itself, follow its chosen strategic direction, and be seen to provide value-adding input. An overarching concern was the need to balance the tactical and short-term focus demanded by the product teams working on sustaining projects, with more strategic input which it was believed would strengthen the group's position within the company and provide benefit from improved usability in the longer term.

This demanded that a sponsor with long-term commitment and vision be found. Someone was needed who would appreciate the need to put in place a culture where usability was made a core element of all products, and not just a knee-jerk reaction to immediate problems, or a palliative for the customer. Achieving this involved considerable effort to establish the group, its vision and its mission. This was managed in five ways:

- *Enthusiastic and untiring backing* from senior managers both in the UK and North America who were prepared to articulate the message at every given opportunity.
- *Presence in debating and interest groups* throughout the organization (e.g. a network management forum), in particular those fora which attracted a mix of sales, marketing and product development personnel, enabling the message to be spread as widely as possible.
- *Circulation of usability related products* to the product development groups, e.g. network management design guidelines and packs describing fundamental design principles. This provided a context for the message that the group was trying to communicate about the importance of usability and how it could be achieved.
- *Provision of quick-fix/quick response assistance.* The moral high ground was not a position that it was viable to take early on. The group needed to prove itself, and provide help where it was needed, thus justifying the value of and need for usability services.
- *Establishing the strategic focus of the group.* This involved making a stand on certain issues, and not responding to areas judged to be out of scope or based on an inappropriate approach. It was difficult to balance this approach with the necessary provision of "quick fixes", but the pressures of being a relatively

small group servicing a large organization meant that requests must sometimes be refused on the grounds of resource constraints if nothing else.

Types of Sponsor

The publicity and goodwill generating activities described in the previous section exposed the group to a number of potential sponsors. Two kinds of sponsor were identified at the product manager level, each with a particular bias which had to be accommodated:

- *Technically biased* – needs to be convinced of the worth of usability and how it could add value. This kind of manager was often dealing with leading edge technologies which he/she believed would address customer requirements on technical merits. We found that this type of sponsor was initially difficult to win over, but frequently became a strong advocate after the first (timely) deliverable, and evidence of the customer's favourable reaction to the user-centred approach.
- *User biased* – already "sold" on the philosophy and believes the technical capabilities of a product are only half of the solution. This type of manager typically responded to pressure from product timescales and budget by demanding detailed proof of the value of usability related services. The prevailing organizational conditions meant that all customer contact had to be mediated by marketing representatives which often severely impacted product timescales and added to the burdens faced by the manager. We found this kind of sponsor easier to make initial contact with, but more difficult to hold to actions required to support the provision of human factors services.

Beyond the Sponsor

Once demonstrable value had been delivered to the sponsors, they quickly turned into champions for the usability cause (at least for a short while). This was very powerful for spreading awareness and acceptance of the work of the design support group throughout the organization. While it was very important for us to facilitate the process of turning our sponsor into a champion, things did not stop there. We found that there were two further things that it was very important to attend to in order to protect our initial position:

- *Deliver to the team members.* In some cases there was a danger that the internal consultants were seen as auditors brought in by the management to assess the team's performance. This negative image could be overcome by spending time with the product group and performing the work in their environment. While it may be easier to administer the services behind closed doors and then deliver the results "shrink-wrapped", this approach does not win trust or co-operation. As consultants we had to get used to using desks while people were away on holiday or even just at a meeting for a couple of hours. Once it was shown that our input was making a significant contribution, desk space and other facilities frequently became available; the first sign of us being regarded as a part of the team.

- *Help the sponsor communicate the usability message.* Often, the usability message seemed to have little meaning at the higher levels of the organization. It was important to help the sponsor articulate the business benefits of the approach by making a clear statement of what had been achieved. We found that a good way to convince the "top brass" was to find ways in which they could observe an evaluation on one of their walk-arounds, or better still take part in one, see part of a focus group, or receive a summary of the findings. We felt that these activities helped take us off the "endangered species list", as we were no longer the latest anonymous fad which could be cut when budget and timescales exerted a squeeze on the project.

First Encounters – Frantically Paddling under the Water

When an enquiry was received or an opportunity identified, the first encounters were handled by the relevant function manager from the design support group. The initial meeting focused on determining the nature of the enquiry, after which the function manager would assemble the team who would explore the proposition, scope and clarify it, and deliver the solution. This team was frequently small, maybe only one or two people in size, and these people acted as the client-service team as well as the technical solution providers.

Defining the Terms of Engagement

Once the service team had been assembled, the detail of the opportunity had to be explored. It could frequently be expected that what the product team had in mind in terms of support would be somewhat different from the kinds of human factors support that we would ideally propose, and in some cases the project would be considered to be so far off track as to require unwinding a full six-months (rarely possible, however desirable it might be). The most commonly encountered problem was that of being asked to provide input in a total vacuum. When proposing a plan of action, it was important to be sensitive to the constraints within which the project team acted. For example, responding that nothing would be possible without a full user-task analysis, would win very few points and probably result in the door that had been so carefully prised open being firmly pushed back closed.

At this point in the relationship, the main objective was to nurture the confidence of the sponsor. This was most effectively achieved by delivering quickly and making as few waves as possible (although often we were paddling frantically under the water). The issue was frequently one of balancing the support that could *practically* be offered with what we would *ideally* like to do. Where the difference between these was large we sometimes felt it necessary to "cover our backs" by recording what we would have done in an ideal situation and noting the implications of deviations from this plan.

In defining the terms of engagement, we found that the following activities enabled us to make significant progress in establishing ourselves with the group without making a rod for our own backs later in the process.

Manage Expectations

We often called a meeting to talk through our initial assessment (and possibly the proposal if we had reached that stage) with the product manager and the product team. This established a shared understanding of what was possible, what would be done, when and by whom. This requirement sometimes came as a surprise to a client/customer, who expected the human factors team to be able to come in, perform the necessary tasks and go without requiring anything of them. It was important to disabuse all concerned of this misconception as soon as possible.

Explain the Role of User Input

We were sometimes asked how we could call ourselves human factors specialists when we patently did not know a thing if we had to keep going to the users to ask them! This kind of challenge was difficult to face calmly, but we found that a well-defined approach to user-centred analysis and design helped us to point out how user access improved the quality of the information we could provide to the product team. Published human factors guidelines and approaches often proved useful to avoid unnecessarily re-inventing the wheel, or when we had to deliver something quickly based on a minimum of information.

Baseline the Product

We always tried to make an assessment, however informal, of where the team and the product were at the beginning of our involvement. This enabled improvements, progress and the worth of the user-centred approach to be demonstrated later on in the project.

Identify Sources of User Information

We were constantly on the look-out for those people in the organization who may have had customer exposure/knowledge. Often we found that there were ex-customers now on staff. Sometimes ex-staff were found to have left to work for the customer, and these opportunities were seized as a useful way of negotiating and achieving user access.

When providing input to leading edge products which were making use of brand new technologies, it was often the case that there were no existing users or well-defined tasks. In these cases we made use of any relevant knowledge from analogous systems and industries to provide information about the likely structure of tasks, and likely usability issues. For example, in the case of telecommunications networks we looked to road distribution systems and the utilities for insights into network representations and management issues.

Identify the Information Needs

Cataloguing the specific issues or items of information that we wished to explore with users, and finding examples of where this related directly to design decisions which were proving difficult was an on-going activity which we undertook in the background. We never knew when we might get the opportunity to ask a question of a user, so having thought about the issues in advance was useful preparation. Throughout our involvement with a product group, we sought things that we could do which would help today, and made sure we were alert to information or opportunities that might help tomorrow.

Support the Reporting Process

We continued to help our sponsor to get recognition from the activities that we were undertaking. Often this took the form of writing progress reports to be included in monthly reports, and being prepared to speak at product group meetings. Sometimes this led to subsequent work, for example a presentation of the results of an evaluation on a graphical network management tool for a particular product group led to the manager of another product group asking us to do a design assessment on another, related, network management product which was facing similar problems representing complex connectivity data.

Getting Access to Users – "You Want to Do *What*?"

In promoting a user-centred process, access to the users to determine requirements and obtain feedback on designs is essential. In our experience, when trying to negotiate such access, we met with two situations that we needed to overcome.

Incredulous Disbelief

Customers in the telecommunications market expect their suppliers to provide the best solution to their problem, without having to help them understand the specific and detailed requirements to be met. In response to this the suppliers did not wish to be seen to ask the kinds of low level, task and process questions required for user requirements analysis. Customer contact over and above pre-planned meetings, receipt of specification documents and handover of deliverables was, therefore, viewed with suspicion by both sides.

This situation was exacerbated by the widely held belief that pre-sale marketing activities had uncovered the necessary requirements and task-specific information. We often found it useful to compare and contrast the kinds of information that could be obtained from managers, user representatives and the users themselves, in order to illustrate why user access was required. This is illustrated in Box 9.1.

Box 9.1: A comparison of the information obtainable from managers and users

Managers/user representatives	End users
Strategic level information	Tactical information
Official procedures (as laid out in company manuals)	Detail of day-to-day working
A list of the people to speak to with strong or the "right" opinions	Local experts
General level processes	Detailed task steps including work-arounds
Company direction	Users perceptions of company direction
Organizational structure	Working responsibilities
Operational figures	Daily workloads
Major issues and operational problems	Low level detail of the problems with the existing system

In tackling the incredulous disbelief situation there were five main things that needed to be done:

- *explain* what information we needed;
- *define* who we needed to get it from;
- *describe* how we would get it;
- *show* what we were going to do with it;
- *illustrate* the benefits that would accrue to the product group and organization as a whole from having it.

In addition to the traditional interviewing techniques used for requirements analysis, we sometimes used video during user access. This enabled us to capture rich information about the context of the tasks and how they were performed. We found the video particularly useful to take back to the product group, to provide detailed context for their design and development activities. In one notable case, we discovered that the developers had never seen the inside of a network management centre, and were unaware of how the system they were developing would be used in conjunction with other systems.

The Wrong Kind of Access

Requests for access to users for the purpose of usability evaluation were frequently interpreted as a request for a demonstration session to managers from the customer organization. In our opinions such an activity was a form of "rubber stamping" usability – a way to claim user involvement without demonstrating the necessary commitment to the process. When faced with such a situation, we had to decide whether to agree to it or not. Although we believed that the only way to obtain the kind of feedback that we needed in relation to a proposed design was to build a working prototype and engage the users in hands-on, task-oriented exploration and testing, we sometimes had to take what was offered.

Where it was not possible to carry out a "proper" evaluation, we used the session to engage the customer's interest, explain the benefits of hands-on testing, agree a follow-up visit and generate an expectation of usability activities in the mind of the client. In many situations the follow up sessions successfully demonstrated that valuable input and a high degree of customer commitment could be obtained from such activities. Such a realization was very powerful in helping to promote the user-centred approach as customer pull is always more effective than designer push.

Delivering the Results – How to Prevent Them Shooting the Messenger

The results of human factors activities were frequently delivered in the form of reports: user requirements reports, design specifications, evaluation reports etc. Considerable sensitivity had to be exercised in writing and delivering such reports.

Tasting the Medicine

Delivering the results of a study should be a rewarding experience for all involved. Early on in our relationship with the product groups, however, we realized that there were many precautions we had to take before this situation could be assured. As the results began to emerge from one of our usability evaluations an atmosphere of tension arose in the design team. Probing revealed that they were nervous of the feedback that they might receive. They had had their system diagnosed, but were now afraid of tasting the medicine. We overcame this by arranging individual feedback sessions. As there was much positive feedback, and the negative feedback had good applicability, the designers themselves were soon requesting a meeting in which the results were presented more openly.

Other activities we found to be useful when delivering the results of our consultancy activities are discussed below.

Provide Interim Feedback

We found that going off-site for an evaluation (or requirements activity) left the rest of the team on tenterhooks. We tried always to telephone back to the product group or email them to let them know we were receiving valuable feedback and helpful insights into the usability of the design. We also tried to avoid making the product team wait until the final report to find out how they did, by giving them personal informal feedback wherever possible.

Present an Outline of the Report

We often made presentations to the sponsor, product team leader and other relevant parties outlining the main findings and general thrust of the report that we were planning to write. This helped us to achieve acceptance of the issues and uncover any political angles which might have impeded incorporation of the results into the design process. Where possible we would involve product group members in the presentation of findings and in contributing to sections of the report where appropriate, in order to increase ownership of the results.

Perform Impact Analysis

Impact analysis (however rudimentary) allowed people to view the results objectively. Two frameworks that can be helpful when performing an impact analysis are illustrated in Box 9.2. We used these with one of the product groups with which we dealt. Specific numbers, definitions and criteria vary between projects, those presented here merely serve as an example. Involving the team in the impact analysis helped to obtain agreement, buy-in and commitment to implement the changes.

Box 9.2: Impact analysis frameworks

The frequency of occurrence (or mention of issues relating to the user interface by the users) was regarded as being a particularly important and useful categorization of the data. Frequency values of low, medium or high were assigned to each of the issues raised. These were determined according to the rules set out in the table below:

Frequency	Number of users affected	Description
Low	2–4	More than one user raised this issue
Medium	5–10	There was a significant incidence of this issue, with between a quarter and a half of the users experiencing it
High	>11	The majority of users experienced or commented upon the issue

Cost to User

The cost to the user was another factor felt to be important when classifying the data. The cost to the user was defined in the following way:

	Causes error	Interrupts task flow	Not learnable	Confusing	Causes irritation
Low cost					Yes
Medium cost		Yes			Yes
High cost	Yes	Yes	Yes	Yes	Yes

An impact analysis framework should be defined for individual projects, based on the agreed project acceptance criteria.

Don't Forget the Customer

Encouraging the sponsor to deliver a version of the report to the customer helped to cement sponsor commitment to the approach. When customers received a courtesy copy of the report, it often resulted in them writing an appreciative letter back commenting upon how well the usability activities had been handled and extending invitations for us to return. We sometimes used these contacts for other activities – for example, in one case we invited customers to take part in design workshops to brainstorm ideas for future, visionary products.

Follow-on Work – once the Wheels Are in Motion

Repeat business or follow-on work was regarded as the highest accolade in terms of providing human factors services. If a group requested "more of the same", this was taken to suggest that they had extracted something of value from our input. During or after a piece of work, there were several events that might be regarded as signalling success and indicating that we might receive follow-on work. These included:

- reference being made to the work in other reports of project briefings;
- the product group asking for information on user tasks before making design decisions;
- requests for the results of the study to be disseminated;
- good coverage in the product group's monthly report;
- invitation to return to the customer site;
- request from the customer for further information on user-centred methods;
- requests for information from higher echelons of management;
- being asked for material for use in a "showcase" activity (e.g. site tour or publication).

Bagging the Opportunity

There were a number of aftercare and promotional activities which we undertook as part of the completion of a project, and which increased our chances of turning an expression of interest into a qualified opportunity.

- *Continue to spend time with the product group* – we placed a member of our human factors group on long-term secondment to a group with whom we had had a lot of contact and whose product direction matched our strategic aims. It was important that we were not seen to disappear as soon as the applause started to die down.
- *Help the sponsor to report on the activity* – we prepared summaries of the work for our sponsor to use in a number of situations including the annual management conference at which corporate successes and strategic directions were discussed.

- *Provide widespread access to the information* – we placed a copy of the presentations and reports on an electronic bulletin board. We made reports back to all parties involved in the project (e.g. marketing). Where possible we did this verbally rather than in memos, email or a formal bound report.
- *Show appreciation for the effort of all involved* – we were instrumental in getting appropriate managers to write a letter of thanks to the customer commenting on the value of their input and co-operation. We also ensured that the product team were recognized for their efforts.
- *Prepare learning material* – within our own group we established a repository of baseline data for comparisons and a resource library. We also prepared "publicity" material such as case studies that could be sent to interested parties.

We found that these activities made the difference between a one-off piece of consultancy and the establishment of a working relationship which opened up new opportunities and set precedents which made subsequent projects with product groups all the easier.

Maintaining Control – Suddenly Everyone Is an Expert

Establishing a relationship with a product group did not mean that the obstacle course had been successfully completed and that a bed of roses lay ahead. Once the product group had been involved with a project, they believed that they knew all about it and that they were adequately equipped to do the job themselves. It was important to keep a keen eye on the situation to maintain control and ensure that disaster did not strike.

For example, in one case, news of one of our usability evaluations spread, and we found two other product groups trying to take the results and design modifications and apply them directly to their own product. They believed that results from one requirements exercise or evaluation could be generalized to another and were therefore unwilling to facilitate user access for their own products, wishing instead to use existing data and recommendations. It was only because one of the development team thought we would be delighted to see how our recommendations were being used elsewhere that we became aware of this problem and could take steps to remedy the situation. In order to avoid these kinds of problems, it was important to define a number of roles for continuing involvement with the product groups. There were several alternative roles which we adopted; some of these are listed below.

Active Involvement

We continued to perform the user-centred design activities required by a product group when we did not feel that they were ready to undertake the tasks, where the new work was significantly different, or when the product group did not want to take on the responsibility themselves. Care had to be taken to ensure that active involvement did not occupy too much of our limited resource, as this would have detracted from our strategic objectives.

Monitor and Manage

Sometimes we handed over responsibility for carrying out the activities, but retained a role monitoring and managing the human factors aspects of projects. Performing this role required a defined process for user-centred analysis and design to be put in place so that the product team could plan their activities. Active contact with the product group had to be maintained throughout the project, although not in as intensive a way as if we had been carrying out the activities ourselves.

Review and Assure

Occasionally we undertook a Quality Assurance (QA) or reviewing role. This was even more remote and required little active contact. This role was only suitable for those instances where a good relationship had already been built with the product group, and the group needed to be assured that they could ask for further assistance if they required it. This kind of approach required us to define the level of responsibility that we were prepared to take for the outcome of the project (and this is what distinguished a review role from a QA role).

Educate

In some cases our role was as nothing more than a trainer. This enabled us to manage the skills transfer process in a formal way. All training followed a structured process which was repeatable. Where possible it also included exercises so that the attendees could practise what they learned. It was useful to put training in place alongside active involvement in the project so that skills transfer could be reinforced and experience built up in a supported environment.

Developing a User-Centred Culture

The previous sections have covered the process from identification of a need, through building the relationship, delivering human factors input and effecting skills transfer. This process helped us to introduce an ethos of user-centred analysis and design and a level of competence into the organization. In order to develop and refine the process, and establish a firm culture of user-centred activity, some further activities were also required. The list below shows some of the activities that can be performed to continue the process and put in place an infrastructure which encourages learning and development in the area of user-centred design.

- *SIG* – establish a Special Interest Group (SIG) who can form a learning network and share experiences.
- *Forum* – set up a regular, formal meeting where user-centred design issues are discussed.
- *Bulletin board* – establish an electronic bulletin board. Regular postings should be made to it by human factors personnel, and the SIG members should be

encouraged to use it. Other interested parties may happen across it while browsing, thus increasing the exposure to the user-centred approach.

- *Speaker series* – invite external speakers to talk about their work and experiences, and have presentations from internal project teams to share the perception that successes are already happening within the organization.
- *Telephone* – telephone members of the product groups for an informal chat and keep in touch with what they are doing. Share news of new work with them.
- *Drop in* – when in the vicinity drop in to say hello, keep up to date with what the teams are doing and ask for impromptu demonstrations. This is a good way to spot new opportunities for work.

Lessons Learned

Traditionally human factors has been a hard sell, and it has seemed that product groups only realize their need for a user-centred approach after they have had their fingers burned. As more organizations adopt a user-centred approach to product development, the sell will become easier. One of the keys to selling and building user-centred activities into an organization's culture, is the recognition that human factors is more than the structured application of techniques, is even more than the acceptance of the user-centred philosophy. Human factors relies heavily on the rigorous and conscientious development of a client relationship.

From the range of experiences gained while consulting to the product groups in the telecommunications organization described, and from experiences gained subsequently in many other organizations and industry sectors, it has been possible to extract some of the salient points of developing an effective client relationship which promotes the adoption and use of user-centred techniques. The success of the relationship is dependent upon:

- significant time spent with the product groups throughout the course of development of the product;
- continuity of contact during the early part of the relationship;
- perceived value and timeliness of your inputs in relation to the product needs and timescales;
- coming up trumps in a time of crisis – sometimes delivering quick (and dirty if necessary);
- helping the product group to get kudos from your work – make it a differentiator for them;
- promoting skills transfer and enabling them to carry out the process intelligently;
- setting up a learning organization with a culture of user-centred activities.

These are simple to administer but take time and determination. These factors enable a successful and profitable relationship between internal consultant and the organization to be cultivated.

Part 4

*The Politics of Expansion:
How to Work Effectively on an
International, Multi-Cultural Level*

10. "Oh, so That's the Way You Do it over There!"

Bridging the Physical and Cultural Barriers of International Usability Testing

Ingrid K. Towey

ABSTRACT

To establish usability testing at the US branch of Glaxo (now Glaxo Wellcome Inc.), we had to work "on the cheap", with few of the formal trappings of usability specialists. No permanent usability labs. No two-way mirrors. No elaborate research to write scripts. Few written documents explaining what we did or why we did it. Our approach emphasized doing quick tests, delivering results, and immediately redesigning the software based on the tests (often the same day).

However, when it came time to internationalize our work and begin to co-ordinate with Glaxo Wellcome UK, this casual, hit-the-ground-running approach became more of a hindrance than a help. Both the US and the UK had established methodologies for conducting usability testing, but our approaches were different, and we did not even realize that they were. In the US we had been so busy getting work done that our methodology existed only as folklore, carried in the heads of a few people, who believed strongly that they were doing it the right way. Becoming international forced us to examine our practices in detail, compare them to the UK's, and write both procedures down. Our internationalization effort forced us to bridge the physical and cultural barriers between our countries and, in so doing, examine ourselves more closely. We are wiser and our work is better as a result.

Introduction

International software design is always a tricky proposition. Developers in different countries tend to have divergent work styles and may follow diverse design methodologies. In addition, the work practices they are supporting can be wildly different even if they and their clients all work for the same company. The physical distances between countries can make it even more difficult to understand each other and work together well. Can we really afford to fly across the Atlantic every time someone needs to talk face-to-face?

It is common enough for usability testing to be tacked on at the end of the project life cycle where few changes can be made to the system. On international projects, this sort of problem can be even worse. Some developers may even believe that the usability testing will "fix" design problems that actually stem from international miscommunication of product specifications. The politics of this sort of situation can be very sticky and require careful handling.

My advice is to make your methodologies for usability testing as explicit as possible. If you have an international counterpart, take time to get to know each other – how you both work, how you communicate, and what your goals are in usability testing. While on an international project, write everything down, communicate frequently at scheduled times with the entire team, and work hard to understand each other. In addition, you need to be flexible enough to adapt your work to the needs of an individual project. You do not have to give up doing usability testing correctly, but you may have to give up absolute control over the testing process.

How Usability Started at Glaxo Wellcome in the US

What is Glaxo Wellcome?

Glaxo Wellcome is an international pharmaceutical research company that specializes in drug discovery research. Using information technology and computing effectively is critical for Glaxo Wellcome to keep its edge in this fiercely competitive industry. But, because information technology does not directly increase the company's bottom line, application developers and usability experts are constantly justifying their existence to prove that they add value.

How Does Usability Fit in at Glaxo Wellcome?

Usability is critical for ensuring that information technology can actually improve the company's bottom line. In an ideal computing environment, our scientists would no longer be aware of the computer – they would see it only as a means to find the information they need. We want to free their creativity to discover new drugs, instead of imprisoning them in our software.

Although the company has hired more usability specialists and interface designers in the last few years, we do not have enough usability staff for everyone to work full-time on a single project. Currently, I receive many requests for usability help (more than I can do, in fact). I struggle between working full-time on one to two projects or bouncing in a haphazard fashion from project to project. Because we have so much usability work to do, many of the technical writers hired for requirements and end-user documentation also double as usability advocates. Writers documenting unusable software are in an excellent position to become extremely aware of the software's problems. Depending on the team, the writers may have some leeway to change the design. Developers are also catching on to usability issues and are striving to design more usable products from the start, but the company still has a lot of room to grow in this area.

Sometimes we have the problem that people accept usability testing, but they do not completely understand what it is. I have had to explain to a number of developers that we are not looking for bugs in the software or features that do not operate as documented. Instead, we want to make sure that the people using a product can do so quickly and easily to accomplish a particular job [1].

How Usability Testing Got Started

Usability first found a niche in the US because the developers are near their clients in an in-house computing organization. Customers are individuals that the developers know and respect. Many of the clients I supported when I first came to Glaxo (before it merged with Wellcome) were PhD scientists in our Research division. We could not deny that they were intelligent and their opinions mattered.

In addition, for much of the software we designed, usage was optional – the software automated an existing manual process that could still be done by hand if the system was too difficult to learn. For a developer, it can be very sobering to see a piece of software sit idle after he or she has spent weeks or months designing and coding it. Some programmers figured out quickly that the problem was not the client or even the performance of the system, but its usability. The clients would complain about glaring colours, incomprehensible text, and screens that did not help them perform business tasks. The developers knew they needed help.

I was first hired in Scientific Computing to write technical documentation for these difficult systems. It soon became clear to both my manager and to me that the more unusable the software, the more difficult it was to write a manual to describe it. My role quickly expanded to include user interface design, platform standards, and eventually usability testing. We realized that we wanted to put the documentation into the user interface, instead of spending a considerable time and effort writing manuals, quick start sheets, and on-line help [2]. If it takes reams of instructions to explain the software's functions, the software is too hard to use. The end user should be able to figure out the basics from trying to use the software with minimal instructions.

If a Product Needs too Much Documentation, Something Is Wrong

Once we really started to tackle usability issues, we stumbled across another problem. Sometimes we would design software that seemed important at the time but did not fill a real need or support the way our clients worked. Two developers in another department became familiar with contextual design (CD) and decided it might be useful for Glaxo (contextual inquiry (CI) is one small part of CD).

CD focuses on knowing your customer and then using that knowledge to drive the design of the system and the user interface. "Great product ideas come from a marriage of the detailed understanding of a customer need with the in-depth understanding of technology" [3]. Because of our interest in CD, several US people became CD coaches and began to guide teams in CD. This methodology enabled us to design usability into the entire software design process from the beginning. By using customer-centred design practices at the beginning of the software development lifecycle, we can alleviate the pressure on usability testing to "fix" usability problems that stem from requirements gathering. CD has been useful and effective but also a difficult change in our existing software design paradigm.

Changing the Software Design Life Cycle Can Be a Daunting Process

Local politics drove our early usability work...

Project Profile: The Vmax System
Software name: Vmax
Type of team: US only
Developed by: US only
Type of usability testing: Electronic prototype
Description of software: Runs laboratory equipment that analyses tissue samples

Why We Did the Vmax Usability Testing

Our first usability testing was with the Vmax System. My goal in doing these tests was to have proof that the design was not usable and needed rework. The original Vmax was supposed to emulate pushing buttons on the front of the actual laboratory machine, and the first design had that general approach.

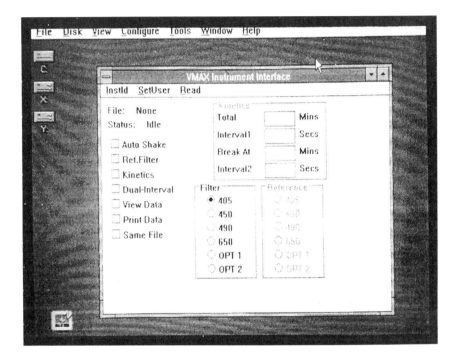

Figure 10.1: The Original Design of the Vmax System

We were still getting complaints about the usability of the product, and scientists who had used the system for several months still tended to make many mistakes. Some of the problems were obvious: for example, the check-boxes on the left were just a jumble of different functions. Some were tasks to perform, whereas others were particular modes that the machine could run or options for formatting the data file that the machine produced (for example, Same File meant that the next run would be saved in the same data file). In addition, the software was not very reliable, and often both the computer and the laboratory machine had to be rebooted in the middle of a run.

A developer in my group got the job of redesigning Vmax, and it was my assignment to help him and write any necessary end-user documentation. When we completed the first iteration of the design, I was not pleased with it, but the developer was tired of having several people tell him how to design his system. He was no longer willing to listen to our opinions. I had recently attended a conference where I had seen a usability test performed on stage, and I knew that usability testing could prove my point. Our boss agreed that we could usability test it, if we set up the tests that week, ran them in one day, and redesigned the screens the following day. This was an aggressive timetable that would not impact our delivery date. We borrowed a vacant office, set up a computer and spare Vmax machine, and scheduled five clients to test the system. I wrote up scripts and arranged a video camera. We were ready to roll!

Although the new system was more intuitive than the original, the clients still had problems during the tests. For example, they were unsure where they needed to go on the screen to begin each new task. Based on their comments, I came up with two different screen designs in Visual Basic. The developer then picked the one he liked best. One innovation in the new screen was that it had a floating task panel that showed the tasks to perform in order.

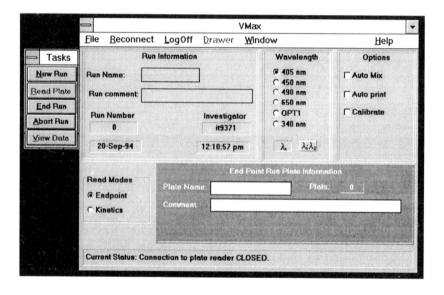

Figure 10.2: What the Vmax Screen Looked Like after Usability Testing

The new system required ten pages of documentation (the old manual had been 50 pages long), was very reliable, and received few complaints. As a pay-off for the improved usability of our products, we found that our systems were requiring much less documentation than they had previously (5). Suddenly, I was not just a technical writer any more – I was making the transition to being a user interface designer and usability specialist. Usability testing had made a difference to the software and to the direction of my career.

Developing a Standard Methodology in the US

All of the early projects for which we performed usability testing followed a pattern similar to the Vmax project. Eventually, I was following a standard methodology based on the politics of my environment.

- Someone would call me or come by my office with a usability testing request. If the request came from outside my department, I would clear it with my boss. (I have always received many requests from outside my group – departments are not usually willing to sacrifice headcount to hire a usability consultant, even when they realize the importance of one.)
- As quickly as my schedule permitted, I would plan a time for the tests, often borrowing an office or conference room near my desk. We have no dedicated space for usability testing – it is still living on the fringes of the software development life cycle. As I developed a backlog of project work, setting up quick tests became more difficult. I had much more work as a usability specialist than I had ever had as a technical writer!
- Since I did not always have a role in designing the software, I would take time to become familiar with it. Then, I would write up scripts, have the developers review them, recruit end users, and test the software myself using the scripts. Because usability testing was frequently tacked on at the end of the project, I often did not see the software until it was almost ready to deliver.
- I would run the tests, videotape or audiotape them if I could, and have the developers observe, where practicable. The videotapes and audiotapes would provide proof of my observations to the developers – these tapes offered the evidence I needed to help me to influence the system design. As any usability expert will attest, not all developers can bear to have their software evaluated. One developer got up in the middle of a usability test, stood over the screen, pointed out which buttons to click, and explained the logic of his design in detail. He excused himself before the next test, explaining that he did not have the objectivity to stay and watch.
- I would write up a tactful report of the main usability issues with my ideas for redesigning the system.
- I would give the report and videotapes (if any) to the developer and his or her manager or have a meeting to discuss the key issues and possible resolutions. This methodology was basically quick-and-dirty usability testing, and the entrepreneurial atmosphere of Research and Development at Glaxo US made this type of work style possible. I would usually work directly with a project leader or developer who requested usability testing. At most, I would ask my boss for permission to do the testing. We did not usually appeal to any higher authority.
- In the next several years, other departments within the company began their own usability testing efforts. But, many of them based their work on what I had done, and we rarely needed to co-ordinate our work anyway. My "methodology" remained in my head and largely undocumented, although I trained two people that worked with me. Then, Glaxo and Burroughs Wellcome merged, and our Information Technology (IT) departments were reorganized along international lines.

Internationalizing Projects and Approaches

The Goals of Internationalization

The main goal of internationalizing our IT groups was to avoid duplication of effort. Why should we design the same piece of software on both sides of the ocean? We could save money by developing the software once and installing it in both the US and the UK (assuming that the US and UK clients had the same work practices to support). But, to internationalize, the US and UK software teams had to work in a similar fashion and we had to understand where we differed. Without this understanding, our attempts at collaboration could look like outright opposition.

The Formation of the Usability and GUI Skill Centre

As part of merging Glaxo and Burroughs Wellcome, four usability specialists in the US and UK were moved into a common, international group, the Usability and GUI Skill Centre. For the first time, we all reported to a single department head. We were excited and interested in working together. Lesley Trenner (LT) the UK Lead Specialist for the Skill Centre, and I had communicated informally for years. We had written emails, spoken on the phone, and even had a video-conference. LT and I knew we wanted to work together and that we shared many of the same goals. When we met in person during team building in the UK, we explicitly named the following as our Skill Centre goals:

- Integrate usability and usability testing into every phase of the design process (we were both tired of trying to tack on usability at the end of the project life cycle).
- Spread basic user interface (UI) design principles and UI consistency across the company. We knew we needed a new UI style guide that could tie together the US and the UK and the Glaxo and Wellcome parts of our identity. In addition, we had the political motive of wanting to establish ourselves as authorities on usability and design.
- Publicize a wider definition of usability and GUI design. All four of us felt strongly that user interface designers and usability specialists needed to be an integral part of the software design team and not just the "GUI police".

Even at this point, we began to realize that our common goals helped to obscure how different our approaches actually were. LT's work emphasized GUI reviews of software, whereas I had focused on designing user interfaces and leading contextual design teams. LT had concentrated on promoting usability by training developers and managers in usability testing. I was more interested in being a user advocate. I thought of myself as a guerrilla usability tester – my goal in usability testing was to get enough ammunition during a test to justify redesigning the software. I thought that the improved software would promote usability on its own. Both our methods were actually effective, just different.

The VOLUNTEER Project: Our First International Usability Tests

Project profile: VOLUNTEER
Software name: VOLUNTEER
Type of team: International
Developed by: UK contractor
Type of usability testing: Electronic prototype
Description of software: Manages laboratory notebook data

Our first international collaboration on the VOLUNTEER project, sharply highlighted our different working styles and approaches. VOLUNTEER was a complex system with an awkward user interface. We were not responsible for redesigning it, simply for reporting the test results, so neither LT nor I were really focusing on the usability issues we thought most important. In addition, we were brought in when the product was almost finished. These circumstances made the testing stressful and accentuated the weak spots in our partnership. Moreover, LT and I had hidden assumptions that only came to light during the actual usability tests.

Methodology Used

As we prepared for the tests, everything seemed to be going fine. As far as I knew, LT was following my standard methodology:

- LT requested my help for the US half of the VOLUNTEER usability testing. Because this work was not included in my quarterly plan, I asked my boss if I could participate, and she said yes.
- LT scheduled the dates of the tests and had the VOLUNTEER team in the US schedule the conference room. The VOLUNTEER team was also responsible for setting up the equipment.
- LT wrote the usability scripts and instructions for moderating the tests and sent them to me. She also recruited the end users who would be participating in the tests. Since I did not have a role in designing the software, I took time to become familiar with it and worked with the US team to run through the scripts on the actual system.
- The other US usability specialist and I showed up early for the scheduled testing with our laptops and audiotape recorders. We assumed we would be running one or two tests at a time. The tests were supposed to take 45 minutes, so we expected to be able to run three during the afternoon time slot.
- We knew that LT would be writing up a report of the test results as soon as we could send her our logs.
- LT was also responsible for distributing the report to the US and UK members of the VOLUNTEER team.

We were prepared. Or so we believed. The first indication that something was wrong was that the equipment was not set up on time. The US VOLUNTEER team had problems getting everything set up in the conference room, so we started late and the test participants had to wait. We were also confused when all three test participants showed up at the same time. I quickly asked one of them if we could reschedule him. Since the equipment was not completely set up, he did not mind. Several members of the US VOLUNTEER team were also in the room, and they observed while we ran the tests, although we wondered why so many team members were there. At this point we knew the testing was not going smoothly, but we did not know why. Because of the five-hour time difference, the UK had already gone home for the day, so we could not call LT to ask.

What Went Wrong?

The next day LT and I talked at length, and we began to figure out the problems. LT had assumed that we could test all three participants at the same time and that the VOLUNTEER team would conduct the actual testing. My colleague and I would then be available to float among the three usability tests that were taking place. LT usually ran usability tests like this in the UK, so she had several trained developers on whom she could rely to conduct the testing. Unfortunately, the US VOLUNTEER team had never been formally trained, and I had worked with only one of them before. They had not had enough training to run the usability tests on their own.

LT was also surprised that we had taken notes on line and audiotaped the tests, although she was pleased with the thoroughness of our notes and the exact quotations from the participants. It turned out that she did not usually have problems with equipment set up because she conducted tests in IT training rooms that had computers already set up. After this discussion, LT and I realized that we needed to become more aware of each other's standard working practices and try to harmonize them. As far as we were concerned, the crisis was over, and we had started to solve the problem.

How International Issues Amplify Small Problems

Unfortunately, we still had some political fallout coming. A UK manager sent my boss an email complaining about the US testing. He believed that I was a purist and inflexible and was upset that one of the clients had been "turned away" from the testing. Once again, the time difference worked against us. I received the email in the afternoon – everyone in the UK had already gone home. I quickly responded to the major points in the note. However, because email is not a good way to settle conflicts, I told him that I would call him in the morning. After we talked on the phone, he understood better what had happened.

At this manager's request, I asked the test participants for a critique of the testing. As it turned out, the client who was "turned away" really did not mind having the test rescheduled. Most of the concerns he expressed were about the software and the delivery schedule. The fact that the results from the US and UK tests were in almost total agreement also helped to satisfy this manager that we had actually done a good job.

The differences in LT's and my approaches to usability testing came from the difference in our reasons for conducting the tests. LT considered them primarily a tool for selling programmers on usability, whereas I thought the tests should focus on redesign. LT believed that actually seeing users struggle with the software was more persuasive than anything she could say about the importance of usability. In my interactions with developers, they had always been willing to believe my reports. In *Brit-Think Ameri-Think*, Jane Walmsley suggests that the British must have proof that something is better before they try it. In contrast, Americans tend to love something simply because it is new [4]. LT and I began to wonder if our different strategies actually came from the differences in the cultures around us.

How Can We Fix it?

LT and I knew that the kind of hidden assumptions we ran into on VOLUNTEER could sink us the next time we tried international work. As a result, we decided to have a series of teleconferences where we would discuss in detail how and why we conducted usability tests. From these discussions, we developed a Usability Testing Starter Kit that we could distribute to other people conducting usability tests and that we could use ourselves for international and local testing.

Because of heavy workloads, we had to turn down a lot of requests for help, and we felt that the kits could help people get started for themselves. However, putting the kit together also gave us an excellent opportunity to examine what we each did and analyse why we did it. We wanted the Starter Kit to be comprehensive without becoming a separate book on usability testing. It covers the following topics:

- people to contact for help with usability and GUI design (US and UK);
- task analysis;
- resources for GUI design (a bibliography and a reference to the Skill Centre's Intranet web page);
- detailed instructions for the different phases of usability testing: selecting the number of people to test at a time; recruiting test participants; writing scripts and questionnaires (including samples of both from our work); summarizing the usability tests in a final report;
- tips for international usability testing;
- ways to plan usability into projects from the beginning.

In putting together the Starter Kit, we really had to come to terms with the differences in our work styles. The international section outlines our advice on how to avoid the pitfalls of the VOLUNTEER project (see Box 10.1).

Box 10.1: The Usability Testing Starter Kit

Tips for International Usability Testing

Is it Worth it ?
Performing usability testing internationally can have its benefits:

- The testing may help you realize that parts of your system (for example, icons or terminology) are not meaningful cross-culturally.
- Testing can help ensure that an international product fits the work practices of all the countries involved.
- The users in all the countries affected will feel more invested in the system and more involved in the design process.
- The wider set of testers makes it easier to find general usability problems.

However, making usability testing international has all the same pitfalls as any international effort:

- It takes extra time and money to co-ordinate the testing.
- Extra communication and planning are necessary.
- You need to meet the people running the tests in the other countries ahead of time. Video-conferences and phone conversations are a poor, but sometimes adequate, substitute for face-to-face meetings. It may be helpful to travel internationally to bridge the gaps.
- You have to trust your counterparts in the other countries.

Some projects may not be appropriate for international usability testing, or you may want to test different parts of the application on different sites. Base these decisions on the project's overall usability criteria and your specific objectives for doing usability testing.

Hints and Tips Based on the VOLUNTEER Project

Pick a Leader
Someone has to be in charge of the usability testing effort. This person must drive the testing and communicate the final results. He or she must:

- Communicate the goals of the usability testing to the usability team and participants.
- Prepare a single script to be used at all tests.
- Co-ordinate recruiting testers and observers internationally. Although the leader may not be able to do all of the recruiting alone, he or she should know ahead of time who all the testers and observers are and why they have been chosen.

- Communicate the results (for example, by writing a report or having someone else write it).

Discuss Objectives and Plans by Communicating Regularly
- Schedule regular (twice a week) teleconferences or video-conferences.
- Schedule teleconferences immediately after each usability testing session. Debrief each other on your successes and failures. Were there any surprises?
- Set ground rules for the team and make sure the entire team understands them (for example, all team members might agree to review the usability report within two days of receiving it).
- If a conflict arises, telephone the person in question immediately. Do NOT try to settle international disputes via email. Email can make small misunderstandings mushroom into disasters.

Plan and Prepare Together
The only effective remedy for the difficulties of international usability testing is preparation.
- Take time to get to know your counterparts, understand the software you are testing, and familiarize yourself with the usability testing script.
- Use the same script internationally. It may be necessary to allow some local variations but these will make analysis of the results harder.
- Plan when the sessions will be held. Holding them at the same time may not be feasible (due to time differences, etc.), and it may not be desirable to have all your support people busy at the same time. If you wanted to test international communications or speed, then you might plan for the sessions to overlap.
- Make sure it is possible to set up the necessary equipment and network connections in all the countries involved ahead of time
- Allow for differences in time zones
- Plan usability tests so that you can communicate with the other countries involved during the testing. Confusion and misunderstandings can then be cleared up immediately and the test results will not be jeopardized.
- Plan time into the testing for a teleconference afterwards. If possible, plan so that you can teleconference immediately, so that no one will have already left for lunch or home.

Current Developments

Since VOLUNTEER, we have run several international projects, although LT and I have not collaborated directly on them. We have referred to the Starter Kit on several occasions. International projects continue to provide challenges in terms of international travel, maintaining consistency in gathering requirements from users and managing US and UK expectations. Below I describe our work on the MedTrack project for which we developed a usability testing "hybrid" which helped minimize some of the difficulties of international usability testing.

Project profile: MedTrack
Software name: MedTrack
Type of team: International
Developed by: US-based team
Type of usability testing: Version 1 – GUI review; Versions 2 and 3 – paper prototypes
Description of software: Provides a GUI front-end for international clinical trials data stored on a VAX mainframe

MedTrack's History

The MedTrack clients for the system were looking forward to moving from the VAX mainframe into a GUI environment and very receptive to the change. Although no one performed formal usability testing on the original electronic version of the new system, two members of the MedTrack team reviewed the GUI for usability and conducted user acceptance testing. This testing was to ensure that all the features worked as described although the clients were also encouraged to note any usability problems. Based on this review, system requirements were refined and screens redesigned. The team worked with a group of expert users (from both the US and UK) who committed to take time to help with the usability testing and design. A few representatives came from every department that had a stake in the software. This group of users worked extremely well together and agreed on many of the major issues.

What Can We Do Better in the Next Version?

The MedTrack team was pleased with how their usability efforts had worked for version 1, but, the system still had a few usability bugs, and the team needed a clear plan for adding new features for version 2. They felt they needed help working on the UI design for version 2, so they asked me to consult. I reviewed the user interface and used contextual design (CD) techniques to help them model the existing structure of the system. I then recommended they prototype the new screens on paper and usability test their paper mock-ups with their expert users.

Inventing a Usability Testing Hybrid for International Testing

The MedTrack team had a special problem in usability testing their paper prototypes: they wanted to make sure all the expert users saw the system at the same time and could interact and discuss the additions, but these users were extremely busy. It was hard to even get them all in one room at the same time and, with many of them in the UK, it was not practical to schedule standard one-on-one usability tests. Typically, the US-based MedTrack team travelled to the UK for only a short time (a week or less), and one-on-one usability testing would not allow them to interact with all the expert users for the new system.

In response to these political and physical constraints, we designed a hybrid between usability testing and a demo.

The team made large paper prototypes on flipcharts that an entire room of users could see. (Paper prototypes are often about the size of a standard piece of paper. This smaller size makes them more portable and fairly comparable to the size of a computer screen. As with other usability tests, testing paper prototypes is commonly done with one or two end users at a time.)

One expert user at a time tested the paper prototype while the MedTrack team observed and moved the pieces of paper to simulate a computer system. A new expert user would rotate into the tester role for each new section or window of the system. Most of the expert users then got a chance to experience the look and feel of the new system and to take part in real usability testing.

The rest of the expert users observed and recorded any comments on Post-It notes. They would mark a note as either a usability issue, a business issue (a problem in how the work was currently done), or a design idea for improving the system. All the expert users could then contribute to the usability testing and design process without overwhelming the single user in the front of the room with their comments.

The team would put the notes up on the wall and discuss each note at the end of the usability testing. They would also cluster notes that appeared to be related. Sometimes, they would even run through the prototypes again to give the expert users another opportunity to speak up. These techniques ensured that all the users felt heard and that the team understood the message behind each note.

The Political Benefits of This Usability Testing Hybrid

This testing style met the political goal of guaranteeing that all the expert users contributed to the design process and that the UK and the US users were equally involved. In addition, the MedTrack team was not sacrificing a major goal of usability testing: making sure the development team saw the users doing real tasks with the UI. Instead, the expert users extended the observations of the team. Moreover, the testing style maximized the amount of exposure the UK expert users got to the product. The tests also uncovered a number of usability and design issues before the system was coded electronically. For example, the team had designed a tab dialogue to handle choosing defaults. This dialogue failed in usability testing, so they came up with an alternative design. The developers then coded from the final paper mock-ups.

The new system has continued to receive kudos for its usability. The MedTrack team has recently completed paper prototyping and usability testing on version 3 of the system. The MedTrack project manager, emphasized the importance of early usability testing on paper prototypes: "What you did for us has really paid off. It is really, really keen and important. We hardly ever get a call about how to use it [MedTrack] . If the front-end is not usable and simple, it's not going to fly… I know now that if there are too many training issues with a piece of software, something's wrong."

Lessons Learned

As a result of our international experiences over the last few years, we have many words of advice for accomplishing international usability work within a company:

- Make sure the intent and methodologies for usability testing in all the countries involved are as consistent as possible. Take time to clarify the work processes each country uses for testing.
- Make every effort to communicate frequently with the teams performing the work in other countries (via teleconferences, video-conferences, and international travel, if possible). Take time to get to know the usability people and end users internationally and keep everyone informed. Make sure you have the right people as stakeholders early.
- Develop a handbook of the similarities and differences in your work practices (like our Usability Testing Starter Kit). We encourage everyone to take the section on international usability testing from our Starter Kit and use it as blueprint for this kind of work in your own companies.
- Be willing to design novel solutions to international issues (the MedTrack usability testing hybrid). Be flexible and aware of problems as they arise.
- Before you travel internationally for requirements gathering or usability testing, plan which end users you will work with and why they are the best choices.

The most critical piece of advice I have for international usability work is:

- Take the extra time to plan every stage of your work in excruciating detail. You will not be sorry.

References

[1] Joseph S. Dumas and Janice C. Redish (1993) *A Practical Guide to Usability Testing*, Ablex Publishing Company, Norwood, NJ.
[2] Marc Rettig (1991) "Nobody Reads Documentation", *Communications of the ACM*, vol. 34, p. 7.
[3] Web page for InContext Enterprises Inc. (http://www.incent.com/CDP.html).
[4] Jane Walmsley (1987) *Brit-Think Ameri-Think: A Transatlantic Survival Guide*, Penguin, New York.

11. *Spreading the Word: Introducing Usability Evaluation on an International Scale*

How to Integrate Your Services into High Level Marketing Objectives

Joanna Bawa

ABSTRACT

A method of performing comparative usability evaluation was developed at PC Magazine UK and subsequently transferred to the USA – and later to Germany and France. As the method developed in different countries, many lessons were learnt about the importance of presenting usability data, the purpose of a usability report, the objectives of those who are reading it and the merits of different styles of conducting and analysing a test. Distinct international attributes are less important than global "human" factors in successfully conveying a message about a complex subject such as usability, but nonetheless, different countries have different markets, expectations and needs. These things can represent difficulties, but they can also be made to work in favour of the usability function.

Introduction

New products and new forms of technology-based interaction and communication create a need for new ways of evaluation. A comprehensive analysis of usability nowadays requires more than a critique of the interface but must take into account a range of factors, including competing products, user preferences and changes in the wider working and social environment. This breadth of factors also applies to those organizations designing, developing and marketing software and technology products, and those, like PC Magazine, which evaluate and review these products.

This chapter considers the extent to which the usability evaluation process can be adapted according to the business need and integrated with marketing activity to achieve objectives which meet the needs of more than one area. In particular, it looks at the benefits and difficulties of transferring usability skills within an organization but across national boundaries, to achieve mutual gains without generating internal competition. It also considers the higher level impact that a well-marketed usability function can have on an organization, and how, in turn, it is possible to identify marketing activities that support the development and maintenance of a usability function.

Ziff Davis and PC Magazine

Ziff Davis is a media company specializing in the dissemination of information about technology. A privately owned company for many years, it was sold in 1996 and is now owned by Softbank Corporation. Ziff Davis's original focus was – and in many ways still is – print magazine publishing, its flagship publication being PC Magazine, the highest circulation technology publication in the world. The company owns a large number of computing and technology publications which are available around the globe, and has recently expanded its media interests to include television and the Internet. Irrespective of the medium, its purpose is to inform its readership of new developments in all areas of technology, in as rigorous and objective a way as possible. This has led to the development of some of the most detailed hardware testing methods available, for personal computers, printers, monitors, modems, scanners, networks and other hardware and peripherals. These tests are carried out in laboratory conditions and are used to determine a huge range of performance indicators which, in conjunction with an expert review, enable prospective buyers to identify their preferred product with greater accuracy. This lab-based approach to product reviews has become the hallmark and most significant differentiator of Ziff Davis generally and PC Magazine specifically.

Testing software has always been more difficult. Performance indicators for software are harder to define and comprise a smaller proportion of the overall "value" of a product. Things which typically indicate "good" results for hardware, such as high speed, often indicate a mixed result for software. Fast software may be good software, but it may equally be software with limited functionality, or a sparse and non-standard interface. It might equally be an indifferent product with a powerful computer driving it. There are further difficulties – people rarely want to use software for a single, definable purpose (unlike, say, a printer) but tend to have a number of things they would definitely like to do and a vague notion of other possibilities which may or may not become relevant in the future. Few elements of software functionality can be measured in a meaningful way, or presented as information which is useful to individuals trying to choose between similar, competing products. For example, although it may be easy to measure, it is not particularly helpful to inform buyers that two word processing packages include a mail merge function, but one can cope with 7000 addresses while the other can only cope with 6000. Nor is it particularly interesting to note that one of them can hold nine documents open simultaneously and the other one ten. These things may be readily quantifiable, but they are not useful or interesting to users seeking to make an informed choice between products.

These difficulties were compounded by the sudden explosion in the range, size and complexity of business applications software that occurred following the tremendous success of Microsoft's Windows operating system. A vast number of software programs appeared in the early 1990s, all claiming to take advantage of the Windows graphical user interface and the power of the x86 microprocessor series of personal computers which evolved alongside it. The challenge of measuring and evaluating such software using PC Magazine's objective, quantifiable approach multiplied out of all proportion, while the actual information produced diminished in quantity and quality.

A New Way of Evaluating Software: the Need for Usability

This was the situation with PC Magazine's product testing labs when Ziff Davis established a London office in 1991. Within the established framework and mission of the magazine, the London office was given full responsibility for developing its own approach and procedures, with the resources and encouragement to develop existing test methodologies and bring in new ones where appropriate. The hardware performance testing lab was, and still is, the best equipped comparative evaluation facility in the UK, run along the same lines and with the same approach as its US parent. The software lab was a question mark. PC Magazine's staff were aware that this question mark could either be seen as a daunting problem or as a tremendous opportunity. To achieve the latter, it was necessary to identify an attribute, or series of attributes, of business applications software that were important and meaningful to prospective users. It was also necessary to develop a means of measuring these attributes quickly and accurately, in a way which yielded reliable, valid and replicable information.

Academic versus Pragmatic Considerations

"Usability", still an emerging concept in 1991, was readily identified as the best expression of the quality or attribute of software which the software testing lab required. Even without the term appearing in the literature, some similar term would eventually have been coined to describe the combination of qualities that are commonly used to define usability: intuitiveness, learnability, ease of use, and of course, user satisfaction.

In the PC Magazine model of usability, however, a unique combination of requirements was identified. Any form of usability evaluation had to take place within rigid guidelines and according to a tightly defined methodology – in order to comply with the magazine's established testing philosophy of absolute rigour and objectivity. Of course, much of what constitutes "usability" defies such classification and relies almost exclusively on softer, subjective measures. Such a methodology would also have to be quick and easy to implement across a large number of products, since a monthly publication imposes a tight, inflexible deadline, without which no magazine would appear. Those usability testing methodologies in existence tended to be drawn out and time consuming, requiring large numbers of participants in order to achieve statistical validity, performing tests and analyses which could go on for days or even weeks. And in every case, the result of such testing was sufficient data only to comment on the appropriateness of one or another relatively small detail of a single product's interface.

A significant and related problem was the dearth of research literature discussing the possibility of *comparative* evaluation, which was the central requirement of the magazine, and indeed, the vast majority of the magazine's target readership. PC Magazine exists to compare similar (and therefore competing) products, evaluating the merits of each according to some benchmark and using objective data to distinguish between them on a range of criteria. The end result of any kind of magazine-based usability evaluation would, therefore, have to be data which reliably and consistently discriminated between like products – sometimes a large number of like products – in terms of their usability.

These requirements seemed at first to be contradictory and mutually exclusive, not to say complicated and potentially overwhelming. As a process with its roots in academia, usability testing lacked any kind of pragmatism or recognition of business need; as a product development methodology it lacked any immediate relevance for the PC Magazine comparative function. Nonetheless, some method for analysing the comparative usability of similar software products was needed, which would not only serve the immediate publishing need but would also support and enhance the established procedures of PC Magazine (see Box 11.1).

Box 11.1: Development of the comparative methodology

The comparative approach to usability was defined by the very specific requirement of the organization, outlined above. The first step was to conceptualize the approach as a broad and shallow one, slicing snapshot views of many products at once. This is in contrast to the deep and narrow approach which characterizes traditional or "classical" usability evaluation (or development testing, as we later came to call it, to distinguish it clearly from comparative testing). Next, drawing upon as much existing knowledge as could be found, a four-step procedure was drawn up which would allow the usability lab to review several products at one time in a reasonably structured, coherent, repeatable, useful and informative way:

- *Task analysis*: research into the type of product being tested, involving discussion with users and vendors to identify the key tasks undertaken, by whom, and in what context;
- *Test design*: the usability test relied on task analysis data to compose a series of exercises for the testers which represented "typical" behaviour. Although every test comprised separate sub-tasks, these sub-tasks were sequenced and designed so that altogether, they led to a single, meta-task wherever possible.
- *Test implementation*: the test sessions were designed so that each product was looked at for at least half a day by at least four people. Testers and products "rotated" in an organized sequence to control for start-of-test nerves and also end-of-test boredom. Throughout each product

test, testers recorded their experiences in a structured format, and were formally debriefed afterwards.

- *Data analysis*: results were both quantitative and qualitative. Quantitative data included time and accuracy (productivity); errors and help references (intuitiveness) and satisfaction, derived from a questionnaire. These three main indices contributed to the overall usability score. Quantitative data was used to support the more revealing qualitative data – what the testers actually said. Thus, data was ultimately presented as a series of detailed tester comments and lab staff observations, backed-up by actual measurements and scores.

- *Data presentation*: every month the results of the tests were published in the magazine. Information about the test itself and its objectives, together with a brief outline of the testers, was supplied, before the detailed results appeared. Products were compared on the various tasks in the test, and each good or bad point about each product was supported by the qualitative data from the interviews and supported by the quantitative scores derived in the lab. The style of writing was rigorous but non-technical: there were no wild assertions or unsupported criticisms; and reported material was interwoven with anecdotal material from the interviews. Overall, the Usability Report comprised about a third of the total comparative review, the other two thirds being a Performance Lab report (purely technical matters) and the expert review, carried out and written by an individual with specific expertise in that product group.

"Any Use to You?": the Response of Readers and Vendors to Usability Reports

The first comparative reviews of product usability excited little attention in the readership. Feedback about the contents of a magazine is notoriously difficult to get, and even more difficult to rely on or respond to until a large-scale formal attempt is made to determine reader views. Normally, this is done by conducting a series of focus groups with representative samples of readers across the country and polling them for detailed opinions of different magazine sections.

Focus groups on PC Magazine's use of usability testing after a year of publishing a usability report every month revealed an interesting result. When asked what the magazine lacked, most readers expressed a strong wish for more information about usability-related issues, typically asking for "more detail about whether a product's any good at what it claims to do", or "some kind of field testing showing whether or not the people who buy these products can actually understand them". When it was pointed out to these people that such information was there within the magazine in the form of a usability report, they expressed amazement, even though they had been subscribing to the publication for at least a year.

Closer analysis revealed two main problems with PC Magazine's usability data. The first was one of terminology – almost nobody in the focus groups had a clear understanding of what "usability" meant, and when discussing usability issues were more likely to talk in terms of *understanding, user friendliness, ease of learning*, or *liking*, making no connection between these terms and the term "usability". The second problem was one of presentation. This proved to be a general issue throughout the magazine, which presents the highest proportion of facts about products per paragraph, of any similar publication. This inevitably leads to a dense and rather dry writing style, which supports the magazine in its role as a reference work rather than an entertaining read. So, although a full explanation of the terminology and the methodology is included in every report, its presentation tended to signal "boring background detail" rather than important explanatory information, and was therefore left unread.

By contrast, the response of software vendors to the usability report was more immediate, more detailed and more positive. Enthusiasm was linked directly with awareness: companies with some established investment in usability testing readily recognized the value of the usability report; less committed companies were supportive but had difficulty seeing how the issue related to them. Overall, however, the effect of PC Magazine's usability reports served to generate a mutually beneficial cycle of awareness in usability testing and a greater usability output from vendors – or at least, the drawing of attention to "usability" or related terms in their marketing literature. From the focus groups it was possible to draw three important conclusions:

- Awareness of the vocabulary of usability is low, especially amongst those to whom it is arguably of greatest relevance.
- Awareness of the ideas and objectives associated with usability is high – vendors and users do understand that the important attributes of software have less to do with speed and performance and more to do with softer, comprehension and interaction-related issues. These issues are often poorly articulated and rarely translated into specific policies or activities.
- Usability data needs to be presented in a way which enables readers to make their own links between perceptions of what constitutes good quality, easy to use software, and what experts refer to as usability. As such, usability data must educate about usability as much as it must inform about the properties of a given product.

"Any Use to Us?": the Internal Response to Usability Evaluation

The success of the comparative methodology in generating meaningful, consistent and discriminating product data ensured that the lab and its services soon attained a secure place in the magazine's battery of tests. Not only did the usability lab produce an important new layer of product information for the readership, it also marked the magazine out from its competitors in terms of the quality and depth of product review it published. Ultimately, this latter fact proved to be far more important in ensuring the long term viability of the usability lab than the testing itself – it is always worth considering the potential marketing value of a usability evaluation function in any organization.

The task of marketing a magazine is very similar to that of marketing any other product or service. It has to be targeted, its potential user-base (or readership) carefully researched and their needs understood. The product must meet those needs in a timely and appropriate manner, offering the functions, services or information which are demanded. A well-marketed product is aware of its competitors, seeks to carve out a unique niche for itself in which it can compete most effectively, and hones that competitive edge by developing or acquiring an elusive USP – unique selling point – that its competitors cannot match.

As anyone who has ever browsed the newsagent's shelves looking for technical enlightenment will surely agree, the computer magazine market is a particularly crowded one. On any day, tens of publications jostle for room, offering computing information. Each is targeting a different type of person, each presenting slightly different information in a slightly different way. To the reader, however, this is not always obvious – the claims appear to be the same and the covers are indistinguishable. A genuine USP is highly sought after, and for PC Magazine UK, the usability lab became just that.

Usability: a "Unique Selling Point" for Many Products?

At about the same time that usability testing was taking root in the UK, a related marketing issue arose with the parent company's US-based publications. In 1993, PC Magazine was one of two distinct Ziff Davis publications in the UK (the other being PC Direct); in the USA it was one of ten. When an organization develops several products which are fundamentally similar (because of, e.g., its history, expertise or resources), additional research and marketing effort is required to differentiate these products sufficiently from each other, as well as their competitors. In the USA the Ziff publication, PC/Computing, was struggling to achieve a niche distinct from that of the better established PC Magazine. PC/Computing is aimed less at those who choose or specify technology and more at those who use it, therefore it focuses less on the technology and more on applications of the technology. Even so, it covers the same products in the same markets and utilizes some of the same lab resources as PC Magazine. In order to define its niche more clearly, something else was needed – something which would support the magazine's focus, but in a way which would not push it into a bracket already covered by a different publication. As was the case for PC Magazine UK, usability testing proved to be the solution to these challenges.

Taking Usability to the US: New Lab, Same Company

I was seconded to PC/Computing for three months to help establish a usability lab there, an experience which yielded many insights into the politics of usability within an organization. The first and most noticeable was simply the difference in the amount of money available. With a circulation of 800,000 in 1993, PC/Computing was nearly ten times larger than PC Magazine UK was at that time, generating more than ten times the revenue. Resources available for developing the publication were therefore substantial. Secondly, support was high because the usability proposition had already, to some extent, proved itself. The request to build a usability lab had been generated by a senior figure within Ziff Davis (the Editor-in-Chief of PC/Computing and formerly Editor-in-Chief of PC Magazine UK), and was therefore a high priority item. His interest was twofold – on the one hand he had presided over the launch of the usability lab in the UK, and eventually agreed that it had proved to be useful and effective. On the other hand, his new remit at the helm of PC/Computing required that he redefine the magazine's niche more clearly, making a new usability lab an ideal way of achieving this.

The Consultant from **Where?**

Arriving in San Francisco from London as a usability consultant to an established magazine has two effects. The first is that you feel utterly terrified, daunted and inadequate, the second is that, at the same time, you feel important, needed and slightly superior. The first lesson, which I learned early on, is to completely discard both these feelings, since neither are even remotely accurate.

After the first few days of mutual confusion, enquiry and introduction, it became apparent that the sooner one can identify those people to whom one is of direct relevance and interest, the better. From that point on, the most important thing to do is effectively communicate one's goals, purpose and intentions to them, so it becomes easier to form a team of enthusiastic individuals sharing common objectives. This is an important lesson: in the early stages of my time there I found a team of competent and knowledgeable individuals who were enthusiastic about the concept of usability evaluation but cautious of a person whose role and credentials were unclear to them. Even though we belonged to the same organization, I realized it was naive to assume that their knowledge of activities in London was even partial, or that they should even be interested. The most important lesson associated with establishing a lab in the States (indeed anywhere) was, therefore, to talk to everyone involved as soon as possible, not only to find out about them but to let them find out about you.

Once initial anxieties had been put to rest, it became clear that support for the new lab was substantial. Keenly aware that PC/Computing was a natural platform for user-centred testing, the magazine staff formed a team which was anxious to put some usability practice into place as soon as possible. In keeping with the UK lab's humble origins, the first usability test (of the latest versions of the then independent WordPerfect word processing program and Microsoft Word) took place in a vacant meeting room using computers borrowed from around the magazine offices. Magazine staff gathered to listen and watch as the first team of testers were read the standard explanation of the testing procedure (including the repeated assurance that they themselves were not being tested), and the purpose of the test. Despite the relatively uneventful testing, high levels of interest were apparent in the number of drop-in visitors the "lab" experienced during the first day, and another crowd gathered to hear the debriefing sessions with the testers afterwards.

During this stage I realized how easy it is to "forget" that testers are human – on more than one occasion, interested parties would conduct loudly whispered conversations in the usability testing area about the fascinating behaviour of the testers, as if oblivious to them as hearing, feeling people. Gentle reminders to step outside always sufficed at these moments, but it was a clear lesson to me that a "lab" conveys a special atmosphere, and those who work in one, in whatever capacity, acquire a curious aura which distances them from non-lab people. After a three-day testing period, sufficient data had been gathered to begin the less spectator-friendly process of analysis, at which point the team dropped to myself and one other person – the primary usability appointment.

What Tells the Story: Numbers or Words?

Analysing usability data is a difficult task for a number of reasons. The analysis must be done in a way which is credible, reliable and valid, faithfully reflecting the procedures and experiences of the testers to most effectively gain a "true" result. It must also be done in a way which delivers information which has real meaning for those who later read it – it is no good providing data accurate to seven decimal places if it describes an experience or function which has no bearing on the product's usability. Furthermore, when it comes to usability, it is meaningless to provide quantitative data without also providing a qualitative explanation. Why did testers find one product so much more satisfying than another? What factor or combination of factors led them to these conclusions? In what context were they working when a "satisfying" experience occurred? Towards what goal were they proceeding? It is possible (even likely) that different testers might have very different experiences yet still agree that one product is more satisfying than another – but quantitative data will not reveal this.

It was at this point that the first disagreement emerged between my key associate and myself. He was a trained physicist and statistician with an interest in human factors, whereas I am a psychologist with computing expertise. This led to two very different opinions of the relative merits of quantitative data within the usability evaluation process. He favoured a rigorously scientific approach, with every task and user action described as a complex statistical representation, lending authority and credibility to what would otherwise have been very "soft" data. I preferred a reduced role for quantitative data, relying on simple measures to establish general trends, which could then be used to support the (more important, in my opinion) soft verbal data. In particular, with relatively few subjects testing the products I was unhappy about placing too heavy an emphasis on statistics, thereby implying a higher degree of certainty about our findings than could be reasonably said to be the case. Our different backgrounds made it difficult for either one to convince the other, and our debate reflected many of the issues which have always plagued usability evaluation. It was a poignant picture of usability at the crossroads – is it an art or a science? Who does it help? How is it best presented? Can it be done in a way which supports higher objectives, namely, those of the parent organization?

Usability Data Is only Part of the Picture

The apparently irresolvable dilemma which gripped my associate and myself in the privacy of my office became far less intractable once the wider team was brought into the discussion. Compiling a complete feature for publication within the magazine requires the efforts of many, and more often than not, each person must rely to some extent on the work of others. The products we had reviewed were also inspected by labs staff and expert users, each with a particular angle of interest and different goals. Their findings were then channelled to an overall Reviews Editor whose job it was to compile the final report, drawing on data from all three sources. Unlike PC Magazine UK, PC/Computing does not publish exhaustive details of its testing procedures and findings, but relies on a single, lengthy report which draws on highlights of its tests. It was therefore vital that the data emerging from the usability lab could be readily understood by non-usability experts, that it made concise points which were not covered elsewhere, and that it fitted into the overall layout of the magazine without requiring extensive amendment. With these factors pressing upon us, it soon became apparent that a written summary of verbal protocols, analysed for themes and trends, and accompanied by a brief supporting summary of quantitative scores, was our best chance of getting good and accurate coverage of our evaluation in the published report.

What Does Usability Data Look Like? How Much Is Too Much? (Or Too Little?)

In itself this raised another question, which PC Magazine UK with its greater emphasis on testing and a larger proportion of pages devoted to this subject did not have to face; namely, that of presentation. What does usability data look like? Given the PC Magazine experience, what was the best way to present such data in a way which would make it recognizable and meaningful to readers, without losing too much detail and hence the essence of the lab? The problem was compounded by the PC/Computing magazine model, which did not require lab staff to write their own reports (as in the UK), and instead gave that function to an editor who had a number of data sources to take into account and was unlikely to have experience or knowledge of usability.

The biggest risk was that usability data would be misinterpreted, inappropriately edited, misrepresented or ignored altogether. This put additional pressure on the usability team to compile information into a format which made it readily accessible to non-expert editors, who further compressed it to make it appealing to non-expert readers. My concern then switched to the other extreme – that by oversimplifying our data to improve "digestibility", it would not be discernible that any formal evaluation had occurred at all. By reducing a week's worth of testing to a few crisp sentences, all the effort of the test designers, testers, observers and analysts would go to waste and PC/Computing would lose the competitive advantage it required.

Resolving this problem required the input of usability staff, editors and designers in a process remarkably similar to that faced by Web site designers today. Achieving a balance between visual appeal, editorial integrity, fact-based credibility and bite-sized readability is very hard to achieve; and in many ways requires some form of "meta-usability" analysis (a term now appearing in the literature, particularly with reference to the Web). The PC/Computing solution was to rely heavily on verbal protocol data for the written reports and accompany these throughout with pictures of the testers, supported by "sound bite" captions of their comments in bold text enclosed in speech marks. Quantitative data was converted into scores along the same lines as those used in PC Magazine UK and presented as at-a-glance bar charts. Throughout the magazine, plenty of references were made to the new usability lab and a light-hearted column, the "Usability Hall of Fame" was started to encourage readers to think about and describe their own usability horror stories. The effect was marked: PC/Computing soon became known as a proponent of the idea of usability, and usability data was scattered throughout its pages in a range of eye-catching ways. Unlike PC Magazine UK, however, it did not acquire the association with a lab-based methodology, since these processes were largely hidden from readers.

The Wider View: Marketing and Competitive Considerations

PC/Computing fully embraced the concept of usability, and did not hesitate to draw it into its repertoire of marketing and promotional tools. From the beginning, the main purpose of the usability lab was to provide the magazine with a better-defined market segment and a more effective means of appealing to software vendors, advertisers and readers alike. On both counts it has achieved its goals. Although all usability professionals recognize that good usability work relies on a trained and perceptive mind rather than a cluster of video cameras and a mixing desk, PC/Computing understood that non-usability professionals do *not* know this. Their lab is considerably more elaborate than the work requires, but the lab works just as hard as a marketing tool as a usability lab.

One argument commonly used to say "no" to usability testing is that it is purely an overhead, a luxury which can be dispensed with when times are hard. Although this is not always true, it may become so as product developers increasingly study aspects of design and usability as part of other courses, obviating the need for usability specialists. The collision of consumer demands with business software has brought in a whole new range of product development opportunities which are being snapped up by designers rather than usability folk, since the traditional usability adherence to goal-centred, task-oriented testing simply does not apply to consumer gadgets. Such losses are losses to usability, as well as to the market.

Spreading the Word Internationally

The inauguration of PC/Computing's lab was greatly helped by a huge wave of promotional literature, announcements and demonstrations that, coupled with the magazine's own intensive editorial coverage of the area, soon established PC/Computing as *the* usability publication in the USA. Shortly after I returned to the UK, the German equivalent, PC Professionelle, began to develop its own usability lab, and later, France's PC Expert established (in a true, French, linguistically pure way) its own "laboratoire d'ergonomie". As a result of this international spread of labs, the company as a whole was able to conduct genuine international usability testing, with labs across the world engaged on common evaluations. The most successful was a review of videoconferencing technology, with German and English testers carrying out real-time videoconferences in the respective labs. Despite a set-up and scripting task of mammoth proportions, the raft of cross-cultural usability information we derived from this testing was of such high quality it remains relevant three years later.

Conclusion: Usability Must Get Tough

Efforts to bring usability out of its ivory tower and into the unforgiving world of business frequently reveal it for the fragile creature it is. It is still unfamiliar to too many companies and individuals who should know it well and take it for granted, and it has not really succeeded in securing an automatic place in the product development process. Why is this? Do we, as usability professionals, guard it too jealously and veil it too heavily in our own jargon? The experiences recounted in this chapter suggest that perhaps we do.

In an age of digital information (indeed, on a magazine concerned almost exclusively with digital information), we still need something to see, touch and experience through our senses in order to be truly impressed by it. Usability is not a concrete concept, but it still needs to be made concrete in order for non-practitioners to grasp it with their hearts as well as their minds. This means using it as a marketing tool; applying its findings to less high-minded pursuits, such as The Usability Hall of Fame; finding new ways and new methods to apply it, which may not survive rigorous academic scrutiny but will get usability the hearing it deserves; playing the political games which will distance it from the ivory tower and its jargon and bring it closer to the commercial goals of organizations and the hard-nosed decision-makers who wield the power. The price for doing so is that usability may lose its status as a black art which draws on a mix of esoteric sciences and sensitivities; and instead line up alongside the more mundane practices of marketing, advertising and selling. Rather than retire, hurt, to academia, it is time for usability to sharpen up its act. We all know what it means and what it can do – but it must become more robust and more realistic if it is to survive.

Lessons Learned

- No usability lab can survive in isolation, but must understand and support the goals and objectives of its funding organization. This is the only way commercial usability testing can hope to survive for long enough to become established (or better still, able to earn its keep directly).

- It is vital to understand the perceptions other people have of usability, whether they be customers, readers, patrons or interested passers-by. As this chapter shows, most people have an incomplete idea at best, and as a result will often respond to usability issues in a misinformed way.
- The role of a usability consultant is rarely an easy one. It is not enough to know your subject material, you also have to understand where you fit within your new team, what their expectations are and what can realistically be achieved.
- Transferring usability skills across international boundaries depends far more on typically human things than any sort of national character. Communication, understanding and common goals are paramount, although an idea of prevailing market conditions in the different countries is also useful.
- Usability evaluation has a lot to contribute to the commercial world, but it must come out of its ivory tower to do so. Although its roots in academia are vital, it is equally vital that it sacrifice some of its more esoteric ventures and claims in favour of more robust, cost-conscious practice.
- Usability testing conducted across international boundaries can yield data which is greater than the sum of the data derived by two individual labs in different countries. Despite a shrinking world, there are plenty of cultural traits and expectations which a usability evaluation can reveal like no other test.

12. *Standards and Style Guides – a Cross-Cultural Perspective*

Tom Stewart

ABSTRACT

This chapter explains why standards are important in helping to improve the usability of systems, and describes the key standards which can be used to support system development. It goes on to discuss the problems of incorporating such standards into system development procedures, drawing on a real situation within an organization where the development team and the users were divided between offices in Germany and The Netherlands.

Introduction

Inconsistency in the user interface can be a major source of error, confusion and user discomfort. This is enough of a problem within most organizations. In an international organization, where the common language is not the first language for most users, inconsistency can be the final obstacle to successful system use. However, avoiding inconsistency is not easy. Few systems are designed in isolation or as a single integrated development. Historical precedence reduces the options open to designers and excessive "standardization" across common requirements may prevent systems from being truly suited to any individual user or task. International standards can help by providing a basis for consensus which is external to the organization and by representing agreed "best practice". But incorporating standards and style guides into the organization's development procedures raises its own problems. Indeed, many people see standards as an unwarranted constraint on their freedom to develop their own solutions and designs. There are also national differences in attitudes to standards in general. In Germany, most customers check for the appropriate stickers on products to show that they meet and have been tested to appropriate standards. In the UK, few people would recognize the stickers and would certainly never think of checking for them.

Why Standards Are Important in Improving Usability

System Concepts, founded in 1981, is a London-based management consultancy specializing in human factors. Our blue chip clients are mainly based in the UK

157

but increasingly we work in Europe and worldwide. We see our role as supporting our client's business by improving the relationships between people and the technology they use to work. System Concepts is not just a company name, it is also an idea. The idea is that a business system comprises components interacting for a purpose, though more typically there is often too much emphasis on technology – which is simply one of the components. We argue that more attention needs to be paid to other components – people, organization and environment – and to the purpose for which they interact – the business and individual tasks and objectives.

But it can be difficult to persuade organizations to shift their focus from technology to whole systems. Publicly available standards can be an enormous help and so we have a company policy to support national and international standards work through active participation in several committees, particularly ISO/TC 159/SC4 Ergonomics of Human System Interaction.

Although designing usable systems requires far more than just applying standards, we find that standards, especially those based on International Standards, can be a significant vehicle for improving systems. They can be used for

- encouraging consistency;
- promoting good practice;
- acting as a basis for common understanding;
- ensuring an appropriate prioritization of user interface issues;
- supporting the fulfilment of legal requirements.

Consistency

Most users have horror stories to tell about inconsistency between systems and even within the same system. For example, pressing the Escape key in one place may safely return you to your previous menu choice. In another place, you may be unceremoniously "dropped" to the operating system, the friendly messages disappear and you lose all your data. In one of the mainframe based systems in our client organization, the F3 key provided help in one subsystem and aborted the transaction in another! Such inconsistencies seem almost deliberately designed to create user error and confusion. Standards and style guidelines provide a consistent reference across design teams or across time to help avoid such unpleasant experiences. Indeed, in other fields, consistency, for example, between components which should interconnect, is the prime motivation for standards. It is certainly a worthwhile target for user interface standards.

Good Practice

In many fields, standards provide definitive statements of good practice. In user interface design, there are many conflicting viewpoints about good practice. Standards, especially International Standards, can provide independent and authoritative guidance. International Standards are developed slowly, by consensus, using extensive consultation and development processes. This has its disadvantages in such a fast moving field as user interface design and some have criticized any attempts at standardization as premature. However, there are areas where a great deal is known which can be made accessible to designers through appropriate standards and there are approaches to user interface standardization, based on human characteristics, that are relatively independent of specific technologies.

The practical discipline of having to achieve consensus helps moderate some of the wilder claims of user interface enthusiasts and helps ensure that the resulting standards do represent good practice. The slow development process also means that standards can seldom represent the leading edge of design. Nonetheless, properly written, they should not inhibit helpful creativity.

Common Understanding

Standards themselves do not guarantee good design but they do provide a means for different parties to share a common understanding when specifying interface quality in design, procurement and use. The client organization discussed in this chapter, like other users, uses standards to set appropriate procurement requirements and to evaluate competing suppliers' offerings. Their suppliers use the same standards to check their products during design and manufacture and to provide a basis for making claims about the quality of their products.

Appropriate Prioritization of User Interface Issues

One of the most significant benefits of standardization is that it places user interface issues squarely on the agenda. Standards are a serious business and whereas many organizations pay little regard to research findings, few organizations can afford to ignore standards. Indeed in Europe, and increasingly in other parts of the world, compliance with relevant standards is mandatory in major contracts.

Fulfilment of Legal Obligations

In 1990, the European Community published a directive (90/270/EEC) on the minimum safety and health requirements for work with display screen equipment. This directive obliged member states to transpose it into national legislation by the end of 1992. These laws, regulations and administrative provisions form part of the national health and safety legislation which is legally binding on most employers in Europe. Although the Directive was aimed at employers, many seek to pass on some of their responsibilities to their suppliers and demand guarantees from them about the suitability of their products, both hardware and software.

The requirements are listed in an annex to the directive and are worded rather vaguely. Meeting relevant standards therefore, particularly ISO 9241 which is discussed later, is one of the best ways of demonstrating good ergonomic practice.

The Client and the Nature of the Problem

The client was a European organization with major offices in a number of European cities. Each office was staffed by nationals from throughout Europe and English was used as the predominant common language, although it was the first

language of only a few of the employees. The organization had a unionized workforce and the work was moving from being paper intensive to an increasing
dependence on computer-based systems. These systems were mainly designed by
third party suppliers under contract to the different offices. There was, therefore, a
wide variety of different styles and ages of computer systems used by most
employees. The increase in screen working was beginning to cause concern for the
staff representatives and the publication of the display screen directive acted as a
focus for the organization to start to take ergonomics seriously.

We were invited to support a newly formed ergonomics committee and work
with its members to develop an internal infrastructure to promote good ergonomics. From the start, we proposed to use International Standards to underpin our
strategy. The organization was receptive to this approach and our first task was to
brief them on the standards which are, or soon will be, available in this area.

What Standards Are Relevant to Usability?

There are two different types of international standard which are relevant. The
most fully developed are those which deal with hardware ergonomics. However, in
the longer term, the more important ones are those which are still being developed
to deal with software ergonomics – how the software of the interface and the
system match the characteristics of the users and the tasks they wish to perform.

International standards are developed over a period of several years and in the
early stages, the published documents may change dramatically from version to
version until consensus is reached. As the standard becomes more mature (from
the Committee Draft Stage onwards), formal voting takes place and the draft documents provide a good indication of what the final standard is likely to look like.
Table 12.1 shows the main stages in the development of International Standards.

Table 12.1: The main stages of ISO standards development

WI	Work Item – an approved and recognized topic for a working group to be address-ing which should lead to one or more published standards.
WD	Working Draft – a partial or complete first draft of the text of the proposed standard.
CD	Committee Draft – a document circulated for comment and approval within the committee working on it and the national mirror committees. Voting and approval is required for the document to reach the next stage.
DIS	Draft International Standard – a draft standard which is circulated widely for public comment via national standards bodies. Voting and approval is required for the draft to reach the final stage.
FDIS	Final Draft International Standard – the final draft is circulated for formal voting for adoption as an International Standard.
IS	International Standard. The final published standard.
Note: Documents may be reissued as further CDs and DISs	

Although draft standards are usually publicly available from national standards
bodies, they are not widely publicized. We used our inside knowledge of standards

under development to help our client start to use such draft standards as part of their internal processes. This gave our client and its suppliers advance warning of future requirements but there was always the risk that the draft could be dramatically changed. We therefore had to be very clear at all times just how much reliance could be placed on the publicly available documents.

The main standard we used was ISO 9241 which is concerned with office work with visual display terminals. This is a 17 part standard which has been under development for more than a decade. A few parts are published, but most are still in various stages of draft. The standard covers both hardware and software issues. Table 12.2 shows a list of the parts and a note of their status in mid 1997. Note that as part of the creation of the single European market, most parts of ISO 9241 are also published in parallel as European Norms (EN). These replace similar national standards in member states of the European Union (EU) and the European Free Trade Association (EFTA).

Table 12.2: Parts and status of ISO 9241 in June 1997

ISO 9241 Ergonomics requirements for office work with visual display terminals (VDTs)	
Part 1: General Introduction	IS/EN
Part 2: Guidance on task requirements	IS/EN
Part 3: Visual display requirements	IS/EN
Part 4: Keyboard requirements	3rd DIS
Part 5: Workstation layout and postural requirements	3rd DIS
Part 6: Environmental requirements	2nd DIS
Part 7: Display requirements with reflections	FDIS
Part 8: Requirements for displayed colours	FDIS
Part 9: Requirements for non-keyboard input devices	3rd CD
Part 10: Dialogue principles	IS/EN
Part 11: Guidance on usability	FDIS
Part 12: Presentation of information	DIS
Part 13: User guidance	FDIS
Part 14: Menu dialogues	IS
Part 15: Command dialogues	FDIS
Part 16: Direct manipulation dialogues	DIS
Part 17: Form filling dialogues	DIS

Hardware and Environmental Ergonomics Standards

The most straightforward standards from a procurement point of view cover user interface hardware which may be bought on its own or as a system component, for example a keyboard, to be attached to some system. The proposed purchase can be checked against the specification in the appropriate standard and this gives the purchaser some confidence about the usability of the product.

Standards making is a slow process, partly because of the need for consensus and partly because it takes some time for stability to emerge in any new technology. This means that formal hardware ergonomics standards may not be available to support the procurement of newer interface devices. In such cases, requiring equipment manufacturers to demonstrate evidence of the usability of their products provides the most effective route for ensuring good ergonomics quality. ISO 9241 Part 11 offers guidance on specifying or assessing usability in this context.

Software Ergonomics and User Interface Standards

There are a number of standards which provide guidelines on good practice for the design of the dialogue between user and the interface software. Since the "right answer" is usually heavily dependent on the context, it is often not possible to provide guidelines which permit strict compliance checking. Even so, it is usually possible to check whether such guidelines have been breached in a significant way. For example, a standard containing guidelines on good dialogue design principles may warn against screen clutter without giving precise values for the number of open windows which may be regarded as reasonable. For a typical office user performing a document formatting task, it should be obvious that an interface which requires ten overlapping windows which fill the screen is breaking this guideline. Checklists based on such guidelines can be useful during procurement even if strict compliance cannot be assessed.

Developing an Effective Standards Policy

Having briefed the ergonomics committee on the standards which they could use, our next task was to agree a strategy for introducing the ergonomics programme. The committee contained representatives from many different parts of the organization, including trade union representatives. Management and unions initially adopted opposing views on principle. However, we spent considerable amounts of time and effort working together with the different representatives to discuss every obstacle. Our major strength was that we were external and independent. Management felt comfortable because we seemed to be practical and were using internationally agreed standards to support our recommendations. Their interest in standards was primarily as a means of inhibiting the wilder claims and ideas of individual staff members.

The trade union representatives felt comfortable because we were working to improve their members' working conditions by improving the usability of their systems. They too were reassured by our use of, and involvement in, internationally agreed standards. Their interest in standards was quite different to management and was based on their desire for official recognition that poor ergonomics and unusable systems could be significant problems for their members. Eventually, after several iterations, we agreed to draft a high level policy statement which could be supported by senior management and also by the trade union. The principle was that this document would be couched in very general terms and be supplemented by a number of specific working documents which would contain the technical content.

Working Documents

The working documents formed part of a Project Manager's Handbook being developed by the organization covering a number of technical and contractual matters as well as the ergonomics issues. Table 12.3 shows the titles of the working documents.

The documents deliberately cover a wide range of issues including hardware, software and procedures. They were published to all employees in the organization as part of a structured training programme which started at senior management level with short briefings and worked down through the hierarchy to practical sessions for all levels of staff.

Table 12.3: Working documents to support high level policy statement

Document Number	Title
1	Ergonomics requirements for the procurement of display screen workstations in xxxx
2	Procedure for addressing usability requirements in system procurement and development
3	Guidance on involving users in the development and implementation of systems
4	A user's guide to workstation ergonomics
5	Working environment questionnaire
6	User interface style guide

The implementation of the hardware ergonomics policies was not difficult. The organization already used published standards and purchased high quality equipment. The additional standards were therefore relatively easy to incorporate and apply.

However, the software and organizational policies were much more complex and several, more general, issues arose which may be of interest and relevance to other organizations.

Political Hurdles and Standards Implementation

Challenges

User interface standards and style guides are particularly important where large systems are being developed by different teams. Once the overall system is integrated, inconsistencies within the user interface can be difficult to resolve and can lead to errors, inefficiencies and frustration. Many organizations are turning to consistent user interface standards to avoid such problems and to allow easy transfer of staff between departments and increased interworking across traditional organizational boundaries.

One of the early issues concerned the difference between a user interface *standard* and a user interface *style guide*. Some of the ergonomics committee would have liked to develop user interface standards which would be mandatory across the organization in order to avoid the kind of inconsistency problem with function keys mentioned earlier. However, there were others who argued that it was more realistic to aim at a style guide which could recommend good practice but which could permit deviation if circumstances required it. After much debate, it was recognized that the extensive installed base of inconsistent existing systems and the distributed way in which systems were procured or developed, made a single mandatory standard unrealistic.

The senior management committee responsible for information technology (IT) raised the question of the additional costs of such a style guide. It was pointed out that the costs need not be high. All system developments require design decisions. Therefore, there was no reason why good design decisions made using a style guide should be any more expensive than the normal ad hoc design decisions for user system interfaces. Indeed in most cases, there would be savings in time and effort required because some design decisions had already been made.

One of the problems in the organization was a general lack of communication between the geographically remote and independent operating units. When systems had to be developed to support two such locations, there was a tendency for one site to become the dominant partner and the other to feel that their requirements had been underestimated. The style guide was intended to improve this inter-site communication.

Solutions

Few organizations have the infrastructure, internal control or the stamina to enforce strict interface standards. In this organization, it would have been all too easy for individual developers to allow variations to creep into their designs – there was very little communication between different development groups and much of the detailed code writing was carried out off-site by contract programmers. There was also a culture of "not invented here" when anyone tried to introduce new ideas, especially those concerned with the way individuals work. The majority of the workforce were highly qualified individuals with strong views about technical issues. There were already many different systems and subsystems with little obvious similarity or consistency. New systems could easily be developed in isolation with totally contradictory features. Typically, these would only be discovered at the user acceptance testing stage and by then the time penalties for correcting them would have been difficult to cost justify. Nonetheless, it was felt that there would be significant benefits in developing an enterprise-wide, high level User Interface Style Guide for new systems. The key benefits were seen in terms of maintaining best practices, interworking, staff mobility and efficiency of procurement, design and maintenance.

The senior management committee responsible for IT raised the question of the additional costs of such a style guide. This is a common issue raised with human factors consultants and although it is not difficult to present cost benefit information which supports whatever is being proposed, in our experience this may not solve the problem. Whilst cost-justification should be expected, it is sometimes the case that the specified "evidence" is out of line with the normal decision-making processes in the organization. For example, when estimating the benefits, we may get asked for "proof" through the question "has this been done elsewhere and how well did it work?". Asking for such proof is often another way of saying "I do not believe you". This means that it is probably not enough simply to provide the evidence asked for (for example by saying that organization X saved 15 per cent in the first year by implementing this idea). When faced with such "proof", a sceptic will respond by saying there are sufficient differences between organization X and themselves that the figures cannot be relied on. If you then try to show other similarities between the two organizations, the sceptic will find some other weakness.

A more constructive approach is to spend time persuading them that you understand their problems and show that what you are recommending will help them directly. We therefore pointed out that the costs associated with the style guide need not be high.

It was pointed out that the most significant benefits of adopting an enterprise-wide style guide would be improved consistency of user interfaces which in turn could reduce user errors and learning times. Increased consistency was also likely to increase the acceptance and hence the utilization of new systems. The re-use of design elements from a design library could also contribute to savings. Of course, the mere presence of a style guide would not ensure consistency. Designers would have to choose to conform or be disciplined to conform for the benefits to be achieved.

We recognized that one way of encouraging them to follow the guide was to support it with a code library and provide lots of good examples for designers to follow. We were also aware that there were conflicting requirements in the organization, which would take some time and discussion to resolve. For example, there were quite different styles of working in the different locations, partly due to national differences in attitudes to work and partly due to technical differences in the nature of the work. In The Netherlands, the majority of the users were familiar with using complex database search engines and often developed their own small pieces of software to help them with their own tasks. There was a culture of sharing these small programs but only within limited groups of colleagues. There were wide differences in the way different individuals worked. In Germany, there was a different regime and the software tools were much more disciplined. Individuals were not encouraged to use their own programs and were often prohibited from so doing. There was also more use made of support staff, sometimes to operate the systems for the more senior staff. We found that the presence of a style guide was likely to bring such issues to the surface earlier in the development process. We believe this reduced overall development time and cost. Experience in many organizations suggests that the cost of making changes in systems increases significantly as the development process continues.

The guide took the form of a high level statement of principles, a list of approved proprietary platform standards, an agreed organization-wide subset of these standards, an icon and function library, a glossary of organization-wide terms and an interactive demonstration to illustrate the various preferred interface styles. The complex task of gaining contributions and approval from all parties proved to be an opportunity for addressing other, related communications issues.

One of the problems in the organization was a general lack of communication between the geographically remote and independent operating units. Although the staff were all highly qualified and relatively well paid, the management style in the organization was very hierarchical and there was little encouragement for more human activities. They had to be persuaded that some face-to-face meetings were necessary and that videoconferencing was not sufficient to develop co-operation, trust and team working. When we suggested that the group responsible for the guide might meet up the night before (with half having travelled from the other site) for dinner, this was greeted as a surprising idea. In fact, once we started encouraging such social interaction, the project groups started working together far more effectively. There was a tendency for the different nationalities to stick together socially and trying to build more coherent project teams was not seen as a priority by senior management.

The guide was clearly an organization-wide initiative and not the exclusive property of any one site. Everyone therefore felt entitled to contribute to its development. Indeed, it was quickly recognized that not taking part could lead to specific interests being ignored. The process of developing, reviewing and agreeing the style guide was therefore in itself a positive process in improving communication between sites with different national and cultural viewpoints. Commenting on the style guide became a relatively safe way of making general comments about the development process. In some cases, small cross-site subgroups would be set up to deal with specific queries, improving working relationships enormously.

The interactive version of the style guide was an extremely useful vehicle for encouraging designers and users in The Netherlands and Germany to simulate their systems long before hard design decisions were made. Thus it was possible to bring together mixed groups to review ideas and even to test out these ideas with potential users. Whereas previous discussions between these groups had tended to take the form of each side expressing their views and then agreeing to differ, the sessions which involved the demonstration systems and the practical feedback from users greatly focused attention on real differences. These real differences could then be discussed and resolved in a reasonably calm and positive manner.

The main sources of cost were the cost of developing and maintaining the style guide and supporting it with a design library. The cost of checking new designs for compliance became incorporated in the normal review and quality assurance procedures.

Lessons Learned

- Although few organizations have the history, the infrastructure or the stamina to impose and police rigid user interface standards, style guides can be developed to reduce the unnecessary variation caused by dispersed design teams and extended system development timescales.
- The process of developing, reviewing and agreeing style guides can be a positive one for enhancing organizational communication, especially across traditional organizational barriers.
- The use of examples, code libraries and interactive demonstrations greatly enhances the effectiveness of the style guide as a means of encouraging conformance.

- In practice, it is better to motivate and encourage designers to follow good examples in style guides than to rely on post design monitoring and policing operations.
- International standards are slowly being developed which address many different aspects of user interface design – both hardware and software. These standards can be used to provide support for in-house measures.
- Senior managers are more likely to take style guide and user interface issues seriously if they know that there are public standards which support them. Such standards can also help organizations meet their legal obligations in European countries and this is likely to further increase senior management enthusiasm and commitment to improved user interface design.

References

For further information on the availability of ISO standards, contact BSI or your national standards organization.

The British Standards Institution, 389 Chiswick High Road, London W4 4AL, UK. Telephone: +44 (0)181 996 9000.

13. Usability Practice in the United States: Perception versus Reality

Patricia Dorazio

ABSTRACT

Many usability professionals argue not only to justify a usability presence, but also to gain management commitment to integrate usability activities throughout the product development cycle. In Europe, there is sometimes a perception that more American companies practise more usability work and spend more money doing so; in this chapter, I look at usability from an American perspective and explore the perception and the reality of usability practice in the United States. I also offer some tips and techniques from those practitioners successful in making usability happen within their organizations.

We only See What We Want to See

Each day of our lives we are faced with a myriad of information, some useful, some not. As humans, it is up to us to take in this information, process it and make sense of it. We use past information to decode images and to relate new experiences to old, for past experiences largely determine what each of us perceives. This is equally true for computer users – many come to Windows 95 with some basic knowledge of windowing systems and manipulation techniques. When faced with Windows 95 for the first time, these users see a somewhat ambiguous graphical user interface, complete with new terminology (My Computer, My Briefcase, Explorer), visual cues, and an on-screen taskbar. To use this version effectively, these users must rely on past experiences with previous windows applications and apply that knowledge to working with a graphical user interface. Soon users realize that Windows 95 is very similar to previous versions of Windows, and they then feel confident to proceed with normal tasks and manipulations.

There is general agreement that perception is a gathering and an interpreting of information; and once meaning is realized, we react accordingly. Therefore, our perception of reality is directly related to our environment, our experiences, the quality of information we receive, and our interpretations, be they accurate or in error; and at times it almost seems impossible to differentiate between our perception of reality and reality itself.

The Perception of Usability Practice in the United States

Perception involves a conscious awareness of what is around us and our making sense of it. We are challenged by a sea of information, and though we are trained in the information-gathering/interpreting process, we can, of course, misconstrue or even manufacture information to satisfy our natural curiosities. In fact, because we are fallible, we can imagine what is not really there, make erroneous assumptions, or attribute what we want to a particular situation. When we see something that is not really there or when we misinterpret a situation, confusion sets in; we cannot accurately discriminate between what we have actually seen (the reality) and what we have imagined (the perception). When our perceptions go awry or when we make errors in the perceptual process, the end result is a perceptual error, an *illusion*.

Sometimes our perception of something becomes the "constructed reality". The perception of usability in the United States is a constructed one: we have constructed our idea of usability practice in the United States from company publicity, from the usability reports we see touted in the trade journals, and from the history of human performance engineering. We have read about, seen, or heard of American companies doing usability (often referred to as "usefulness", "learnability", "efficiency of use", or "usability engineering") and, therefore, producing usable products from that accumulated information we perceive an explosion of usability practices in American businesses and industries.

This leads me first to address the perception of usability itself.

Perception 1: What does "Usability" Mean in the USA?

When I asked employees in a variety of industry sectors (consumer products, computer hardware, computer software, consumer applications, business software, telecommunications, financial services, online services, industrial products, to name a few) to tell me of the usability work or practices within their organizations, I got a wide range of responses. Usability specialists, engineers, program developers, and technical communicators are doing everything from classical human factors and ergonomic controlled testing (a systematic collection and analysis of data during development) in a very sophisticated laboratory (with its central focus on analysing statistical data) to a quick "hallway" review of a particular product or project and, finally, to a validation of product development efforts. In a recent usability survey conducted by the Usability Professionals Association (UPA), respondents performed "multiple types of usability evaluations", including competitive evaluations, design walk-throughs, field studies, focus groups, lab tests, prototype studies, and surveys [1].

Additionally, most people I spoke with had misunderstandings about when usability should be applied to the development process. Most usability specialists and managers stated that usability practice in their companies occurred at the end of the development cycle; there it would do the least damage (translation: impact the schedule), and any changes would have to wait for future releases. However, usability specialists in almost all companies argued for early integration of usability in the development life cycle, pointing out that "not considering usability in the early stages of development often slows the product release" [2]. So what does this all mean? Quite simply, each one of us involved in usability has a different perception of *what* constitutes usability and *when* it should occur, though almost everyone I spoke with claims to "do usability" to some degree at some point in the development process. Perhaps it is just this claim of doing usability that leads people to perceive companies (and management) in the United States have not only readily accepted usability as a standard practice, but also have committed money and resources to continue the practice.

Perception 2: Reporting Usability Results

In looking at usability in practice in companies and organizations throughout the United States, I became acutely aware of the many aspects of a successful usability program, but none as important as promoting successes and making usability results known – and making them known in a *big way*. Those employees directly or indirectly involved in usability in companies in the United States tend to tout usability results both inside and outside the company, especially when usability input has directly led to decisions related to product or documentation redesign and improvement. It is this notion of "bigness" (i.e., tell the world) that leads outsiders to view the United States as a culture of "bigger is better". The United States has more software industries, more information technology (IT) development, more chances for companies to grow and prosper, and simply greater and better odds for success. Hence the perception that because usability results are reported in a variety of ways (i.e., internal reports, technical reports, research studies, journal articles, formal usability reports, usability reviews, redesigned prototypes, highlights tapes, "white papers", etc.), one can conclude there seems to be more usability work practised in the United States than in other countries.

Let me cite some examples. At IBM, NASA, Apple's Human Interface Design Center, and Philips, to name a few, usability results, good or bad, are provided to all people involved in software development. Results are typically reported in meetings, reports, oral presentations, email messages, diagrams, video, electronic data and paper sketches. And because the development teams tend to be informal, members not only hear and read about usability findings, but they also discuss those findings and hold meetings to decide major issues, to recommend changes and to set priorities.

Is Usability the Same as Quality?
Usability successes are widely publicized in professional and trade journals and at professional conferences. At the 5th Annual Usability Professionals Association Conference in August 1996, for instance, many usability professionals from the

United States and from the rest of the world shared information about usability methodologies and successful studies at their respective corporations. And, not surprisingly, usability in recent years has been closely aligned with Total Quality Management (TQM). Why? Because TQM, according to most of its advocates, is greatly influenced by the quality of design and the conformance to customer demands, requirements and needs, the very same underlying principles of usability. Because usability success implies user-centered design and/or ease of use, the end result is a quality, usable product. And nowadays a quality product brings more recognition (and reward) to a company than does its reputation or history.

Is Usability Catching On?

All of this "usability talk" gets around. Inevitably, the competition becomes aware of the usability practices of others. Ironically, it is this talk of usability practices and successes, growing bigger and better by the moment, that fosters an intense competitiveness among companies and industries. For instance, if Company A is "doing usability" and is successful at it, then Company B cannot afford *not* to do usability. As word gets around that Company A is spending a certain percentage of its development budget on usability, Companies B, C and D are pressured to jump on the bandwagon and allocate the same amount, or even more. In this case, Company A drives an entire industry. It is this competition that has led to more focus on every competitive aspect of a product, including its ease of use.

Perception 3: American Companies Build it Big

The simple fact is that no evidence suggests that usability is bigger or better in the United States, or that it is even more readily embraced in the United States than in other countries. Although the absolute numbers of practitioners is larger, the proportion is not – if anything, usability is no better or worse than anywhere else.

Nevertheless, Americans invest and spend a lot of money, and this is particularly true of corporate America. Jakob Nielsen notes that American companies have increased their usability engineering budgets from 3 percent (for non-military systems) in 1971 to 6 percent in 1993 [3]. He also notes an increase in the number of trade journals that include usability in their product reviews.

Additionally, American companies have a reputation for spending large sums of money building sophisticated usability test laboratories, complete with video cameras and one-way mirrors. For example, American Airlines spent over "$700,000 to be exact – on a two test-bay, 3000 square foot facility", with "a large sum of that money spent on network communications to equip the lab for testing all products developed company-wide". Sun Microsystems has "four usability engineering laboratories in Mountain View, California, and Colorado Springs, Colorado. The Usability Engineering (USE) laboratories each include: an observation room (where the usability engineer runs the studies and others watch); a usability room (a large room for the studies that can be configured in multiple ways); and an equipment room. In addition, there are storage rooms for furniture, equipment, and videotapes". The cost of furniture and lab equipment alone for Symantec Corporation's usability lab in Cupertino, California, totalled approximately $55,000. IBM's very impressive 14-room Atlanta usability laboratory, in addition to having an evaluator's room, a control room and an observation room, "simulates the working environment in which the product's end user operates… In recent evaluations the evaluators' areas…have simulated working environments for computer integrated manufacturing, desktop publishing, medical, and personnel management products. [Additionally], the evaluator's area contains software, documentation, furniture, and any special hardware that may be required to evaluate the product. The area may also contain a telephone, which can be used to simulate calls to a customer support hotline".

The UPA survey cited earlier indicates "the most frequently mentioned items [in usability labs] were video cameras and voice recorders…46 people indicated that they have one-way glass, which does usually mean a physical space set up for usability evaluations (and/or focus groups)." Other frequently mentioned items include a scan converter and video editing equipment [4].

More than likely it is the announcement of the steadily-growing budgets and investments American companies are making on elaborate physical usability labs that leads others to believe there is a greater emphasis not only on usability testing, but also on integrating usability methods at many points throughout the product development cycle, from the early conceptual phase through the product release phase.

Perception 4: Usability Is a Team Effort

A common element emerging in those organizations reporting results is the idea of the team approach to usability. But this idea runs contrary to two widely-held usability perceptions:

- usability resides in a separate department;
- usability is the developer's domain.

First, according to many human factors engineers in large American software corporations, usability practices have traditionally been confined to a separate department of "human factors engineers" and only tangentially linked to product development. These engineers have well-defined roles and responsibilities and are usually called upon at the end of the development cycle to "test" particular products. At this stage of development, however, most human factors engineers feel their role is restricted to "giving the official approval or thumbs up". In other words, they "simply validate development efforts rather than generate usable designs early in the development life cycle" [5]. And because many of these human factors engineers are usually physically located some distance away from the product designers and developers who seem to get all the attention, human factors engineers seldom feel like part of the development team. Rather, they are viewed as outsiders, as "consultants" with lots of responsibility, but with little authority or power to contribute significantly to product design.

Second, though product design comes about as a result of the input of many skilled people, the tendency in American software corporations is to have product developers or managers (usually engineers or computer programmers) assume ownership of the product. These technically-skilled people are the chief decision makers, responsible for all product-related decisions, including those related to resources, schedules, changes and modifications, and, most importantly, functionality. It is a product's function, what it does and how it does it, that remains the sole concern of product owners; and it is their position that:

- the more function a product offers its customers ("function creep"), the better that product will be, despite the fact that customers may not want or ever use those particular functions;
- if an application is functional, it is usable;
- whatever testing performed is for functionality improvements, not for usability (i.e., cosmetic) issues.

Despite the perception of individual ownership of products, most American software companies develop products as a team, consisting of representatives from various departments, including documentation, product and development planning, engineering, programming, marketing, quality assurance, usability, and so on; though not in the habit of working and thinking as a team, each member feeds customer ideas back to developers, thus encouraging a sense of teamwork while ensuring equal input into product design and development. This team approach more often than not fosters a collegial spirit and a sense of responsibility for all those who design software applications to serve customers' needs. Many of 1996's UPA conference participants addressed the idea of team development and testing, offering up the "human" side of usability testing throughout the product life cycle. From their own experiences, many believe a team approach brings a tangible quality to usability; team members who view usability "as a cumulative attribute of a product" [5] now exercise some "leverage" within the corporation. And with leverage comes the further selling and staffing of usability.

This brings usability to a full circle: after realizing that almost every American company has someone doing usability at some point in the development life cycle and after using the team to bring usability issues to the forefront and to discuss or publicize usability test results, the natural perception is that many American software companies have come to grips with what usability is all about. The usability specialists and human factors engineers I spoke with have faced and surmounted the many obstacles presented to them, and they remain champions of the cause. They continue to work as a team and to report results, further selling everyone on the idea of usability. Sceptics, especially project managers, are slowly buying into the usability idea and (reluctantly) supporting the cause with monies and resources, further shoving usability into a visible limelight.

Other Reasons Why the USA Is Perceived as the Leading Usability Practitioner

In addition to those discussed above, there are a number of historical explanations to support the perception that American companies readily embrace and practise usability. After the war ended, psychologists played a bigger role in equipment design. Their work was largely supported by the government, and the results are in numerous in-house technical reports. In 1949, the Ergonomics Research Society and the Human Factors Society were formed; both professional organizations promoted work in human performance and the application of research findings to product design and development.

Historically, usability (using people to help design products) can be viewed as a natural outgrowth of human performance engineering. As tools, equipment and entire systems became more complex, it became clear that industrial engineers could no longer avoid history and omit users, their requirements and their limitations from future product development. Determining user needs and characteristics when system objectives and specifications were still being written became a natural and crucial step in the first stage of systems development. To reinforce this idea, companies such as IBM distributed guidelines for product development [6]; these guidelines not only accounted for strategies for product development (i.e., product and programming objectives, functional and logical specifications), but they also took into consideration usability activities. Usability was included to provide a framework for the design and test of each hardware and programming product or system; this framework considered product usability objectives, user requirements, work activities and task analyses when designing prototypes. Over time, obtaining user input, testing performance levels and measuring user satisfaction became integrated into the development cycle companies implement today.

Some human factors engineers earning PhDs in cognitive or experimental psychology offer another explanation of usability acceptance in the United States: early Human-Computer Interaction (HCI) research was conducted mainly in the United States at prestigious research universities and funded largely by giant American corporations and/or by the government. In terms of HCI research, the early focus centered on application ease of use: what kinds of applications are required for varied audiences performing different kinds of tasks and what is an acceptable level of human performance when using the computer to perform daily tasks? Much of the research started with and continues today on the information-processing aspects of computers and the "look and feel" of the human-computer interface. The plethora of HCI textbooks and research articles, with a large percentage of studies detailing user-centered design, has placed the emphasis on more end-user involvement early in the development process.

Parallel to this 20th century HCI research was the increase in end-user computing (both on the mainframe and on personal workstations). Almost everyone is somehow affected by the computer. The highly successful entrepreneurship in the computer and semiconductor industries in the United States (known as the Silicon Valley phenomenon) fostered intense competition among many companies in the commercial world on the west coast. In fact, much of the early work in usability started on the west coast, where software companies had a greater awareness of the importance of usability involvement. Add to that a large American market and a profitable American economy, and you have everyone appearing to "do usability" because it breeds product acceptance and company profits.

The Reality (Common Practice) of Usability in the USA

Faced with a glut of information, it is easy to see only what we choose to see, ignoring what is often unpleasant, unfriendly and ugly. But that only gives us a narrow view, a view "through rose-coloured glasses" and we know the world is not that pleasant, beautiful or perfect. Such is the case with the reality of usability practice throughout the United States. Presented with an ambiguous (and often confidential) image of usability in the United States, it is easy for people to "construct a false perception" about the common practice of usability.

Americans claim products are safer and easier to use, but perception and reality differ. In gathering information for this chapter, I quickly learned that the perception held by those outside of the United States regarding usability practices is indeed not the reality. The bottom line, again citing the UPA survey, is that *some* product changes get implemented and there exists *some level* of support throughout American companies and organizations for usability testing.

Common usability practice indicates quality and usability are getting confused and, though TQM principles do include understanding users' needs and requirements, this clearly is only a small part of usability practice. Unfortunately, many companies in bringing new products into the marketplace practise the "checklist method of development'; if at any time designers bring users in to comment on or participate in the design of new products – or to involve users in any way – then designers claim to have practised usability and feel free to check off (completed) that part of the development process. The fact remains that when companies say they do usability, what usability activity is done comes as a result of an uphill struggle by an ever-decreasing group of usability specialists. Yes, something is better than nothing, but clearly implementing only one part of usability is a far cry from actually doing usability.

Let us talk about realities here:

Reality 1: Usability Is a Type of Marketing

Many American companies are combining technologies and resources to create hybrid products and departments, rather than create a single product line or have centralized groups with dedicated responsibilities. As a result, usability departments have been greatly downsized; more often than not, usability personnel have been integrated into product development departments. Consequently, their roles have changed dramatically. Many are charged with enhancing marketability and ensuring acceptance in the marketplace. In other words, they are responsible for quality and for facilitating the development process to ensure quality, not necessarily usability testing.

Reality 2: Usability Must Be Cost-Justified

In an age of downsizing and company re-engineering, many usability practitioners, unfortunately, must justify their existence every step of the way if they are to keep their positions and leverage some impact on product development. The fact is that many usability specialists spend a lot of time proving their worth. They continually

- explain what usability is and educate decision makers;
- size up the situation to determine what the climate is for introducing usability testing within a particular development cycle;

- gather and convene usability champions on regular basis;
- maintain usability momentum;
- gain credibility by being satisfied with small, incremental changes to the development process; and, most important
- show tangible payback to the organization, either in terms of increased profits or improved user satisfaction levels.

Reality 3: Not Everyone Outside the Business "Gets" Usability

Usability specialists in the company are often viewed as "usability police", who, as a LAN administrator stated, "scream, holler, push, nag, and pull the loudest for a greater emphasis on usability testing, interface design, interface standards, and refining the development process to call for greater user involvement starting earlier in the development cycle".

Reality 4: Usability Is Usually Forced Rather than Invited into the Product Development Process

Usability practice in the United States occurred as a direct response to the rising complexities associated with technological advances. Initial usability efforts grew out of pockets of research. Researchers at Xerox PARC and Apple spearheaded efforts to develop landmark systems that were not only easy to use, but capitalized on the graphical interface and the way users manipulate data and images: "Computers should be designed for the needs and capabilities of the people for whom they are intended" [7].

Reality 5: American Usability Practice Lacks Standardization

While American computer companies were enhancing the computer interface theorizing on ways to change users' attitudes towards the computer as a tool, European researchers were focusing on the ergonomic aspects of the physical equipment, in particular the computer keyboard and the terminal. Europeans remained concerned with developing standards, with making measurable assessments, and with imposing a set of rules that could formulize computer design and usability testing.

Reality 6: Usability Budgets Are Usually Small

While much has been made about the monies spent by (large) American companies to build elaborate usability laboratories equipped with one-way mirrors, data-logging software and a large resource staff, usability testing, as Dumas and Redish point out, does not absolutely require all of this. In fact, you do not even need a physical lab. The truth is whatever usability practice that does take place, more often than not, happens on a "shoestring budget" with limited resources and equipment, if any at all.

Reality 7: Customers Do Not always Know What They Want

American corporations have been slow to learn that a heavy focus on the customer expectations alone does not guarantee a quality or usable product, or even product leadership. Unlike the Japanese competition, American companies spent time and energy pleasing customers at the expense of delivering a usable, "value-added" product. As Michael Treacy and Fred Wiersema note in *The Discipline Market Leaders*, customers only *hone* the judgement of market researchers and leaders; customers can help get the details right, but customers cannot define the next product breakthroughs.

Reality 8: Pressure to Measure Usability Can Dilute its Effectiveness

In jumping on the "quantify and measure usability" bandwagon, corporate America has been less than successful in logically pinpointing usability and quality in less-structured product design work. Yet American companies continue to track requirements and apply hollow findings to product design and measurable outcomes. This oblique focus actually deters developers from a usability fundamental, that is, creating and fostering customer relationships, directly or indirectly, throughout the product life cycle so that customers can expect an unsurpassed, ever-improving product designed to meet their needs. That is the "value" that customers covet from successful corporations.

For obvious proprietary reasons, usability information is not readily forthcoming; nevertheless, what little evidence we get suggests some measure of usability does occur in American corporations and organizations, but not to the degree that companies would like us to believe. The realities discussed above indicate that corporate giants like Compaq, Kodak and SABRE Travel Information Network [8], to name a few, do take users and their feedback seriously when designing new products or revising old ones; for these companies and others like them, obtaining user input is a must in developing usable products that serve human needs and requirements. Other companies like Digital, Bellcore, IBM, Microsoft, Attachmate and GE Information Services [9] have integrated usability into the product development cycle, fully realizing a positive impact on the product and on users' attitudes.

On the other hand, some companies present an ambiguous and confusing picture: though they perceive usability to be important, usability activities in their organizations quite often, in fact, take a back seat to marketing a product's "bells and whistles". Even with the best intentions for recognizing usability contributions, these companies remain steadfast in the belief that it is still a product's functionality, not its usefulness, that sells and yields increased profits for company shareholders. These companies inevitably trade off usability for further research and development and, ultimately, corporate profits, a company's bottom line. Unfortunately, ignoring usability considerations often magnifies product flaws and brings about customer dissatisfaction, not to mention a less-than-ideal position in market leadership.

Fostering Receptive Attitudes to Usability

Usability does happen within American companies, both large and small, and many usability practitioners, managers and consultants have shared with me their secrets about convincing the "powers that be" that usability is a good thing. The UPA survey shows that usability activities in some companies have moved away from the end of the process only to be integrated throughout the product development cycle. But just how do you get support for this integration? How do you sell usability within your organization? How do you get others to "buy into" the value of usability testing process and make the usability investment?

There are many aspects to usability, but key to building a successful usability testing program is educating company personnel about the usability testing process, finding a leader and prominently aligning usability within the organization.

Educate Others

Many small companies believe in "diving in" by retaining outside usability consultants, but most usability advocates recommend a more conservative, in-house commitment to educating its employees. It is not hard for people to become familiar with usability, for a large wealth of information exists and is available for the asking. The educational process can include inviting psychology or human-computer interaction experts to present informal talks, sponsoring on-site workshops or seminars, establishing a "usability bulletin board" that highlights usability's key issues and ramifications, touring usability labs, and joining online discussion or news groups. Those truly sold on the usability idea may seek appropriate educational training by attending formal classes, professional workshops, or enrolling in certificate or degree programs.

Find a Leader

Once people within the organization share, talk and think about usability – essentially, realize a group of usability-focused people exists – usability gurus, those passionate about spreading the word, clearly emerge. And within that group of usability "evangelists" undoubtedly emerges a leader, a true champion of the cause. With some luck, this usability leader will also be a fairly senior-level employee, someone management respects and someone who can work cohesively with a multidisciplinary team, especially product developers and engineers.

Usability leaders, traditionally, strategically start bringing usability to the product forefront by:

- selecting the right product for a pilot study;
- naming a usability team, a cross-section of people from various departments;
- developing a short-term plan that concentrates on the chosen product;
- launching a pilot test;
- inviting management to attend and view this pilot test or to view a highlight videotape of the event.

Though usability success depends on many factors, without a doubt, none is as important as the role of the usability leader. Many usability crusaders directly correlated usability success with the position the usability leader holds within the company. Choosing a well-connected leader who is in a position to make decisions and who exerts some power sends the correct message: usability practice is important to design and development issues. Usability sells, and can be a "product differentiator...for usability translates into bigger profits for the company that has paid more attention to user needs" [10].

Organize and Align

Usability is a value-added service, not a functional mandate. And because of its precarious nature, usability demands a co-ordinated and cohesive effort from *everyone* involved in product development, including representatives from software, hardware, documentation, marketing, quality assurance, training and support, advertising, sales and promotion. Just where to align usability is not only a company decision, but also a political one as well. (See also Chapter 1.)

Depending upon the organizational climate of the company, the relationship among the departments involved with product development, and the variety of products produced, usability can either reside within product development itself (decentralized) or be a totally independent function with ties to all products and projects (centralized). In the first situation, usability is closely aligned with product development; usability practitioners can provide design guidelines and user interface technologies as product families evolve. In the second situation, usability practitioners belong to an identifiable group of professionals with stated responsibilities; as such, they actually influence company-wide product development and can develop stronger, more widespread allegiances. In either case, it is important to note that an entire organization's perception of the importance of usability practice depends on departmental or management commitment to it (i.e., how usability is funded, how many resources are allocated to usability).

Conclusion

This chapter relays firsthand the perceptions and the realities of usability practice in the United States, with emphasis placed on perceptions of usability in the United States, on possible explanations for those perceptions, and on the inevitable realities or common practices of usability in the United States. Through the experiences of those who have successfully (and patiently) overcome the usability hurdles, it becomes possible to learn the techniques these practitioners have applied for making usability happen within their organizations.

Most companies have a predisposition to usability. Usability can and does happen, regardless of the company or the political atmosphere. It takes dedicated personnel and a dynamic atmosphere. That is the one true reality behind usability practice in the United States.

Acknowledgements

Information gathering takes a considerable amount of time, and I owe many thanks to friends, acquaintances, and "unknown faces" who contributed to the writing of this chapter. I would also like to acknowledge colleagues for performing a number of edits on a number of drafts. Thanks to all for the guidance, feedback and support.

References

[1] Janice Redish (1997) "UPA survey shows who we are and what we do", *Common Ground*, vol. 7, no. 1, p. 5.
[2] Larry Fix and Alan Bitterman (1996) "Managing Concerns About Process Speed", in *Making Usability Happen*, User Interface Engineering, North Andover, MA, p. 7.
[3] Jakob Nielsen (1994) "Usability Laboratories", *Behaviour and Information Technology* vol. 13, nos. 1 and 2, p. 3.
[4] Janice Redish(1997) "UPA survey shows who we are and what we do", *Common Ground*, vol. 7 no. 1, p. 6.
[5] Larry Fix and Alan Bitterman (1996) "Overcoming the Hurdles", in *Making Usability Happen*, User Interface Engineering, North Andover, MA, p. 23.
[6] Michael E. Wiklund (ed.) (1994) *Usability in Practice: How Companies Develop User-Friendly Products*, AP Professional, Boston, p. 7.
[7] Robert W. Bailey (1982) *Human Performance Engineering: A Guide for System Designers*, Prentice-Hall, Inc., Englewood Cliffs, NJ, p. 193.
[8] IBM IS and CG/IS and TG Development Guide, Section E, Part 52, IBM Endicott Product Security, Endicott, NY, May 1997.
[9] Jenny Preece (1994) *Human-Computer Interaction*, Addison-Wesley Publishing Co., Reading, MA, p. 5.
[10] Michael E. Wiklund (ed.) (1994) *Usability in Practice: How Companies Develop User-Friendly Products*, AP Professional, Boston.

14. *Round the World in 18 Days*

Lessons from an International Usability Tour

Susan M. Dray and Lawrence R. Rowland

ABSTRACT

Before going ahead with international usability testing, it is important to understand and evaluate the elements which will contribute to its success. Some of these are organizational and political in nature, others are related to logistics, still others to international and cultural factors. This chapter provides a first-person account of a set of international usability evaluations which were dubbed the "Round the World Usability Testing Tour". In order to test the usability of a new oscilloscope, Hewlett-Packard tested it on users in the USA, Switzerland and Japan. The chapter gives a graphic account of the kinds of problems encountered – from seemingly minor technical difficulties to major differences in culture – and how these were overcome.

Introduction – Events Preceding the "Round the World Usability Testing Tour"

One of the authors (LRR) was working to ensure a highly usable user interface (UI) on a new oscilloscope. Results of international focus group work had been studied during the conceptual phases. Rounds of focus group testing and task analysis conducted around the United States had provided insight into the big problems encountered by users, and the result had been some fairly radical changes in the design. Radical enough to make management willing to entertain the possibility of international testing of the prototypes.

As the plans for the coming years support developed, the question of confirming the fundamental design decisions came up. Suggestions included a series of benchmark tests against competitive instruments, to "prove" the superior design of the product as well as more informal testing in the form of iterative structured walk-throughs interspersing small numbers of subjects with design modifications. The issue of international reception of the design was raised, as some of the early focus group work had been done internationally. Without any firm commitment, the request to "cost out" the project was made.

Lacking prior experience in international testing, LRR was reluctant to undertake such a costly project without adding someone with expertise and experience in international work to ensure its success. Susan Dray (SMD) was identified and contacted and we jointly came up with ballpark estimates of costs, and generated a proposal. This was accepted and the "Round the World Testing Tour" project began.

Planning the Process

The planning looked easy. After all, how much complexity could there be? At a conceptual level, all we had to do was:

- decide on the countries to visit;
- pick a couple of weeks to make the visits;
- arrange for focus groups centres to be used for testing;
- arrange for test subjects;
- make the flight arrangements.

Conceptually, it was not that difficult but specific logistics were complex, far more complex than doing testing in just one site, or just one country. As we began the detailed work of planning this study, there were many twists and turns, typical in international testing. For instance, we heard:

- "Can't test that week. That week is Golden week in Japan"
- "Oh, no, that's Friar Tuck day in Zurich"
- "No, we don't use one way mirrors anymore at the Swiss facility"
- "You need three stops to make an around the world airfare"
- "You do have carnets (passports for the equipment) don't you?"
- "Who is the name of the rep in Tokyo? Sorry, he is not in the office this week".

Needless to say, it was not as simple in reality as it seemed like it should be. It never is. But, with the help of a good travel agent and focus group companies in San José, California; Zurich, Switzerland; and Tokyo, Japan, and the tireless efforts of the team to juggle all the focus group arrangements, the plan was finalized. Here is what the plan looked like in the end:

- Pilot the test in Colorado using internal subjects
- Do a software rebuild based on pilot results
- Run a US group in San José, California
- Do a software rebuild based on San José results
- Pack up the gear in three transit cases and
- Fly to Zurich, Switzerland
- Recover on Friar Tuck day (a local Swiss Holiday)
- Test for two days
- Rest over the weekend
- Test another day

- Pack up all the gear
- Fly to Tokyo, Japan
- Recover the rest of the day
- Test for two days
- Fly out the evening of the last test day
- Fly back to Colorado.

It certainly was longer than we originally thought, but we had a plan. However, "there's many a slip, 'twixt cup and lip".

Doing the Study

Developing the Test

The test environment was somewhat complicated by the nature of the task domain. Using the oscilloscope is not the dominant task for our user population. We were aiming at design engineers doing debugging. We needed to successfully trigger the debugging response, while not presenting a situation too complex to be mastered by a "typical" engineer. Too easy a task and the debugging was not engaged; too complex and it could not be presented, much less solved, in the time available for testing. Beyond that, the test design was standard. We did all those things we always do for a usability evaluation:

- develop the task list;
- develop test stimuli (in this case, instructions and signals from programmable signal generators to feed the oscilloscope we were testing);
- develop briefing scripts and debriefing questionnaires;
- develop subject profiles;
- revise, based on inspections of the design.

We anticipated that we would use our standard methods, and adapt them as necessary. It turned out that in Switzerland we were fine. Japan, on the other hand, required some modifications. But that comes later.

Pilot

The pilot testing went smoothly. We ran into the typical "never done it before" problems and adjusted the test stimuli and reworked some of the instrument software. After three or four subjects we could actually make it through a test without the instrument locking up. By the time the pilot was over we were ready to take advantage of some customers visiting the site for an unplanned test to get some semi-real data. Smooth sailing.

Round One: San José, California

With the results of the pilot testing incorporated into the oscilloscope software, a couple of weeks after the pilot we were in San José. Two levels of management were there, helping us set things up. The division manager showed up during the testing to see what was really going on. Field sales people and marketing representatives were there. This was an amazing show of support. With all the illustrious observers, we learned the art of "walk-throughs as theatre" – this was a major instrument project, with an extensive testing program, so it was extremely visible and very interesting to those behind the mirror. Of course, they were not necessarily the most impartial observers for a usability evaluation. And it was also important to give somewhat more information in front of the mirror so that the people in the back would have a sense of what was happening. This was a judgement call – possible contamination of subject data had to be balanced against observers in the back room knowing what was going on. Some written questionnaires became verbal debriefings because we needed to accommodate observer schedules, and we were less rigorous than we normally are in collecting certain statistics. But the buy-in and political gains for the entire usability process outweighed any notion of "rigorous science" and, on balance, we felt that this was the right direction to tilt.

Then we ran into our first real wrinkles. Firstly, we had forgotten the informed consent forms. Thanks to a laptop and printer, we had them before the test. Secondly, the pilot had been done with the signal generators in the same room as the subjects. In San José, we had a test room separated by a one-way mirror from the observation area. The test administrator (LRR) was in the room with the evaluators, but the signal generators were in the other room, along with the engineers who understood how to interpret the display on the instrument. Running the test without communication with the "back room" was clumsy. A quick trip to the electronics store provided us with a technological fix – a "bug in the ear" radio link between the back room and the subject area. Advice and information could be relayed to the test administrator without disrupting the subjects. This proved to be extremely valuable in the testing, especially when we went international.

Round Two: Zurich, Switzerland

Another few weeks (and a final turn on the software) and we were off to Zurich. The first day was spent shaking off the jet lag; trying to stay awake while your body tells you it is time to rest. After walking around Zurich for a few hours we hit the first big snag. Neither of the two instruments we had would fire up. Cases came open, boards were reseated, connectors reconnected. No luck. Phone calls and email crossed the Atlantic. "Try twisting here and poking there"; "Is there voltage on this?" – Voltage? Did anyone bring a voltmeter? (Luckily, yes.) Finally one scope was up and running. Boards were on the way to fix the other one.

The next day, we discovered some of the test stimuli were not the latest version. While engineering took off for a train ride, the human factors group worked on new stimuli. Luckily, the same laptop and printer that had saved the day in San José with the consent forms saved the day again. We whipped up a new set of stimuli, or test cases, and printed them out in the hotel room. The third day we moved gear to the focus group and set up for testing. The video equipment they provided was supplemented with the kit we had brought. We found out that the informed consent forms were not appropriate for the local culture, so we had to rewrite them, with the focus group people advising.

We started testing, using the protocols developed in the US. Since our subjects knew English, it worked. During debriefing, we found that some of the subjects had difficulty expressing responses in English so the focus group facility contact translated for us. After the second evening of testing, we headed back to the hotel. The next morning we left for the airport and Tokyo.

Round Three: Tokyo, Japan

The Land of the Rising Sun. The train ride from the airport was dazzling. However, we also found out that Japanese public transport is not friendly to people with handicaps (in the form of 70-pound transit cases). There were stairs everywhere. After the train ride to Tokyo, we gave up on the local trains and subways and took two taxis to the hotel. We had to use two because of the transit cases.

More fighting jet lag. Then off to the focus group to set up equipment. All the technology worked. But the protocols had to change. We did not speak Japanese and the subjects did not speak English, as they had in Zurich. A moderator from the focus group had agreed to administer the tests. We moved to the back room, reviewed the protocols with the moderator and found some confusion. The moderator read the test instruction to us, translating back into English, we read her the original English. She agreed the translations did not match and we worked on retranslating. Neither informed consent form was appropriate for the Japanese culture, either – in fact the very concept of informed consent was unfamiliar. So we had to invent one that would work. We had simultaneous translation, but could not always track who was saying what, due to the pace of conversation and the translation lag. It took total concentration to follow what was happening.

A further unexpected problem was that our "bug in the ear" no longer worked. Not a technical problem, or a cultural one – they thought the idea was great. But the bone structure around the ear is different in Orientals! Luckily, the focus group had similar technology. However, the moderator wanted to have Japanese, not English, pouring in her ear during the test. So we had one of the Japanese engineers talking to her. This led to an another translation issue and messages from our group had to be slowed down. After the first night of testing, she decided to allow one of us to talk to her directly, on the condition that he would talk slowly and clearly, which he did, and the testing sped up. We learnt two lessons from these experiences: all legal and process documents should be translated before doing international testing; people are different and that is why we test internationally. Anticipate differences and be flexible.

We changed the protocols to accommodate a very different style of moderator and a different way of presenting tasks. The moderator was not a technical peer, as had been the case in previous tests. Interaction with the users was less technical and technical clarifications required more time. However, while we dropped a few tasks from the set to allow more time for the others, the same measures of success were available and the pre-test and post-test questionnaires were preserved (after re-translation). Perceived ease of use and subjective acceptance measures were still collected after the tasks.

We weighed these changes carefully. We did not want to compromise the Japanese results either because we rigidly stuck to a style and protocol that was not culturally appropriate, or because we modified it too liberally. Knowing how much we could change without "breaking" it was a judgement call based on experience. In retrospect, we could have changed it somewhat more, and probably should have. For instance, because Japanese subjects have an aversion to stating things as yes/no answers, some critical debriefing questions were never answered. We should have designed them for clearer answers. The Japanese data set had some gaps but, on balance, we felt that the data we did collect was of high quality and was representative of the market.

There were some unexpected changes to the plans that worked to our advantage. For example, at first, we were quite worried because none of the Japanese support engineers could act as evaluation moderators, so we had to use a moderator from the facility. How would it work to have Japanese engineers talk to a non-technical, young woman? This actually turned out to be a brilliant stroke of luck. Our moderator was a very gifted Japanese woman, who was able to pick up the nuances of usability evaluation quite quickly. She understood that we were looking for problems, and helped the engineers to show her things in a way that indicated to us when there were problems, without making them "admit" problems. Also, because she was a woman, she was able to ask questions and get answers that would have been very difficult to get had she been a man. She was able to allow the engineers to "teach" her so they could talk to her more honestly without involving "losing face", because she was female. Exploiting this kind of gender advantage was certainly not in the plan, but it worked wonderfully!

We conducted the tests, but lost one set of subjects we had planned on. After the last day of testing, we packed up and headed directly to the airport from the focus group facility. Exhausting though it had been, the Round the World Usability Tour had been a big success.

How International Usability Testing Changed the Product

Many changes were made in the product as a result of the testing. It is, perhaps, a measure of how successful the testing was regarded by management that the results of the testing are considered proprietary by the funding division and therefore cannot be detailed fully here. However, a few general results were:

- A major restructuring of the menus. The groupings and naming conventions were revised to allow more rapid access to underlying functionality.
- A follow-on project was instigated to design the help system instead of leaving it as a part of the main instrument design. A separate round of testing was made on the help system since contents were not available for this round of testing. This included both early design testing based on simulation of the contents and later full-content testing.
- Task orientation was increased in several areas that users had found confusing during testing by repeating control elements in multiple dialogue panels. This

allowed users to modify desired configuration controls adjacent to the initiation of a task rather than requiring them to access separate set-up dialogues.

The Politics of International Usability Testing

Our round the world tour once again reinforced the importance of involving a range of users – be they the end users of a product, or the users of the information generated by a usability evaluation. One of the reasons we were lucky enough to avoid negative political events was because we had communicated with everyone involved regularly during the entire project. In addition, we made trade-offs to ensure that everyone stayed bought in, by incorporating "pet questions" such as "Who do you think should bring out this Oscilloscope?" It was a big "win" for the project that both the section manager and the division manager were able to come to the usability evaluations, in part because we had made it a priority to make the process accessible to them. We split the tasks of running the subject in front of the mirror and managing the process behind the mirror to make sure that both ran smoothly. This was a very conscious decision on our part, since both were vital to the continued success of this project and of usability in general in this division.

Another important political activity for us was making sure that field staff, including both support and sales and marketing, were kept informed and invited to usability evaluations. We found that if these people were involved in the set up of the test, their buy-in was essential, but even if they were not key to the testing itself, it was important for them who we were and why we were there. Often in the past, we have needed to use field people to help us locate potential evaluators or to make local arrangements for us. In this study, even though we were handling the recruiting ourselves in Zurich, the Japanese division was very involved in the recruitment process in Japan. We used local focus group facilities to recruit subjects and host the tests. They were invaluable for providing advice on cultural issues, international travel, translation aid during interviews, and supporting the "nuts-and-bolts" level of administering the tests. We made sure that they were given an appropriate thank you gift for all of their help. In addition, when they were in the States several weeks later, we made sure that their help and hospitality was returned warmly.

It is impossible to over-emphasize the importance of clear written communication. We relied heavily on email, especially with our Japanese colleagues. Email allowed us to copy all of the relevant people and to clarify understanding. It was important for us to remember that we were asking them to speak English for our sakes, and to keep the communication as straightforward as possible.

Equipment: the Nitty Gritty

The technical support of international testing can be quite daunting. Particularly when hardware is under test, carrying equipment is quite a challenge. Not only carrying the device being tested, but all the associated equipment to run the tests and document what is happening. Local people may not know what video standard they use. This is a major issue for testing internationally. NTSC is used throughout the US, but not anywhere in Europe. PAL seems to dominate Europe. The nitty-gritty technical is not something our focus group operators knew, they hire outsiders to do it. If you want video, take the equipment yourself (it constituted about 8 pounds of our three 70-pound transit cases for two cameras and lots of 8mm tapes). Bring lots of extension cords and junction boxes. You will need them all. Set up the entire arrangement, count and label the cords before packing, then pack spares. Arrange ahead of time for local power cords for the equipment you are testing. Always carry at least two of what you are testing. Be prepared to fix anything you are carrying. Usually the testing is done with prototypes, which are somewhat delicate under the best of conditions. Have equipment to do simple fixes and someone who knows enough about fixing what you are testing to work with an expert over the phone lines.

Lessons Learned

It would be hard to capture all the lessons we learned from this international usability testing tour. So much was immediately internalized that it would have required ongoing journaling to catch it all. However, here are some of the significant ones.

- Be polite to everyone. It takes no more time and makes people a lot more willing to help you.
- Keep your sense of humour when equipment or processes go wrong. Smile and move on to what is working. The world will not end if part of the test does not happen. Concentrate on the data you are able to collect.
- Always bring two of what you are testing and still be prepared to fix equipment on the fly.
- Always bring a printer and a laptop. It is well worth the weight.
- Have local people who can support you and on whom you can depend.
- Build in time for plenty of rest and take that time to actually rest instead of sightseeing. You cannot collect good data when you are totally exhausted.
- Write up findings as you go. It is very hard to remember context when you are referring back to the notes that were crystal clear at the time of data collection yet weeks later seem to have been written by a Martian with English as a second language.
- Smile at the customs officials. Most places they are very helpful if they do not feel you are hostile. Remember that American Customs hassle you more than any civilized country does.

Index